50 HIKES
IN EASTERN
MASSACHUSETTS

OTHER BOOKS IN THE 50 HIKES SERIES

50 HIKES
IN EASTERN
MASSACHUSETTS

FIRST EDITION

Madeline Bilis

THE COUNTRYMAN PRESS

A division of W. W. Norton & Company

Independent Publishers Since 1923

All photographs by the author.
Maps by Michael Borop (sitesatlas.com)

AN INVITATION TO THE READER

Over time trails can be rerouted and signs and landmarks altered. If you find that changes have occurred on the routes described in this book, please let us know so that corrections may be made in future editions. The author and publisher also welcome other comments and suggestions. Address all correspondence to:

Editor, 50 Hikes Series
The Countryman Press
500 Fifth Avenue
New York, NY 10110

For more views and vistas from these 50 hikes, follow @50hikesEasternMass on Instagram and tag your own trail pictures with #50hikes.

For information about permission to reproduce selections from this book, write to Permissions, The Countryman Press, 500 Fifth Avenue, New York, NY 10110

For information about special discounts for bulk purchases, please contact W. W. Norton Special Sales at specialsales@wwnorton.com or 800-233-4830

Manufacturing by Versa Press
Series book design by Chris Welch
Production Manager: Gwen Cullen

The Countryman Press
www.countrymanpress.com

A division of W. W. Norton & Company, Inc.
500 Fifth Avenue, New York, NY 10110
www.wwnorton.com

978-1-68268-352-1 (pbk.)

10 9 8 7 6 5 4 3 2 1

To Adam, who has been there every step of the way—literally and figuratively.

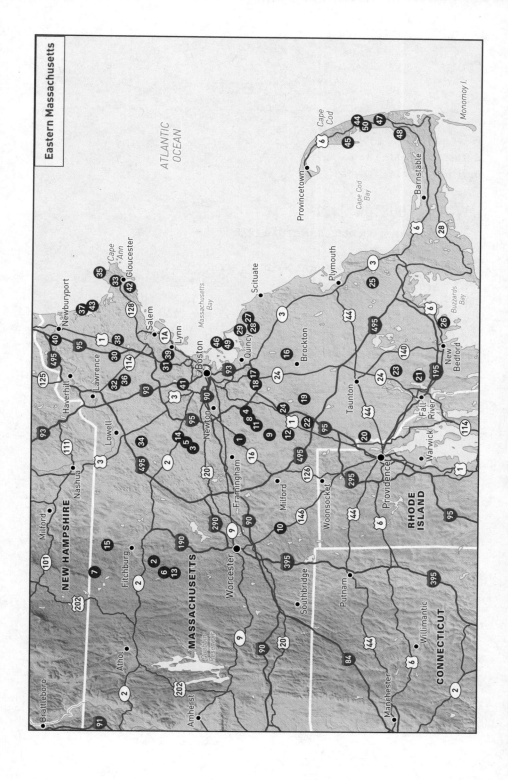

Contents

III. NORTH OF BOSTON | 147

IV. CAPE COD AND BOSTON HARBOR | 209

Hikes at a Glance

Hike	Region	Distance (miles)	Difficulty
1. Broadmoor Wildlife Sanctuary	West of Boston	4.2	Easy
2. Crow Hills	West of Boston	0.75	Strenuous
3. Great Meadows Wildlife Refuge	West of Boston	1	Easy
4. Hale Reservation	West of Boston	2	Easy
5. Mount Misery	West of Boston	2	Moderate
6. Mount Wachusett	West of Boston	3	Strenuous
7. Mount Watatic	West of Boston	3	Strenuous
8. Noanet Woodlands	West of Boston	2.75	Moderate
9. Noon Hill	West of Boston	1.8	Moderate
10. Purgatory Chasm State Reservation	West of Boston	2.3	Strenuous
11. Rocky Woods	West of Boston	2	Easy
12. Stony Brook Wildlife Sanctuary	West of Boston	0.6	Easy
13. Wachusett Meadows Wildlife Sanctuary	West of Boston	5	Moderate
14. Walden Pond State Reservation	West of Boston	2.25	Easy
15. Willard Brook State Forest	West of Boston	3	Moderate
16. Ames Nowell State Park	South of Boston	2.25	Moderate
17. Blue Hills Reservation—Skyline Loop	South of Boston	3	Strenuous
18. Blue Hills Reservation—Breakneck Ledge Loop	South of Boston	4.5	Strenuous
19. Borderland State Park	South of Boston	6.3	Moderate
20. Caratunk Wildlife Refuge	South of Boston	2.6	Easy
21. Copicut Woods	South of Boston	2.3	Easy
22. F. Gilbert Hills State Forest	South of Boston	4	Moderate
23. Freetown-Fall River State Forest	South of Boston	4.15	Easy
24. Moose Hill Wildlife Sanctuary	South of Boston	3.2	Moderate
25. Myles Standish State Forest	South of Boston	3.7	Moderate
26. Nasketucket Bay State Reservation	South of Boston	2.5	Easy
27. Whitney and Thayer Woods	South of Boston	3.5	Moderate
28. Wompatuck State Park	South of Boston	4.8	Moderate
29. World's End	South of Boston	3.2	Easy
30. Boxford State Forest	North of Boston	4.25	Moderate
31. Breakheart Reservation	North of Boston	4.25	Moderate
32. Charles W. Ward Reservation	North of Boston	4	Moderate
33. Dogtown Woods	North of Boston	2.5	Easy
34. Great Brook Farm State Park	North of Boston	2.7	Easy

Dogs allowed	Good for kids	Views	Notes
No	x		A walk through meadows and forests
Yes		x	A brief yet arduous climb
No	x		Half on boardwalk, half on dirt trail
Yes	x		Family-friendly walk around small pond
Yes	x		A trip along gently sloping, well-maintained trails
Yes		x	Exhilarating uphill climb
Yes		x	Steady climb to beautiful mountaintop
Yes		x	Easy hike with high reward
Yes		x	Smooth walk to scenic hilltop
Yes			Risky climb through a ravine
Yes	x		A woodsy walk, then a pondside stroll
No	x		The easiest hike in this book
No			A bracing trip up hills and over brooks
No	x		Historic journey à la Thoreau
Yes		x	Winding walk with a waterfall
Yes			Partially under huge power lines
Yes		x	Steep scramble up rocky hillside
Yes			Trek traversing woodlands and hilltops
Yes			Long walk on old estate with mansion
No	x		Pleasant stroll through Audubon sanctuary
Yes	x		Easy trip to abandoned farm settlement
Yes			Steady climb through boulder garden
Yes			Fun out-and-back through forest
No		x	Up-and-down climb with scenic lookouts
Yes			Bracing journey through scrubby forest
Yes	x		Low-key walk to waters of Buzzards Bay
Yes			Restorative jaunt through forest
Yes			Long ramble through historical woods
Yes	x	x	Picturesque stroll atop harborside drumlins
Yes			Lush forest with wildflowers, glacial erratics
Yes		x	Rocky hilltops and cool, damp forests
Yes		x	Meadows, woodlands, hills, Solstice Stones
Yes			Mysterious wandering among peculiar boulders
Yes	x		Leisurely, family-friendly trip

Hike	Region	Distance (miles)	Difficulty
35. Halibut Point State Park	North of Boston	1.5	Easy
36. Harold Parker State Forest	North of Boston	3.5	Moderate
37. Hellcat Interpretive Trail	North of Boston	1.5	Easy
38. Ipswich River Wildlife Sanctuary	North of Boston	3.5	Easy
39. Lynn Woods	North of Boston	3.75	Easy
40. Maudslay State Park	North of Boston	2.6	Easy
41. Middlesex Fells Reservation	North of Boston	7.5	Strenuous
42. Ravenswood Park	North of Boston	4.5	Moderate
43. Stage Island Trail	North of Boston	1.6	Easy
44. Atlantic Cedar Swamp Trail	Cape Cod and Boston Harbor	1.25	Easy
45. Great Island Trail	Cape Cod and Boston Harbor	6.8	Strenuous
46. Lovells Island	Cape Cod and Boston Harbor	1.5	Easy
47. Nauset Marsh Trail	Cape Cod and Boston Harbor	1.4	Easy
48. Nickerson State Park	Cape Cod and Boston Harbor	3	Moderate
49. Peddocks Island	Cape Cod and Boston Harbor	4	Easy
50. Wellfleet Bay Wildlife Sanctuary	Cape Cod and Boston Harbor	3.5	Easy

Dogs allowed	Good for kids	Views	Notes
Yes	x	x	Quarry views and a rocky coastline
Yes			Smooth tour through woods
No	x		Breezy stroll along seaside boardwalk
No	x		Diverse range of wildlife on view
Yes			Views of city from a stone tower
Yes	x		Pleasant cruise though former estate
Yes			Long trek through rocky hills
Yes	x		Bracing ramble through woods
No	x	x	Wildflowers and sea breezes
No	x		Boardwalk winds through National Seashore
In some parts		x	Stunning journey along beach and through pitch pines
No		x	Salty jaunt around historic fort
No	x		Breezy walk along tidal pond
Yes			Sunny hike around Cape kettle pond
No		x	Island hike with skyline views
No	x	x	Winding walk with stunning bay views

Acknowledgments

Thank you to all my pals, both new and old, who joined me on these 50 hikes: Adam Banks, Emily Huizenga, Tessa Yannone, Rebecca Banks, Keith Banks, Kurt Bilis, Diane Bilis, Jamie Ducharme, Chris Sweeney, Stella Sweeney, Hayley Glatter, Spencer Buell, Jocelyn Hurst, Yiqing Shao, Jen Penningroth, Hudson Penningroth, Kyle Clauss, Brad Lash, Loretta Donelan, Steve Socha, Jackie Socha, Mollie Socha, Dan Socha, Olga Khvan, Kiera Blessing, Jackie Cain, and Rachel Kashdan.

My special thanks to Adam, who not only accompanied me on a whopping 38 hikes, but woke up before 7 a.m. every weekend to drive me to each trailhead. Thank you for lending your extensive horticultural knowledge to me on the trails, for always holding my notebook when I needed to tie my boots, and for the countless slices of pizza we devoured in between hikes. I couldn't have written this book without you.

—Madeline Bilis

Introduction

Eastern Massachusetts is one of the loveliest places on earth. As a native, I, of course, am biased. But I encourage you to find the truth in that statement by using this book as a guide. In these pages, you'll find 50 hikes spanning surprisingly varied landscapes, from the rocky ledges of the Blue Hills Reservation to the sandy stretches of the Cape Cod National Seashore.

This book details some of the most well-known trails beyond Boston, as well as the area's more secret, hidden-gem walks. Eastern Massachusetts is not exactly known for its snow-capped peaks, meaning most of the hikes featured here can be completed in a few hours or less. Trails for all skill levels are included, although the majority of the hikes are perfectly suitable for casual outdoors enthusiasts, with only a few difficult ones peppered in.

The beauty of this guide lies in its endless possibilities for exploration, both on and off the trail. Hikes and trail navigations are described generally, so readers are free to modify or extend hikes as they see fit.

Navigating to the dozens of towns highlighted in this book is also part of the fun. Even though I was born and raised not far from Purgatory Chasm State Reservation, writing this guide allowed me to discover some Massachusetts towns I'd never even heard of. It renewed my innate love for the region, its landscapes, and its character. I learned about native plants, trees, and animals, yes, but I also grabbed a chicken salad sandwich in an old tavern in Gloucester, where I listened to two regulars at the bar discuss the merits of Wahlburgers. One time, I stumbled across a "pug social," in which pug owners from across New England descended upon fairgrounds near Great Brook Farm State Park to simply celebrate their dogs. I also got to poke into centuries-old house museums (the best kind of museum, in my opinion), learn some fascinating Massachusetts history (including a story about a grisly 1900 murder at Breakheart Reservation), frolic through a roadside sunflower field, and sample slices from perhaps one too many Insert-Town-Name-Here Houses of Pizza. Point is, there's a lot to see and do in any one section of this relatively small state. Sometimes it takes getting outside and hitting the trails to help you see it all.

Many hikes in this book make up part of several trail networks: the Bay Circuit Trail, the Midstate Trail, and the Appalachian Trail, to name a few. These longer through-hikes take days—and in the case of the Appalachian trail, months—to complete. If you breeze through the relatively easy hikes outlined in this book, those extended journeys will be a welcome challenge.

Plenty of these highlighted trails also bear the legacy of the CCC, or the Civilian Conservation Corps. Created by President Franklin D. Roosevelt in 1933 as part of his New Deal legislation, the CCC was a federal work relief project that employed millions of young, unmarried men during the Great Depression. From 1933 to 1942, they shaped the country's state parks by blazing trails and

THE BOSTON SKYLINE SEEN FROM PEDDOCKS ISLAND

building recreation facilities. A statue honoring these men can be seen in the main parking area for the Freetown-Fall River State Forest. In addition to state parks, this book features beautiful hikes in properties managed by the Trustees, the world's oldest regional land trust, as well as hikes maintained by the National Park Service.

These 50 hikes use Boston as a home base and are grouped geographically by region: West of Boston, South of Boston, and North of Boston. The fourth section, called Cape Cod and Boston Harbor, features the prettiest coastal hikes at the easternmost points of Massachusetts. Within each region, hikes are ordered alphabetically. However, if you'd like to complete a couple of hikes in one day, take a look at the map at the beginning of the book to get an idea of the trails' proximity to each other. I recommend knocking out the Hellcat Interpretive Trail and the Stage Island Trail in one Newbury trip, the Atlantic Cedar Swamp Trail and Nauset Marsh Trail in one Cape Cod trip, and Rocky Woods and Noon Hill in one Medfield trip. Yet no matter which region you're in, you're bound to see rows upon rows of stone walls. They're a ubiquitous sight in New England, built by early farmers to divide up property and farmland in the 18th and 19th centuries. Put end-to-end, it's said that the stone walls could circle the globe almost four times. See if you can discover which handful of hikes in this book don't feature stone walls.

HOW TO USE THIS BOOK

Each hike begins with an information box containing snapshot information about the trail. That includes the town(s) it's located in, its distance, the time it will take to hike, the elevation gain, the difficulty rating, whether there are restrooms available, whether dogs are permitted, and a short sentence about what you can expect.

To determine times, I compared the time it took me to complete a trail with the time it would take a hiker traveling at about 35 minutes per mile. The result is a rough average of how long a hike will take, including time for taking rests. These times are approximate and will vary between hikers and groups of hikers. You can expect your hiking time to differ based on factors like physical fitness, weather, temperature, and more.

I calculated the distances and elevation gains for each hike using a GPS app on my smartphone. Here, elevation gain is defined as the total number of feet you'll climb during your hike, or the sum of all the climbing done over the course of the trail. Distances were tracked from each trailhead, rather than from the parking lot.

Difficulty ratings are sorted into three categories: Easy, Moderate, and Strenuous. Easy hikes are almost completely flat walking. They're suitable for families with kids and older folks. Moderate hikes may require gentle climbing, but are otherwise more than manageable for a casual hiker. Strenuous hikes should be completed by more experienced hikers. They require sturdy boots with ankle support and offer a heart-pumping workout.

Always check to see if rules about dogs have changed before you head out with Rufus in tow. Similarly, the availability of restrooms is not 100 percent guaranteed. Some hikes marked down as having restrooms may contain port-a-potties rather than freestanding buildings. This means they can be removed at any time.

Following the information box is a set of instructions on how to navigate to a trail's parking lot. These directions flag major routes and highways. You should be able to rely on them alone, though a GPS is recommended. Below it, the address provided is the one you should plug into your GPS, if you're using one while driving. The section labeled *The Hike* brings you to the reason you bought this book. It describes the trail in detail, providing general navigational directions and highlighting history, landmarks, plant species, and more.

SAFETY

Perhaps the biggest threat to Eastern Massachusetts hikers is Lyme disease. Spread by deer ticks, Lyme disease is a serious, and sometimes debilitating, bacterial infection. The disease was named after Lyme, Connecticut, where it was first identified. The only way to protect yourself from Lyme disease is to make it hard for ticks to attach themselves to you. To do that, spray yourself with insect repellent and consider wearing long sleeves and long pants. Some hikers tuck their pants into long socks as an extra precaution. Keep in mind that deer ticks are often hard to spot and can be as small as a poppy seed. Always do a post-hike check of yourself in the mirror to ensure you're free of ticks. They're found in warm, moist places, like the armpits, groin, and scalp. According to the Centers for Disease Control, a tick must be attached to the body for 36 to 48 hours before Lyme disease can be transmitted. This makes a post-hike tick check and shower doubly important. Early signs of Lyme disease include a rash that resembles a bull's eye, flu-like symptoms, and joint pain and weakness. If these symptoms

MAP LEGEND

Described trail			Interstate highway	
Important trail			Secondary highway	
Hike direction arrow			Minor highway, road, street	
Perennial stream			Unpaved road, trail	
Intermittent stream			Railroad	
Major contour line			International border	
Minor contour line			State border	

National/state park, wilderness		P	Parking area
National/state forest, wildlife refuge			Trailhead
Perennial body of water		•	City, town
Intermittent body of water			Overlook, scenic view
Swamp, marsh		Å	Campground, campsite
Wooded area		Ṅ	Shelter
		×	Mountain peak
		▪	Place of interest

occur, head to the doctor right away for antibiotics.

In addition to insect repellent, hikers should wear comfortable boots or sneakers (depending on the terrain), bring more drinking water than would seem to be necessary, and pack sunscreen, a compass, and a raincoat. For the sake of preserving a pleasant hiking experience, always pack snacks. Granola bars, fruit, and other easily transportable items work best. There's nothing worse than a "hangry" (hungry + angry) hiker—and I speak from experience.

Lastly, take every effort to leave no trace of your trip on the trail. There's an old adage: Take only pictures, leave only footprints. Follow it. (Read: Take your garbage with you, don't pick flowers, etc.) This preserves the serenity of the natural environment for future hikers. After all, a hike nurtures the mind, body, and soul—who'd want to rob that from others?

I.

WEST OF BOSTON

Broadmoor Wildlife Sanctuary

WHERE: Natick	
ADDRESS: 280 Eliot Street, Natick, MA 01760	
TOTAL DISTANCE: 4.2 miles	
HIKING TIME: 2 hours	
ELEVATION GAIN: 250 feet	
DIFFICULTY: Easy	
RESTROOMS: Yes	
DOGS ALLOWED: No	
WHAT TO EXPECT: A rambling walk through meadows, forests, and along the banks of the Charles River	

As a kid, the only reason I might hop in a car bound for Natick would be to roam the seemingly never-ending aisles of the Natick Mall. There's more, of course, to this MetroWest town, and Broadmoor Wildlife Sanctuary is one gem hidden in plain sight. Tucked away on Eliot Street, and just a 10-minute drive from the mall, Mass Audubon's wildlife refuge along the Charles spreads out to 624 tranquil acres. It's a sanctuary in multiple senses of the word—the refuge serves as a home for hundreds of different species of animals and birds, yes, but it is also a quiet vacation for a busy mind.

Among the wildlife nesting in Broadmoor are otters, turtles, beavers, bluebirds, hawks, and sparrows. They live in a range of habitats in this single property: by the Charles River, alongside streams, on the shores of a former mill pond, in oak and pine trees, in grasslands, and inside swamps and marshes. By exploring some of the sanctuary's more than 9 miles of trails, you can glimpse this wildlife in its habitat, and learn a bit of land-use history. After all, it wasn't so long ago that a gristmill and sawmill on the property harnessed the water power of a Charles River tributary to operate. Try to envision the mills using the tributary, called Indian Brook, on your walk through the sanctuary.

GETTING THERE

From I-90 W, take exit 15B toward MA-30 and Weston. Take a sharp left onto Park Road, then continue onto Concord Street. Turn right onto MA-16, or Washington Street, following it for 2.8 miles. Turn left onto Washington Street, and after 1.8 miles, continue onto Eliot Street, or MA-16, until you reach the sanctuary. An admission fee of $6 is collected at the nature center.

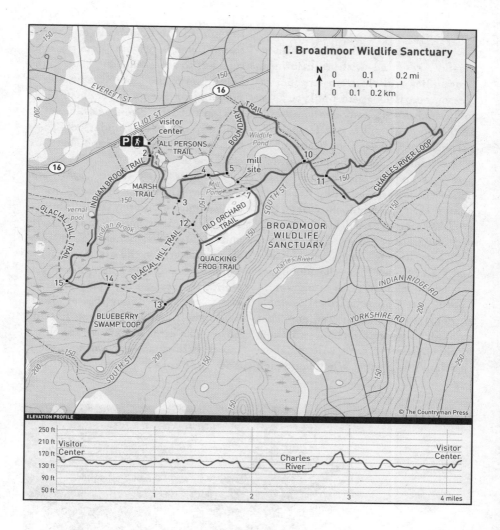

THE HIKE

This hike traces the outer edges of Broadmoor's 9 miles of trails, going from the Indian Brook Trail, to the Glacial Hill Trail, to the Blueberry Swamp Trail, to the Quacking Frog Trail, to the Old Orchard Trail, to the Wildlife Pond Trail, to the Charles River Loop, to the Boundary Trail, and back to the visitor center on the Marsh Trail. As a sanctuary staffer will probably tell you, it's

important to stay on the trails during your visit. Abundant poison ivy closely hugs the paths, and ticks live in the woods beyond them.

Begin your hike by exiting the visitor center and following the gravel path outward. You'll notice blue blazes here, and, later in your hike, yellow ones. The sanctuary makes navigation pretty easy—blue blazes lead away from the visitor center, while yellow ones lead back to it. When you meet the trail's first juncture, turn right onto the Indian Brook Trail. Soon after that, you'll enter a verdant meadow teeming with wildflowers. Dragonflies will zip from blossom to blossom across your path, until you duck into a shady forest. A wooden boardwalk on the right juts out to overlook a vernal pool. The scene is quite beautiful, so it's worth taking a few moments to stop here. Pick up the trail again, and you'll notice it becomes mildly hilly. At marker number 15, turn left onto the Glacial Hill Trail. Then, cross a small bridge over lily pad–clad waters.

In a few minutes, embark on the second trail of your hike: the Blueberry Swamp Loop. Turn right at marker 14 to begin the loop. A boardwalk signals entry to into the blueberry swamp. That means it's easy walking here—tall walls of shrubs dotted with wild blueberries flank the bridge. When you reach the end of the boardwalk and begin to approach a private property line, turn left to start your trip back to the beginning of the loop. By now, you've probably noticed plenty of mushrooms poking out from the thick blanket of golden pine needles underfoot. Their bright red, yellow, and orange hues are quite the sight.

At marker 13, keep right, and begin meandering through woods and swamps along the Quacking Frog Trail. It's leafier here, and tree roots and bright-green moss create a kaleidoscopic pattern on the ground. Emerge from the woods into a field once more. Notice the nesting boxes interspersed across the land. Many tree swallows make their homes in these nesting boxes. The birds are known for chirping cheerful songs and eating insects. They're one of a few species of bird that

THE INDIAN BROOK TRAIL OPENS TO A MEADOW

BRIGHTLY COLORED MUSHROOMS SIT ON THE BANKS OF THE CHARLES RIVER

will nest happily in the close company of humans, and within boxes close to each other.

After traversing the meadow, turn right onto the Old Orchard Trail, where you'll climb another slight hill. Admire the range of old trees here, then prepare to be greeted by two stone walls on either side of the trail. Turn right at the next intersection. (If you've reached the former mill site, you've gone too far.) Continue onto the Charles River Trail, passing by another private residence. Cross South Street and follow it for a few feet before turning right between two trees. The trail is marked with a blue blaze. Enjoy a woodsy walk to the river, and then continue on to trace the banks. Broadmoor borders 2 miles of the Charles, a river that winds through 23 Massachusetts towns before letting out at the Atlantic. Soon, you'll turn onto a trail marked with yellow blazes, signaling your return to the visitor center. Wind through the woods, climbing uphill and then down a rocky path. Ascend a set of stone steps to head back toward the road. Cross it, and continue straight through the two stone bollards on the side of the road. Before you can start frolicking in this meadow, the trail turns into a dense forest. It passes by another private home, and then it swings back around toward Mill Pond. At marker 5, turn right toward the mill site. Notice turtles sunbathing on rocks in the pond, and then turn right again at marker 3. After a series of zigzagging boardwalks, you'll find yourself back at the visitor center.

Crow Hills

WHERE: Westminster and Princeton

ADDRESS: 288 Fitchburg Road, Princeton, MA 01541

TOTAL DISTANCE: 0.75 mile

HIKING TIME: 1 hour

ELEVATION GAIN: 275 feet

DIFFICULTY: Strenuous

RESTROOMS: Yes

DOGS ALLOWED: Yes

WHAT TO EXPECT: A brief and arduous climb up to a rocky summit, with truly stunning views from the top

Long before rock climbers scaled these ledges, Native Americans used the Crow Hills for shelter and signaling, and later a now-abandoned 18th-century settlement called Notown was established at the spot. Remnants of these histories are evident in the ledges—cellar holes, fruit trees, and stone walls can be glimpsed beside the trails. In 1838, the unincorporated area known as Notown was grouped into adjoining towns.

The Crow Hills teem with historical significance. In 1676, a woman named Mary Rowlandson was kidnapped by the Native Americans and ransomed at a spot in the hills called Redemption Rock. Her kidnapping was a major event in the yearlong King Philip's War—a war of bitter fighting in which King Philip, a Wampanoag chief better known as Metacomet, ordered his native troops to raid Southern New England to drive out the colonists. His efforts ultimately did not succeed, and one result of the war was that the Native American presence was wiped out in New England. This opened the door for further colonial expansion. Later, when Mary Rowlandson was ransomed and released, she wrote a book about her time in captivity, called *The Narrative of the Captivity and Restoration of Mrs. Mary Rowlandson*. In it, she described her wish to be released, her travels through the wilderness, and her consumption of horse and bear meat.

Centuries after the war, the state of Massachusetts purchased land in the area in 1922 to establish the beginnings of Leominster State Forest. The Civilian Conservation Corps spent a good portion of the 1930s constructing roads and a park headquarters for the forest. They also developed the area around Crow Hill Pond for recreation.

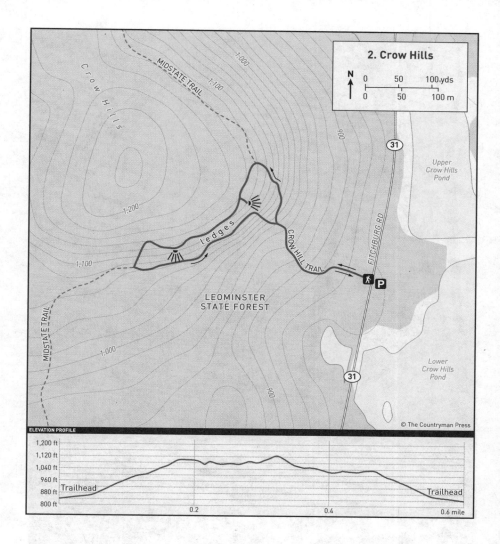

GETTING THERE

From Route 2 W., take exit 28 for Route 31 S. Turn left onto Route 31, or Princeton Road, and follow it until it turns into Fitchburg Road for about 2.5 miles. The parking lot will be on your left.

THE HIKE

This short, sweet, and rewarding journey begins across the street. Cross Fitchburg Road to reach the trailhead. Then take a deep breath, because you'll need all the oxygen you can get as you prepare to climb 275 feet in a few minutes' time. There are two sections to this

STONE STEPS KICK OFF YOUR CLIMB

VIEWS OF CROW HILL POND UNFOLD ATOP THE LEDGES

trail: the initial straightaway from the trailhead and the loop that goes around the Crow Hill. First, ascend the stone steps, then continue to make your way to the bottom of the ledges by following the blue rectangle blazes. You'll know you're about to begin the steepest climb of the trip when you see two signs: one pointing left toward the bottom of the ledges and one pointing right to the top of the ledges. Veer right here and begin your scramble up the rocks. Take extra precautions when it comes to gaining a firm footing, especially if it's drizzling.

Once the trail levels out, you'll begin to follow the Midstate Trail for less than half a mile. It's marked by yellow triangle blazes. Here, the path rims the hill, offering several lookouts along the ledge. Don't get too close to the edge as you appreciate the panoramic views over the treetops. Mount Wachusett (see Hike #6) rises from the green hills in the distance beyond Crow Hills Pond. On a clear day, you can see Boston to the east over the stretch of Leominster State Forest before you.

On your way back down, leave the Midstate Trail's yellow markers for blue ones again. You'll descend into a grove of mountain laurel before making it to the base of the ledges. Scoot along the rock faces, noticing their nooks and crannies. The rocks exhibit plentiful layers in their faces. These layers, or folds, are solidified magma that formed about 380 million years ago.

You'll likely notice hooks in the stone that rock climbers can use to proceed down the rock faces. The spot is extremely popular with climbers, who scale the cliffs after receiving a permit

MOUNT WACHUSETT IN THE DISTANCE

from Leominster State Forest. If climbers aren't active on the rocks during your visit, you are bound to see traces of their hooks and chalk puffs.

Aside from layers and climbers, there's a bit of what appears to be 1800s graffiti on the rock faces, too. Peer into a nearby crevice to see an inscription carved by a group on May 14, 1836. The message is mainly a list of names, such as C. Greenough and A. Baldwin.

Soon after you pass these monumental rock faces, you'll reach the spot where the loop began. Turn right to walk back the same way you came, to reach the parking lot.

Great Meadows National Wildlife Refuge

WHERE: Sudbury	

ADDRESS: 73 Weir Hill Road, Sudbury, MA 01776

TOTAL DISTANCE: 1 mile

HIKING TIME: 45 minutes

ELEVATION GAIN: 79 féet

DIFFICULTY: Easy

RESTROOMS: Yes

DOGS ALLOWED: No

WHAT TO EXPECT: A short walk around marshes, woodlands, a pond, and a river— half on a boardwalk, half on a dirt trail

Great Meadows Wildlife Refuge is one of more than 560 properties making up the National Wildlife Refuge System, which spans from Alaska to the Florida Keys. Overseen by the US Fish and Wildlife Service, the refuge system comprises a vast network of properties established for the sole purpose of protecting wildlife and wildlife habitats. (In its informational pamphlet, the National Wildlife Refuge System calls itself the "most comprehensive wildlife resource management program in the world.")

Great Meadows has two units: one called Concord and one called Sudbury. The units, however, span seven towns: Bedford, Billerica, Carlisle, Concord, Lincoln, Sudbury, and Wayland. About 85 percent of these combined 3,800 acres are made up of freshwater wetlands that line the Concord and Sudbury Rivers. The wetlands are home to more than 220 species of wildlife, ranging from mallards and blue-winged teal to otters, beavers, and white-tailed deer. Beyond creating habitats for these species, the wetlands act as "sponges" that reduce flooding and erosion in the area.

There has been a problem at Great Meadows that biologists are trying to control. Its name? Purple loosestrife. It's an invasive plant from Europe introduced to North America in the early 1800s. The plant features tall spikes of purple petals, and was originally admired as an ornamental flower. In the centuries since it arrived, purple loosestrife has wreaked havoc on these wetlands, choking out the resources that native plants depend on. To prevent the wetlands from being overrun by the flowers, biologists have released galerucella beetles and hylobius weevils in the refuge. These bugs only eat purple loosestrife and have been controlling

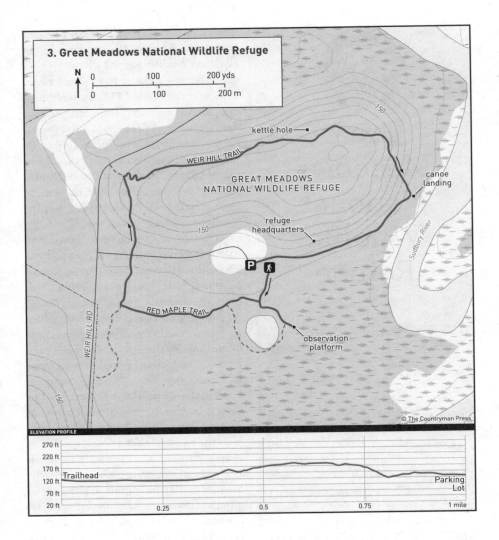

3. Great Meadows National Wildlife Refuge

N
0   100   200 yds
0   100   200 m

kettle hole

WEIR HILL TRAIL

GREAT MEADOWS
NATIONAL WILDLIFE REFUGE

canoe
landing

refuge
headquarters

Sudbury River

P   🚶

WEIR HILL RD

RED MAPLE TRAIL

observation
platform

150

© The Countryman Press

ELEVATION PROFILE

270 ft
220 ft
170 ft
120 ft — Trailhead
70 ft
20 ft

Parking
Lot

0.25   0.5   0.75   1 mile

the flower population without damaging any other living things in the refuge.

On your journey through the Sudbury Unit, you'll traverse Weir Hill, named for the fishing weirs that Native Americans used to use here. According to the US Fish and Wildlife Service, humans first started living on Weir Hill some 11,000 years ago, and tools from the Wampanoag and Susquehanna tribes have been found in the area.

GETTING THERE

From 1-95 N., take exit 26 to merge onto US-20 E. toward Waltham. Turn left toward Stow Street, then turn left onto MA-117 W., or Main Street. After 3.8 miles, turn left onto Old Sudbury Road, then continue onto Waltham Road. Turn left onto MA-126 S., and after 0.5 mile, turn right onto Sherman's Bridge Road. After 0.7 mile, continue onto Lincoln

Road, then turn right onto Weir Hill Road.

THE HIKE

The hike outlined here connects the Red Maple and Weir River Trails. Start out by catching the Red Maple Trail at the end of the refuge parking lot. After only a few minutes of leisurely walking along a wooden boardwalk, you'll arrive at an observation platform on your left. Here, a sign tells the history of the Nyanza Color & Chemical Company, which dumped harmful chemical byproducts into the Sudbury River from 1917 to 1978. In 1983, the river became a superfund site, meaning it was identified by the Environmental Protection Agency as a candidate for cleanup efforts. Cleanup efforts worked to restore the Sudbury as a habitat for fish, birds, reptiles, amphibians, and mammals. Today, on the observation platform, you can view a range of wildlife in the buttonbush wet meadow marsh just beyond it.

When you're ready, stroll down the platform and back onto the trail, turning left. There's also the option to loop around the pond, if you choose. New boardwalks make the Red Maple Trail ideal for families with strollers. As you continue, you'll pass a storage building on your right, and the boardwalk will wind through a leafy patch of ferns.

At the next intersection, turn right for the Weir Hill Trail. Cross Weir Hill Road and head up into the woods. While houses in the distance remind you you're not completely isolated here in the sanctuary, plant signage keeps your naturalist tendencies in check. (Hello, sassafrass.) The dirt trail zig zags up Weir Hill—named for fishing weirs used by the Nipmuc Native American tribe—with a series of steps, then

A NEW BOARDWALK ALONG THE RED MAPLE TRAIL

AN OBSERVATION PLATFORM ON THE SUDBURY RIVER

opens to a mostly flat hilltop. Up here, take care when you peer off of the steep ledge. Bear left to circle a kettle hole in the center of this land, formed 15,000 years ago by a receding glacier.

Another set of steps leads back down the hill, rewarding you with views of the Sudbury River through the trees on your way down. The trail then lets out at a canoe landing on the river, where you can glimpse sunfish, dragonflies, and a variety of bird species. (On my walk, I saw a Great Blue Heron.) Continue on to complete your hike, passing by the refuge headquarters on your way to the parking lot.

Hale Reservation

WHERE: Westwood	
ADDRESS: 80 Carby Street, Westwood, MA 02090	
TOTAL DISTANCE: 2 miles	
HIKING TIME: 1 hour	
ELEVATION GAIN: 100 feet	
DIFFICULTY: Easy	
RESTROOMS: Yes	
DOGS ALLOWED: Yes	
WHAT TO EXPECT: A family-friendly walk around a small pond	

Though Hale is a private nonprofit organization, its nearly 1,200 acres of woodlands are open for the public to explore. In addition to the day camps, educational programs, after-school programs, and event rentals it offers, Hale features more than 20 miles of trails for hiking.

The reservation was formed in 1918, when a man named Robert Sever Hale sought to set aside land to further his goal of providing education that would "develop intelligent, capable, and responsible citizens." He teamed up with the Boy Scouts of America to establish his organization, and today, the property continues to serve the children of Greater Boston.

Hale's property is excellent for families, thanks to its plentiful picnic tables and clean restrooms. While the trail featured here loops around Noanet Pond, be aware that if you'd like to swim in the pond, you'll have to obtain a $20 day pass from the reservation. Call ahead to secure a pass; availability is limited. A word of advice: If you take a dip before your hike, give yourself a good dousing of bug spray afterward.

GETTING THERE

From I-95, take exit 16B to merge onto Route 109, or High Street. Follow it for 1.2 miles, then turn right onto Dover Road. Follow it for 0.3 mile. Turn right again onto Carby Street. The reservation entrance is on the left. Pass the main office on the left and continue to the first paved parking area, also on the left.

THE HIKE

The easiest way to begin this hike around Noanet Pond is by parking at the Cat Rock parking lot. At the part of

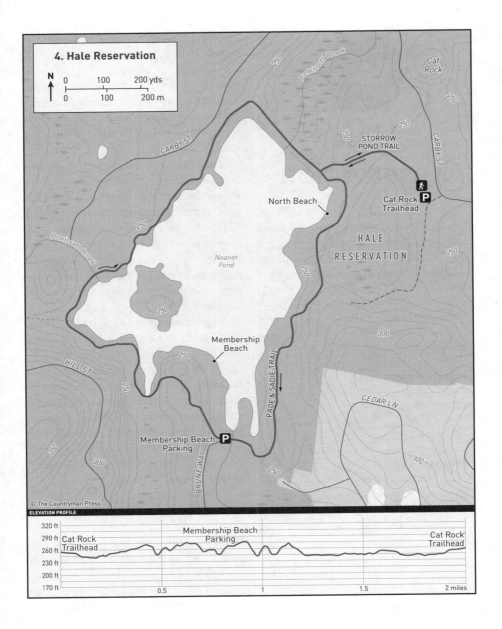

4. Hale Reservation

N
0   100   200 yds
0   100   200 m

Cat Rock

Powissett Brook

CARBY ST

STORROW
POND TRAIL

Cat Rock
Trailhead

North Beach

HALE
RESERVATION

Powissett Brook

Noanet
Pond

Membership
Beach

PAGE & SADIE TRAIL

CEDAR LN

HILL ST

Membership Beach
Parking

BRUNE WAY

© The Countryman Press

ELEVATION PROFILE

320 ft
290 ft — Cat Rock   Membership Beach   Cat Rock
260 ft   Trailhead   Parking   Trailhead
230 ft
200 ft
170 ft
                        0.5   1   1.5   2 miles

the lot nearest the road, there's a gate marking the beginning of the Storrow Pond trail (blue on the Hale Reservation trail map). Begin here, walking down the gravel path until you reach the Page & Sadie Trail by turning left. This is the trail you'll be following, and it is outlined in red on Hale's map. At the outset of the Page & Sadie Trail, walk along the lifeguarded beach to reach the woods. Throughout this hike, the trail will present you with two options: to walk near the water or to venture into the hillier woods above the shoreline. Both options

A BOARDWALK LEADS INTO THE WOODS

POWER LINES ALONG THE POND

are fairly close to one another, so it's up to you, whether you'd like to switch back and forth between a pondside stroll and a more woodsy one.

After a few minutes of walking along the pond, the path veers into the woods and continues uphill. Once you reach the top of the hill, exercise caution on your way back down, as the slope is clutched by roots and rocks. Rounding the next bend will lead you to another parking lot. This is not the end of your walk—simply cross the parking lot to the trail on the other side. It's a straight shot across the lot, so you won't be walking toward the pond here. Enter the trail to the left of the small outbuilding, then bear right. Follow the reservation's red rectangular markers on the trees as you choose between the coastal and hilly

routes. There's a picnic table at the crest of a small hill—a perfect halfway spot to stop for a snack. At the top of the next hill, ascend the stone steps and turn right, then head left to continue around the pond.

The trail then lets out at a paved road. Walk down the side of this road, passing over a small stream, then turn right off of the road and back onto the trail again. This section of the hike passes over several boardwalks and bridges, and past a stone bench. You'll pass by canoes from the Hale Reservation's day camp as you're about to complete your circle around the pond. The hike ends when the trail meets a stone pathway at the side of the pond. At the end of it, you'll see the blue marker to head back to the Cat Rock parking lot.

Mount Misery

WHERE: Lincoln

ADDRESS: 49–81 S. Great Road, (Route 117), Lincoln, MA 01773

TOTAL DISTANCE: 2 miles

HIKING TIME: 1 hour

ELEVATION GAIN: 211 feet

DIFFICULTY: Moderate

RESTROOMS: Yes

DOGS ALLOWED: Yes

WHAT TO EXPECT: A short trip along gently sloping, well-maintained trails

If you've flipped to this page in the hopes of reading about a challenging hike, keep flipping. Contrary to what its name suggests, there's nothing miserable about Lincoln's Mount Misery. In fact, it's not even a mountain—it's a glacially carved hill. Even so, the spot has been affectionately called Mount Misery since at least the mid 1800s.

Some of the earliest references can be found in the journals of Henry David Thoreau, who enjoyed hiking through the peaceful patches of woodland. (The hill is only about 2 miles from Walden Pond—see Hike #14—after all.) One of his Mount Misery entries describes the characteristics of milkweed seed pods in the area. It's the site's tranquil beauty that likely brought him here, as Mount Misery is a road-less-traveled sort of spot.

All 227 acres surrounding the hill are maintained by the Lincoln Conservation Commission, and they have been since 1969. The stretch of land beside the Sudbury River is home to a diverse range of wildlife, from muskrats and painted turtles in its ponds and streams to fairy shrimp and wood frogs in its vernal pools. Song sparrows, American woodcocks, foxes, and otters make a home of Mount Misery's open fields, while wood thrushes and oven birds nest in the large tracts of forest. Even the towering dead trees fallen along the trail provide homes for wildlife like raccoons, salamanders, and flying squirrels.

So why is it called Mount Misery? It's a bit of a mystery. An old newspaper clipping points to two local legends: In the first, a yoke of oxen escaped from a nearby farm in the late 1700s and got themselves stuck between trees. The pair apparently died there. The second legend says sheep grazing on the hill died after falling off of a rocky ledge.

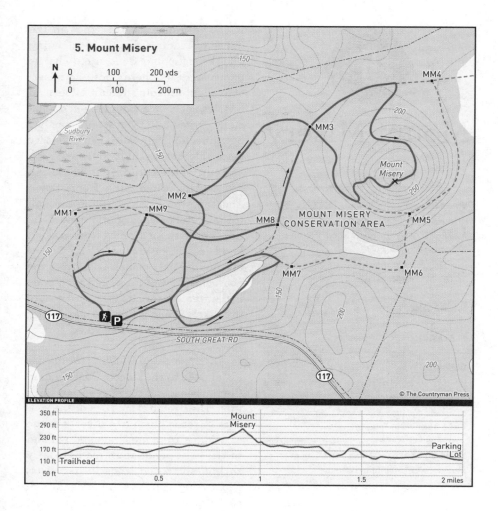

The best origin story, in my opinion, is the one you make up during the hike.

GETTING THERE

Beware of many Google Maps pitfalls if you are using a GPS to navigate. (If you do use Google Maps, "Mount Misery Parking Lot" is the destination you should choose.) From MA-2-W, turn left onto MA-126 S. After 2.4 miles, turn right onto MA-117 W. in Lincoln. The parking lot will be on your right.

THE HIKE

Kick off your visit to the summit of Mount Misery by entering the trail at the left-hand side of the parking lot. The wide dirt path makes for easy walking—that is, until you begin heading uphill. The climb is not steep but rather a steady incline, mixed with bouts of flat walking, that brings you to the top.

Turn right at the first intersection in the trail toward the yellow blazes. Although you've only just left the parking lot, it's peaceful here—the trails are not often crowded, and you're surrounded by oaks, hemlocks, and pines in all directions. At trail marker MM9, turn right again, then continue straight until you reach marker MM8. Here, take a left, continuing straight once more to arrive at MM3. Turn right to start your ascent to the summit, taking care to sidestep tree roots, rocks, and mushrooms.

Your calves may burn as you complete the relatively short walk to the top. (But nothing too miserable, right?) Once you're there, you'll notice there are no views to be had—just treetops in all directions. What looks to be a former foundation also tops Mount Misery, complete with stone cairns inside it.

Start down the path to the left of the former foundation to begin your descent to the base of the hill. At the bottom, turn right, admiring New England's

ubiquitous stone walls on your right and unending trees on your left. You'll arrive at MM3 once more, but instead of retracing your steps to the top of the mountain, continue straight through the sun-dappled woods. Power forward through the next intersection, too, following the red blazes. You'll happen upon a clearing here, dotted with several teepees made of sticks and branches. These structures are a highlight of a Mount Misery walk, warmly greeting visitors in every season.

When you're ready to continue, pick up the trail past the teepees. Then, where four paths meet up ahead, take the one that curves downward toward the pond poking through the trees. At the bottom of this gentle hill, take a right. You'll be circling this idyllic pond before heading back to the parking lot, which is also visible through the trees. Try as they might, the cars whizzing

GRADUAL INCLINES ARE DECEIVINGLY TOUGH TO CLIMB

TEEPEES AWAIT BESIDE MOUNT MISERY'S TRAILS

down Route 117 don't detract from this pond's beauty. When you reach a wooden footbridge in the path, turn left to continue tracing the pond's shores. You'll meet a gurgling runoff of the water before picking up the trail along the pond once more. Keep on this path until you reach the parking lot. You'll be spat out at the other end of the lot, where you began.

Mount Wachusett

WHERE: Princeton

ADDRESS: To reach the trailhead—rather than the visitor center—put "139–173 Westminster Road, Princeton, MA 01541" into your GPS.

TOTAL DISTANCE: 3 miles

HIKING TIME: 3 hours

ELEVATION GAIN: 825 feet

DIFFICULTY: Strenuous

RESTROOMS: No

DOGS ALLOWED: Yes

WHAT TO EXPECT: An exhilarating uphill climb that culminates with panoramic vistas

With over 3,000 acres of land and 17 miles of trails, Wachusett Mountain State Reservation is a land formation that begs to be explored. Its 2,006-foot peak is your hike's reward, offering sweeping views from the Berkshires to New Hampshire to the skyscrapers of Boston.

In addition to offering stunning vistas, the summit hosts an 80-foot steel fire tower and a radio relay station. But beginning in the 1870, the spot was home to a series of hotels. It all started when a man named William G. Morse began selling candy and cigars to hikers and tourists atop the mountain. Apparently, his customers were hungry for more than just views, so Morse built a hotel called the Summit House on this spot in 1870.

Just 14 years later, in 1884, business partners Phineas and Algernon Beaman bought the summit and decided to build a new hotel—a 30-room lodging open for business from May through October. According to the *Worcester Telegram & Gazette*, the place attracted 30,000 visitors per year until it burned down in 1907. The third and final hotel to top off the summit was built by a man named John Mirick. This one only had 14 rooms and closed in the 1930s. Mirick's building stood on the spot until December 1970, when it, too, succumbed to fire.

For your modern-day trip, stop at the visitor center at 345 Mountain Road to grab a map. During my hike, maps were not available, but there are abundant posters with trail information. Many of them have QR codes, so you may scan them with your phone to obtain a mobile map. While it's $5 for Massachusetts residents to park at the visitor center, the reservation's perimeter trails—like the one you'll be hiking—have small, free parking areas. In other words, your trip will be free of parking fees.

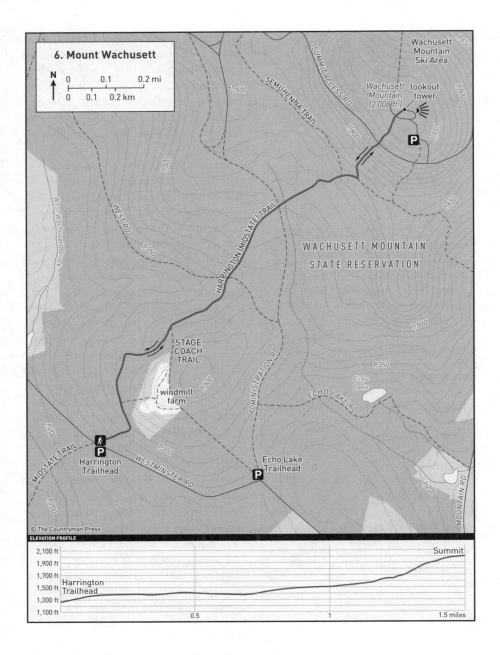

6. Mount Wachusett

N

| 0 | 0.1 | 0.2 mi |
| 0 | 0.1 | 0.2 km |

SEMUHENNA TRAIL

SUMMIT ACCESS RD.

Wachusett Mountain Ski Area

Wachusett Mountain (2,006 ft.)

lookout tower

1,650

1,800

1,850

1,800

1,650

West Wachusett Brook

WEST RD.

1,500

1,350

HARRINGTON (MIDSTATE) TRAIL

WACHUSETT MOUNTAIN STATE RESERVATION

1,500

1,350

STAGE COACH TRAIL

windmill farm

1,500

ADMINISTRATION RD.

Echo Lake

ECHO LAKE RD.

1,200

MIDSTATE TRAIL

Harrington Trailhead

1,350

WESTMINSTER RD.

Echo Lake Trailhead

1,200

MOUNTAIN RD.

1,200

© The Countryman Press

ELEVATION PROFILE

2,100 ft			Summit
1,900 ft			
1,700 ft			
1,500 ft	Harrington		
1,300 ft	Trailhead		
1,100 ft	0.5	1	1.5 miles

GETTING THERE

Follow MA-2 W. toward MA- 140-S. in Westminster. When you reach a traffic circle in Concord, take the fourth exit onto MA-111 N. and MA-2 W. Follow it for almost 30 miles, until you take exit 25 toward MA-2A and MA-140 S. toward Westminster and Princeton. Continue on MA-140 for almost 8 miles, then turn right to stay on MA-140. After 2.4 miles, turn right onto Mile Hill Road. Continue onto Mountain Road after 2.6 miles, then take a sharp right onto Westminster Road. The trail will appear on your right after about a mile.

THE HIKE

As one of Wachusett Mountain's most popular ways up, Harrington Trail is a favorite among park rangers and avid hikers alike. It's also the longest up-and-back hike to the summit, switching between gradual inclines and steep, rocky ascents. To begin, park your car near the Harrington Trailhead, just beyond the gates of the Echo Lake Trailhead on Westminster Road. The entrance to the trail is clearly marked with a brown-and-white sign.

Your journey starts with a bracing climb up a short hill, as you follow the trail's red blazes. It gets your heart pumping before the path levels out, meandering under the cool shade of the trees. This part of the hike serves as a good warm-up for the exhilarating ascent that awaits, as well as a welcome cool-down on your way back to your car.

When you reach a stone wall that lies across the trail, turn left. Here, you'll notice yellow triangular blazes beneath the red ones. These indicate a portion of the Midstate Trail. Continue to follow the red blazes as you sidestep the pointed rocks and thick tree roots that grip the dirt trail. You'll bypass a spur trail leading to a windmill farm. Though it's not included in the mileage of the hike outline here, it's a fun little detour.

At the STAGE COACH TRAIL sign, continue straight. Do the same when you meet the gravel path that is West Road. This trail, like many of the others leading the way to the summit, cross paved roads at points, because visitors are permitted to drive to the summit. Take care when crossing roads like West Road and the upcoming Administration Road. Both cars and bikes will whiz by.

Several footbridges along the way cross small streams. But the type of easy walking a wooden footbridge

A RADIO RELAY STATION

THE VIEW FROM THE TOP

invites won't be available for much longer. Once you pass the sign for the Semuhenna Trail, a scramble to the top begins. Climb up a rocky path toward a trail sign with a map. Turn left here, following the red blazes to the summit. You may need to use your arms and legs to hoist yourself up the rocks at this point. It's quite steep and well worth the effort. When you meet the next paved road, you'll know you're almost there. Take a breather, then stay left to keep on the Harrington Trail. Climb up the boulders once more to reach a rocky clearing, which leads to the summit.

Ah, the summit. Here, you'll find a fire tower, a radio relay station, some viewing areas, signal towers, the ski lift for Wachusett Mountain Ski Area, and a parking lot for car-climbers. The steel lookout tower was built in 2014 to replace a 1966 fire tower. When it was constructed, improvements were made to the summit to enhance visitor experience. You will now find expanded parking and clearly marked pedestrian walkways. The radio relay station, meanwhile, is used by the US Army Corps of Engineers to relay communications to flood control projects across New England.

But enough about the structures atop Wachusett Mountain—it's the views you came here for. As you stand straddling eastern and western Massachusetts, you'll catch glimpses of both from the panoramic vistas unfolding in front of you. To the west, there's Mount Greylock in the Berkshires. It's a whopping 65 miles away, but you can't miss its 3,487-foot peak, the tallest in the state. Yet 50 miles in the opposite direction, the skyscrapers of Boston rise in the distance. Between these two markers, you'll lay eyes on Mount Monadnock in New Hampshire, as well as shorter peaks surrounding it, plus Vermont's Green Mountains.

After you make a tally of the peaks in the distance you'd like to hike, find the HARRINGTON TRAIL sign to head back down the same way you came.

Mount Watatic

WHERE: Ashburnham

ADDRESS: Rindge State Road, Ashburnham, MA 01430

TOTAL DISTANCE: 3 miles

HIKING TIME: 2.5 hours

ELEVATION GAIN: 690 feet

DIFFICULTY: Strenuous

RESTROOMS: No

DOGS ALLOWED: Yes

WHAT TO EXPECT: A short, steady climb to a beautiful mountaintop, then a more leisurely gradual descent

Mount Watatic is a monadnock, defined as a rocky hill or small mountain rising from a mostly level surrounding landscape. (For those thinking of Mount Monadnock in New Hampshire, a "monadnock" is a type of land formation, as well as the name of the Jaffrey, New Hampshire peak that lies less than 20 miles north of Watatic.) The 1,832-foot mountain is one of the highest east of Massachusetts' Connecticut River, making for one of the most invigorating hikes in this book.

This mountain is also not far from Mount Wachusett (see Hike #6), and until the 1980s, it was a similarly popular ski destination in northeastern Massachusetts. Many think that beginning in the 1930s, a rope tow was used to ferry skiers up the mountain. It wasn't until 1964, however, that a company called Mt. Watatic, Inc. was formed. For its opening season in 1965, the company installed a T-bar lift, rope tows, and two trails.

Later, in the 1970s, snowmaking began, and according to NewEngland SkiHistory.com, Watatic billed itself as the "largest night skiing area in Eastern Massachusetts." Double chairlifts eventually replaced those rope tows, and during warmer months, the area became a lively concert venue. The ski area closed down during the 1982–1983 season, in part because of the success of nearby Wachusett Mountain as a ski destination. There was an effort to reopen in the park in the late 1980s, but it did not succeed, due to a lack of funding. In 1997, the remaining buildings at the base of the mountain burned down.

Mount Watatic is still a beloved destination for outdoor lovers; its miles of

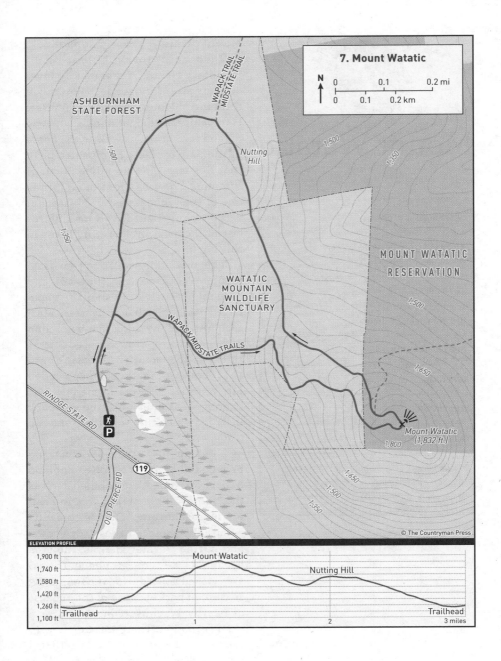

7. Mount Watatic

ASHBURNHAM
STATE FOREST

Nutting
Hill

WAPACK TRAIL
MIDSTATE TRAIL

MOUNT WATATIC
RESERVATION

WATATIC
MOUNTAIN
WILDLIFE
SANCTUARY

WAPACK/MIDSTATE TRAILS

WAPACK/MIDSTATE TRAILS

RINDGE STATE RD.

119

OLD PIERCE RD.

Mount Watatic
(1,832 ft.)

© The Countryman Press

N

0   0.1   0.2 mi
0   0.1   0.2 km

ELEVATION PROFILE

1,900 ft	Mount Watatic			
1,740 ft			Nutting Hill	
1,580 ft				
1,420 ft				
1,260 ft				
1,100 ft	Trailhead			Trailhead
		1	2	3 miles

trails are maintained by the town of Ashby. The spot is also often visited by bird-watchers, being one of the most popular spots for hawk observation in the Northeast.

GETTING THERE

From Route 2 W., take the Abbott Avenue exit in Leominster. Continue on Abbott Avenue, then merge onto Water Street.

Make a quick right onto Bemis Road, and after a half mile, a slight right onto John Fitch Highway. Follow it for 2.9 miles until you reach a traffic circle, where you'll continue straight onto Rindge Road. Follow the Rindge Turnpike for almost 7 miles, then turn right onto Route 101 N. After 0.2 mile, turn left onto Route 119 W., and then drive 1.4 miles until you see the parking lot on the right.

THE HIKE

There aren't maps available at the trailhead marker toward the end of the parking lot, so you'll have to rely on signs and blazes alone during this trip. Right off the bat, you'll see a sign stating that it's only 1.1 miles to Mount Watatic's summit. Save some of your energy, though, as you'll hike about another 2 miles to loop back. For the duration of the trip, follow the yellow triangular trail markers.

The hike begins with a wide dirt trail, which narrows as you enter into a swampy area with a pond. Cross a few wooden boards over a small dam, then enter into an evergreen forest. The climb to the top begins here, with rocky paths and tree root-stepped ledges leading the way. As you forge ahead, you'll use stepping stones to cross a vigorously flowing brook. Then, you'll pass through the middle of a rock that appears to have been split in two. Keep using the jagged rocks and roots to clamber up the mountain, and take breaks to gaze up at the smooth rock face in front of you every now and again.

Soon, a stone wall will appear in front of you, and you'll be reminded of

NO SUMMIT IS COMPLETE WITHOUT A CAIRN

FROM THE TOP, SEE LAND FORMATIONS IN ALL DIRECTIONS

the tireless work the early colonists did to build these. (It's estimated that if all of New England's stone walls were laid out, end to end, they'd circle the globe four times.) Turn right to walk along this wall. Peer over to the other side of the stone wall to see flowering shrubs and plants on the rocks. There's a stark contrast between the two sides—the far side of the stone wall shows what the trail might look like if it weren't constantly being trampled by human feet. Soon, you'll reach a flat area with a cairn and a memorial stone. This isn't the summit just yet, but a peek over the treetops gives a preview of the display of natural beauty that's to come. Continue through the forest, keeping an eye out for blueberry bushes. Once you emerge from the dense forest into a more open area, you'll know you're almost there. One small hill opens to the summit, which boasts views of the Green Mountains in Vermont and the peaks of southern New Hampshire. On a clear day, Boston can be seen in the east, along with the quiet surrounding towns near it. Farms, mountains, hills, and a fire tower lie before you, as the wind whistles. Don't miss the granite monument atop the mountain, which commemorates the area's protection by the state of Massachusetts in 2002. Thanks to the thoughtful people of Ashby and Ashburnham, developers can't wreak havoc on the beautiful spot.

To begin your gradual descent back to the parking lot, continue to follow the yellow blazes until you see a sign that reads WAPACK TRAIL, SOUTH TO 119. This is where you want to go. Head down the hill until you meet a gravel path. Here, there's another sign that says ACCESS ROAD, pointing down this travel path. Don't take it—this is not the trail.

Instead, pick back up to the left to the sign, on the more narrow trail marked by those trusty yellow blazes.

Immediately, it's less rocky here, and less tiresome, too. The steady decline is greener and mossier than the first part of the hike, yet it still crisscrosses some of the area's time-honored stone walls. Not long after leaving the summit, you'll reach the top of Nutting Hill. There are not many views to be had here, just glimpses of treetops. There is, however, a lovely stillness to this place. Soak in the silence before continuing on. A walk along smooth rocks transitions to a dirt trail again, leading all the way down to where you first began the loop up to the summit. Follow the series of signs pointing toward the parking lot. You'll leave the course of the Midstate Trail to walk out the way you walked in, crossing once again over the wooden boards near the pond. Arrive at your car, mere feet from here.

Noanet Woodlands

WHERE: Dover

ADDRESS: Powissett Street, Dover

TOTAL DISTANCE: 2.75 miles

HIKING TIME: 1 hour 30 minutes

ELEVATION GAIN: 343 feet

DIFFICULTY: Moderate

RESTROOMS: Yes

DOGS ALLOWED: Yes

WHAT TO EXPECT: A fairly easy hike with an extremely high reward: panoramic vistas all the way to the Boston skyline

Urbanites in search of leafy solace might consider the Noanet Woodlands in Dover a hidden gem—after all, the Trustees-owned property is only 16 miles outside the city. Locals know better, though, and they tend to get there early, before the 30-car parking lot fills up. Nevertheless, city slickers and Dover residents alike have one person to thank for their suburban outdoor recreation: Amelia Peabody.

Born in 1890, Peabody was chiefly an artist and philanthropist, but she wore many hats. In the 1920s, she began to buy up farms in Dover, including nearby Powissett Farm and the land where Noanet Woodlands now stands. She raised thoroughbred horses, Yorkshire pigs, and Hereford cattle on her land throughout her lifetime. Peabody was also a skilled sculptor, and she studied at the School of the Museum of Fine Arts. Her works were exhibited around the world, including at the 1939 and 1940 New York World's Fairs, the Whitney Museum of American Art, and the Boston Athenaeum.

Over the next 60 years, Peabody continued to acquire farmland in Dover until she amassed an 800-acre estate. She helped establish bridle paths and cross-country skiing trails for public enjoyment, and in 1954, she funded the renovation of the Old Iron Mill dam on her land—a site you'll be able to see during your trip. Upon her death in 1984, Peabody retained her generous nature in her will by donating her estate to the New England Wildflower Society and the Trustees of Reservations. Your walk through the Noanet Woodlands wouldn't be possible without her.

GETTING THERE

From MA-109 in Westwood, turn onto Dover Road. Follow it for 1.5 miles, and

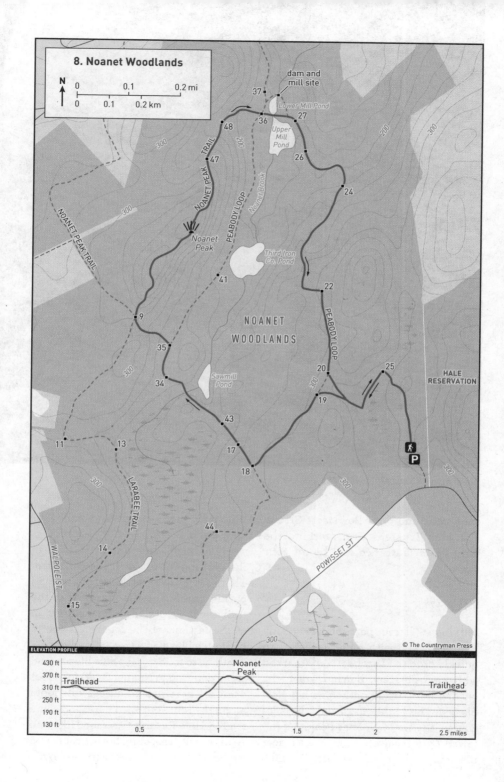

8. Noanet Woodlands

N

| 0 | 0.1 | 0.2 mi |
| 0 | 0.1 | 0.2 km |

dam and
mill site

37

Lower Mill Pond

36   27

48

Upper
Mill
Pond

47   26

NOANET PEAK TRAIL

24

PEABODY LOOP

Noanet Brook

NOANET PEAK TRAIL

Noanet
Peak

Third Iron
Co. Pond

41

22

9

NOANET
WOODLANDS

PEABODY LOOP

35

34

Sawmill
Pond

20   25

19

HALE
RESERVATION

43

11   13

17

LARABEE TRAIL

18

44

14

POWISSET ST

WALPOLE ST

15

300

© The Countryman Press

ELEVATION PROFILE

430 ft		Noanet Peak		
370 ft	Trailhead			Trailhead
310 ft				
250 ft				
190 ft				
130 ft	0.5	1	1.5	2 2.5 miles

LOWER MILL POND AND UPPER MILL POND

then continue onto Powissett Street. The blue Trustees sign marking the parking lot entrance will be on your right.

THE HIKE

This hike will trace parts of the Peabody Loop (marked with blue blazes), turn quickly onto the Larabee Trail (marked with orange blazes), then move on to the Noanet Peak Trail (marked with yellow blazes). The highlight of the trip is, of course, the tip of Noanet Peak. It's followed by a leisurely stroll past a scenic pond and former mill site. The hike concludes on the eastern end of the Peabody Loop.

Head past the ranger station in the parking lot to reach the trailhead. There's a port-a-potty in this second parking area, and the entrance to the trail is just beyond the information sign at the far end of the lot. You'll spot a light blue blaze on a tree immediately—continue to follow these blue blazes (and signs pointing to Noanet Peak) for about a mile. There are countless offshoots along the route outlined here, and some lead to Hale Reservation (see Hike #4). A hike crisscrossing both properties would make a fabulous day trip in Dover.

Larabee Trail. I opted to stay on the Peabody Loop, tracing a short stone wall past trail markers 17 and 43. Large rocks poke out of the gravel here, so don't walk and take notes about the trail at the same time, for example.

Keep left at the fork ahead, then turn left again at the T-shaped intersection just beyond it. Once you see trail marker 34 on the left hand side of the trail, turn right, and then take a quick left for an extremely brief trip along a portion of the orange-blazed Larabee Trail. Mounting these man-made steps is the beginning of your ascent to the main event: Noanet Peak. Your heart rate will pick up here, both in anticipation and from exertion. Turn right at the next sign pointing toward Noanet Peak, and then at trail marker 9, turn right again, up a steep, rocky trail. You'll know you're on the right track if you see a small NO BIKING sign spurting out of the middle of the trail. A yellow blaze on the tree confirms you've made it to the Noanet Peak trail.

Pine needles and tree roots cover the incline that leads to the peak. A glacial erratic on the right side of the path waves you forward. As anticipation mounts, your arrival to Noanet Peak may feel sudden. Without warning, the trail opens onto a gorgeous panorama. Take a seat on the flat rock face underfoot to take in stunning views of the surrounding woodlands. On a clear day, you can spot the buildings of the Boston skyline to the north. The peak is one of the most Insta-worthy spots in this book, so please do snap a pic.

When you're finished basking in the glory at the end of that reasonably easy climb, head down the other side of the peak—it's marked by another yellow blaze. Take a quick right to stay on the Noanet Peak trail, or risk heading down one of the "other trails" indicated

The wide dirt path you're walking along soon crosses a small wooden boardwalk built over a brook. At the end of the boardwalk, turn right and follow the sign pointing toward Noanet Peak. The trail becomes even wider here, laid with gravel to make for easy walking. Turn right to stay within the boundaries of the property, and then at the next intersection, keep left. You'll notice the trails are clearly marked not only with blazes, but with helpful signs and numbered markers, too. Keep following the blue blazes to trail number number 18, then turn right. If you'd like to extend your hike by 1.5 miles, you could continue straight onto the orange-blazed

NOANET PEAK IS ONLY SEVERAL MILES FROM BOSTON

on the Trustees' map. Like your ascent, the descent is relatively gradual. Take care to sidestep the sharp rocks puncturing the trail, then continue a leisurely walk toward Lower Mill Pond and Upper Mill Pond. When you spot a cellar hole through the trees on your left, you'll know you've almost made it.

The clearing in the distance comes into view as two charmingly scenic ponds. The one on your left, Lower Mill Pond, was dammed in 1815 to power a mill for Dover Union Iron Company. It boasted one of the largest mill wheels of its kind in all of New England, and spun day in and day out to help manufacture nails and barrel hoops.

Dover Union Iron dissolved shortly after in 1840, and the dam and mill fell into disrepair. Over a century later, in 1954, landowner Amelia Peabody hired an archaeologist to excavate the site and rebuild the dam. (You can walk to the other side of the pond to inspect the restored dam and still pick up the Peabody Loop to get back.)

If you'd rather not loop around Lower Mill Pond, head straight past the trail marker 36 sign and over the land bridge between the two ponds. You'll spot a stone marker celebrating the 100th anniversary of the Trustees of Reservations. To finish your hike, walk toward the tree with both the blue and red blazes on it, and at markers 27 and 26, continue straight on the blue Peabody Loop trail. You'll cross a few rolling, rocky hills—and bypass a handful of large boulders—before reaching marker 20. Keep straight here. Instead of taking your first right, keep going to veer left. The boardwalk you crossed on your way here beckons you back to the parking lot. Follow the remainder of the blue-blazed trail until you reach it.

9

Noon Hill

WHERE: Medfield

ADDRESS: 170 Noonhill Road, Medfield, MA 02052

TOTAL DISTANCE: 1.8 miles

HIKING TIME: 45 minutes to 1 hour

ELEVATION GAIN: 229 feet

DIFFICULTY: Moderate

RESTROOMS: No

DOGS ALLOWED: Yes

WHAT TO EXPECT: A relatively short, smooth walk up to a scenic hilltop

Like much of the region's mostly undisturbed natural environments, Noon Hill's landscape was carved by glacial movements thousands of years ago. Case in point? The smooth bedrock that tops the hill's ridges. You can picture how a massive glacier imprinted those depressions.

This trail, managed by the Trustees, is a link in the Bay Circuit Trail, though it's a great all-season hike on its own. Because the hike is short and relatively easy, it makes for an invigorating winter jaunt. In springtime, notice the wildflowers flanking the trail, including Canada mayflower and lady slippers, and hear migratory birds singing sweet songs. And in autumn, watch leaves fall from the birch and beech trees there. If you're lucky, you might spot a red fox, a raccoon, a ruffed grouse, or a white-tailed deer.

GETTING THERE

From I-95, take exit 16B. Stay on Route 109 W. for about 1.5 miles. Turn right onto Hartford Street and continue for 3.7 miles. Then take a slight right back onto Route 109, or Main Street, to pass through Medfield's charming downtown. After passing Noon Hill Grill and a Cumberland Farms gas station, take a left onto Causeway Street. Follow it for about a mile until you reach Noon Hill Road. Turn left. The parking lot and the trailhead are on the right.

THE HIKE

Begin your ascension to the 370-foot summit of Noon Hill by passing the trailhead marker just beyond the parking lot. Grab a map from the Trustees' information board—on this hike, you'll trace part of the Yellow Loop for a time,

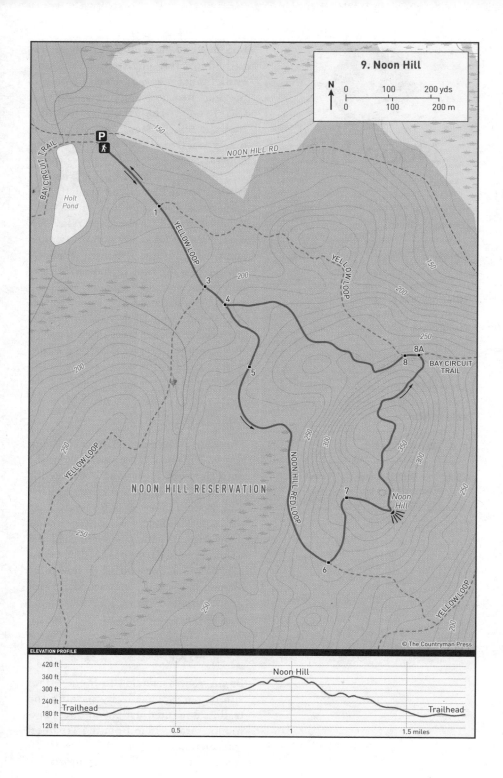

9. Noon Hill

N

| 0 | 100 | 200 yds |
| 0 | 100 | 200 m |

NOON HILL RD

BAY CIRCUIT TRAIL

Holt Pond

150

YELLOW LOOP

1

3

4

200

YELLOW LOOP

250

8A

8

BAY CIRCUIT TRAIL

150

200

5

NOON HILL RED LOOP

250

300

350

300

Noon Hill

250

YELLOW LOOP

200

7

NOON HILL RESERVATION

250

250

6

YELLOW LOOP

© The Countryman Press

ELEVATION PROFILE

420 ft		Noon Hill	
360 ft			
300 ft			
240 ft			
180 ft	Trailhead		Trailhead
120 ft			
	0.5	1	1.5 miles

then turn onto the Noon Hill Red Loop. On your descent from the summit, you'll have the choice between heading back down the Red Trail or the remainder of the Yellow Loop.

The hike along the Noon Hill Red Loop starts with an easy, flat walk. Notice former cellar holes and existing stone walls on your stroll. Once you arrive at trail junction marker 4, you have the choice to either head right or left to begin the Red Loop. For no reason in particular, I went right.

If you do the same, you'll cross a footbridge over seasonal wetlands. The trail then leads upward, passing through groves of American beech and pine trees. The relatively short walk meanders up and around the hill until you reach a set of steps. Ascend the steps,

A PORTION OF ROCKY TRAIL

THE TOP OF NOON HILL

and then turn left to reach the lookout point atop Noon Hill. Here, you'll find a stone bench and impressive treetop views of nearby Walpole and Norfolk. That large circular clearing in the distance is Gillette Stadium, home of the New England Patriots. And next to it, the land slopes toward the Charles River.

The way back down makes for more easy walking. Simply follow the red blazes that lead gently downhill. When you reach trail marker 8A, turn left. Then, turn left again at 8 to stay on the Red Loop. (If you'd prefer to extend your hike, you can keep right onto the Yellow Loop—it also leads back to the parking lot.) Keep along the Red Loop until you reach marker 4 once again. From here, you can retrace your steps back to the parking lot.

10

Purgatory Chasm State Reservation

WHERE: Sutton	
ADDRESS: 198 Purgatory Road, Sutton, MA 01590	
TOTAL DISTANCE: 2.3 miles	
HIKING TIME: 1.5 hours	
ELEVATION GAIN: 190 feet	
DIFFICULTY: Strenuous	
RESTROOMS: Yes	
DOGS ALLOWED: Yes	
WHAT TO EXPECT: An easy walk through a rocky forest, followed by a risky climb through a ravine	

Purgatory Chasm is one of the most unique land formations in Massachusetts. Legend says that's thanks to the devil.

A Native American devil known as Hobomko was said to have created the rocky fissure after he punished an Algonquin woman there for killing a white colonial man. After he carried the woman to the spot, she began to fight back, so Hobomko slammed her head against a large boulder and struck her with his tomahawk. Accordingly, the deep depressions in the rocks represent the places where the woman's head hit the boulders, and the slices show where the tomahawk came down.

Historians know that Purgatory Chasm was really created by dammed-up glacial meltwaters that suddenly gave way and gushed through the rocks. They also know that legend was a tool in the colonists' efforts to convert Native Americans to Christianity. The legend created a gruesome lesson from the woman's murder at the hands of the devil, and it was meant to lure native people to their faith.

Though Hobomko is nowhere to be seen at Purgatory, established as a state park in 1919, the reservation is still extremely dangerous. Almost a dozen people have died there since it became a park, from able-bodied hikers to inexperienced college students. Countless others, meanwhile, have had to be rescued from the depths of the chasm. It goes without saying that hikers should use extreme caution here. Wear sturdy shoes and keep your hands free for climbing.

GETTING THERE

Despite the danger that lies within Purgatory Chasm, it's an extremely popular

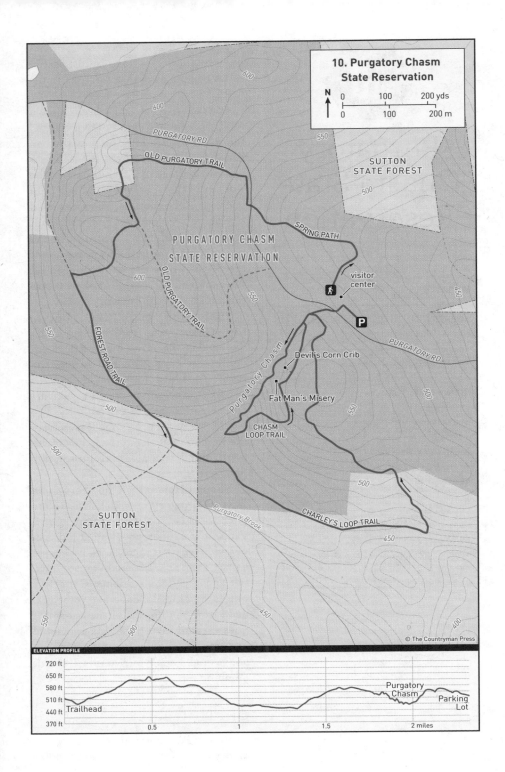

10. Purgatory Chasm State Reservation

N

| 0 | 100 | 200 yds |
| 0 | 100 | 200 m |

PURGATORY RD

OLD PURGATORY TRAIL

SUTTON STATE FOREST

PURGATORY CHASM STATE RESERVATION

SPRING PATH

600

OLD PURGATORY TRAIL

550

visitor center

P

PURGATORY RD

FOREST ROAD TRAIL

Purgatory Chasm

Devil's Corn Crib

Fat Man's Misery

CHASM LOOP TRAIL

500

Purgatory Brook

SUTTON STATE FOREST

CHARLEY'S LOOP TRAIL

450

400

© The Countryman Press

ELEVATION PROFILE

| 720 ft |
| 650 ft |
| 580 ft |
| 510 ft |
| 440 ft |
| 370 ft |

Trailhead

Purgatory Chasm

Parking Lot

0.5   1   1.5   2 miles

DO YOU DARE ENTER FAT MAN'S MISERY?

hangout for hikers and picnickers alike. Get there early by taking the Mass Pike, or I-90, into Worcester. Get off at exit 10A near Route 146, then ride the highway to Sutton. Take exit 6 for Purgatory Road, and after half a mile, turn right onto Purgatory Road. A $5 parking fee is collected in the reservation's parking lots.

THE HIKE

This hike has been cobbled together from a series of trails circling the chasm. I chose to warm up by hiking around the rocks first, then I embarked on the Chasm Loop Trail second. Of course, you can feel free to explore the reservation's trails in any order you like, given that the longest one is only a mile. But for a longer walk followed by an invigorating climb, follow these instructions.

First, grab a map from the visitor center, so you can see the labeled trails. As an overview, we'll be starting along Spring Path, then connecting to Old Purgatory Trail, Forest Road Trail, and Charley's Loop. At the end of Charley's Loop, we'll turn into the chasm via the Chasm Loop Trail, for the second part of the hike.

Begin by picking up Spring Path behind the visitor center. It starts as a paved walkway, and winds past a vernal pool and a spring house, a small stone structure built in 1926. The trail then heads uphill. When you see a sign pointing left for the continuation of Spring Path, don't follow it. Instead, continue straight to reach a connecting trail. Walk past a park outbuilding and up a gravel driveway, then cross the road to begin the next leg of your journey: Old Purgatory Trail. Bear right to start along this

THE CHASM

next trail, following orange blazes on the trees. Here, the hike becomes more moderate in difficulty as you creep farther into the woods. Use the abundant rocks littering the ground as stepping stones as you climb up and down the hilly landscape. When you see a sign marking the continuation of Old Purgatory Trail, turn right instead. You'll descend a rocky ledge down to the forest floor as you make your way to the Forest Road Trail. Another left and the trail flattens out into a gravel road. Catch your breath here before turning onto Charley's Loop, a dirt path marked with yellow blazes. Here, admire the rocks on either side of the trail—the stacks of flat slabs resemble plates of pancakes. In springtime, keep an eye out for wild violets growing near the path. You'll soon see the chasm to your left, offering a glimpse of what you'll be climbing into in just a few minutes. Charley's Loop ends across from the visitor center parking lot, but you'll want to turn left to begin part two: the Chasm Loop Trail.

While the Chasm Loop Trail is surprisingly short—it's only half a mile long—it's highly treacherous. Use extreme caution when climbing rocks and peering over ledges. The trail is dangerous, and over the years, several hikers have died from falls into the chasm. Make sure your hiking boots are tied and belongings are secured before you begin.

Start the second part of your hike by following the blue blazes. Almost immediately, you'll have to use all four limbs to make your way through the chasm's crevices and down into the ravine. A wooden boardwalk waits at the bottom of it. Cross it over a gurgling brook, and rest easy for a moment. The trail tapers off here, becoming temporarily less treacherous. Massive flat rock faces greet you on your right, donning an impressive display of moss and lichen. Turn right to traverse another boardwalk, then scramble up a rocky hill to make your way back to the top of the chasm. Treetop views of the forest, as well as the chasm, await you up here. Take a short detour to experience Fat Man's Misery, an extremely narrow crevice you're invited to squeeze your way through—if you are brave enough, that is. (Full disclosure: The author was not brave enough.) To enter, inch down a steep ledge into the claustrophobia-inducing cavern and emerge from the other side with a newfound appreciation for the wide-open spaces this book has introduced you to. Just beyond this landmark, there's another point of interest called the Devil's Corn Crib. It's another narrow passageway, albeit a less frightening one. All of the rock formations and their cheeky nicknames are worth checking out if time allows.

The exit to the parking lot is easy enough to find as you continue to follow the blue blazes. Don't let your guard down as you scramble up and down the rocks. Injuries, and incredible rocky views, are around every corner.

Rocky Woods

WHERE: Medfield	

ADDRESS: Rocky Woods Reservation
Entrance, Hartford Street, Medfield, MA
02052

TOTAL DISTANCE: 2 miles

HIKING TIME: 1 hour

ELEVATION GAIN: 140 feet

DIFFICULTY: Easy

RESTROOMS: Yes

DOGS ALLOWED: Yes

WHAT TO EXPECT: A journey through
diverse landscapes, from an invigorating
woodsy walk to a pondside stroll

Former logging roads crisscross this Trustees of Reservation–owned property known as Rocky Woods. Beginning in the 1700s, colonial settlers started to clear the land here, reaping timber from its plentiful forests and in turn birthing a burgeoning timber industry. Later, those same logging roads were used to transport granite from a quarry within the reservation, cut from the land's sharp granite ledges.

While the rugged terrain of Rocky Woods can be attributed to glacial movement during the last Ice Age, its six ponds are a more recent addition. They were carved into the landscape as a safety precaution for the growing logging industry. The threat of fire always loomed in the dry woods, so the ponds' water could thwart blazes whenever necessary.

Aside from a healthy logging industry, the surrounding area was home to several mills. Rocky Woods' adjoining property, Fork Factory Brook, was the site of a series of steel mills. They mainly forged pitchforks, hence its name.

Today, Rocky Woods is part of the Charles River Valley Management Area. The Trustees allow dogs on the trails within the 491-acre property. Families hiking with kids can rent out "adventure backpacks" free of charge from the Rocky Woods Ranger station. Available on weekends, each backpack contains binoculars, a magnifying glass, a field guide, a bug box, and a few other goodies.

GETTING THERE

From I-95, take exit 16B. Stay on Route 109 W. for almost 6 miles. Turn right onto Hartford Street, and proceed for about 3 miles until you reach a tree-lined road with stone walls. You'll see a blue

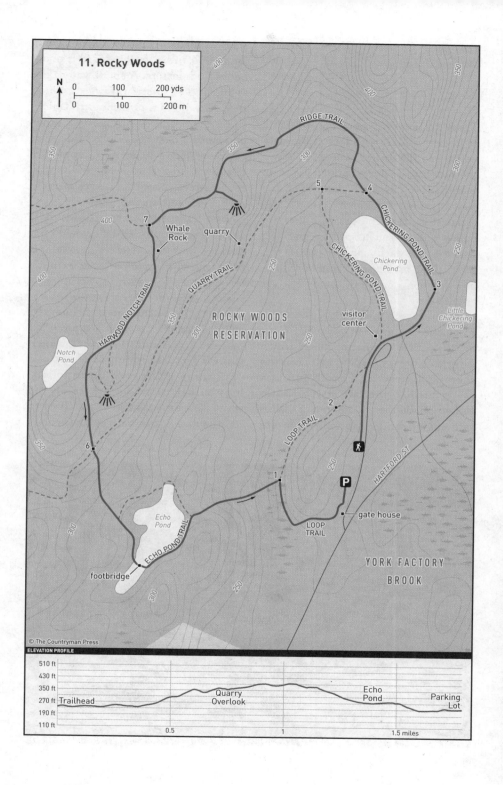

11. Rocky Woods

N

0   100   200 yds
0   100   200 m

RIDGE TRAIL

CHICKERING POND TRAIL

7

Whale Rock   quarry

QUARRY TRAIL

HARWOOD NOTCH TRAIL

ROCKY WOODS
RESERVATION

5   4

Chickering
Pond

Little
Chickering
Pond

3

CHICKERING POND TRAIL

visitor
center

Notch
Pond

2

LOOP TRAIL

6

P

1

Echo
Pond

LOOP
TRAIL

ECHO POND TRAIL

footbridge

gate house

HARTFORD ST

YORK FACTORY
BROOK

© The Countryman Press

ELEVATION PROFILE

510 ft			
430 ft			
350 ft		Quarry	Echo
270 ft	Trailhead	Overlook	Pond	Parking
190 ft				Lot
110 ft			

0.5   1   1.5 miles

Trustees sign marking the entrance to the parking lot.

THE HIKE

There is plentiful parking available at Rocky Woods, with lots at the gate house and the visitor center. However, the Trustees of Reservations requests that visitors pay $5 for a parking day pass. Trustees members, meanwhile, can park for free. A kiosk near the gate house allows you to print a parking pass for your dashboard—members can input their member ID number while non-members can pay the $5 fee via credit card.

After paying and parking near the gate house, I started my hike by following the path to the visitor center, which is set on a grassy playing field near the shores of Chickering Pond. Restrooms are located to the left of the visitor center. Inside the log cabin-like visitor center and ranger station, there are small exhibits about the Rocky Woods landscape, with a variety of kid-friendly books and posters. A small water tank is home to an Eastern Newt—of which there are hundreds in nearby Chickering Pond and the property's other ponds—and beside it, a bluebird's nest can be seen on display. Just beyond the exhibition area, a wood stove with surrounding seating warms hikers on chilly spring and autumn mornings.

Exit the visitor center to follow a short trail around Chickering Pond. After a few hundred feet, a small platform with a picnic table extends toward the pond, allowing for a quick snack break before entering the woods. Continue following the trail—marked as Red Trail on the Trustees' provided map—to arrive at trail marker 4, which signals the beginning of the Ridge Trail. Take a right and begin following the yellow trail markers on the white pine and oak trees. Living up to its namesake, the path in the woods

WHALE ROCK

MUCH OF ROCKY WOODS IS FLAT WALKING

soon becomes rocky, indeed. Notice the small brook cascading over rocks to your right, then cross over the water to continue up the trail. Then enter a shady area, formerly part of the quarry. Once several huge boulders come into view, take a left around the bend, then make your way up a small hill. A path veering left leads to the trail's first lookout. Follow it for a few feet to see the quarry. Turn around and head back down the run-off path to get back onto the Ridge Trail.

The next landmark makes itself visible about 500 feet further, just after trail marker 7, which signals the transition to the Harwood Notch Trail. A long, smooth boulder called Whale Rock beckons you to climb it. Use caution, and your hands, to help you reach the top. It offers a similar view of the quarry. Further down the Harwood Notch Trail, there's the option to take a short detour to another lookout point. The short loop's vantage point frames treetop views of the woods, but

nothing more. To get back onto the trail, take a left when you reach the small pond and admire the rock formations to your left and right until you arrive at trail marker 6.

Trail marker 6 marks the beginning of the Echo Pond Trail. There is a detour on this section of the yellow loop, thanks to the pond's busy beaver population. The beavers caused Echo Pond's water levels to rise over the trail's footbridge, so the leisurely walk down to the pond becomes a bit strenuous once you reach the out-of-service bridge. The detour is not clearly marked, but as long as you traipse close to the water's edge, you'll reach the other side of the pond where the foot bridge would have let you out. The trail then splits. You can either turn left to continue along the yellow trail back to the visitor center, or turn right to head to the gate house. I headed to the gate house, veering left once more to reach the information board in the parking lot.

Stony Brook Wildlife Sanctuary

WHERE: Norfolk	
ADDRESS: 108 North Street, Norfolk, MA 02056	
TOTAL DISTANCE: 0.6 mile	
HIKING TIME: 30 minutes	
ELEVATION GAIN: 30 feet	
DIFFICULTY: Easy	
RESTROOMS: Yes	
DOGS ALLOWED: No	
WHAT TO EXPECT: A short, leisurely stroll through a wildlife-rich habitat	

This property, jointly owned by Mass Audubon and the Department of Conservation and Recreation, spans 104 acres. It's a nature-filled paradise now, but it once was a hub of industrial activity. In the early 1700s, a dam was built here to power a series of mills, including grist mills, sawmills, and cotton mills.

In 1932, the last of the mills to operate at the site, owned by the Woolen Company, declared bankruptcy. According to Mass Audubon, the property was sold twice and then eventually purchased by a woman named Agnes Bristol. She donated the property to the state and Mass Audubon in the late 1950s and early 1960s for preservation.

Nowadays, Stony Brook is known for its All Persons Trail, a universally accessible trail that features a sensory post-and-rope component as well as braille and tactile signs. Tactile maps and audio guides are available at the visitor center as well. The highlight of the short, 0.6-mile trail is its newly improved boardwalk, which leads over wetlands, marshes, and ponds. Here, you'll see a range of wildlife, including birds, beavers, and turtles.

GETTING THERE

From I-95, take exit 9 to merge with Route 1 going toward Foxboro. Follow Route 1 for 2.8 miles, then take a right onto Water Street. After a few hundred feet, turn left onto Summer Street. Drive for about 2 miles, continuing onto Everett Street. Then turn right onto MA-115 for 2 miles. Turn left onto North Street, and the visitor center will be on your right.

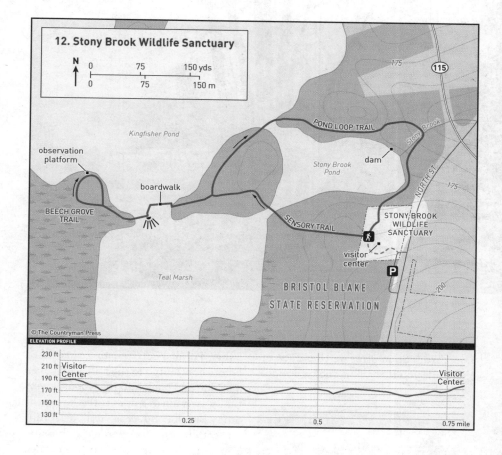

12. Stony Brook Wildlife Sanctuary

N

| 0 | 75 | 150 yds |
| 0 | 75 | 150 m |

Kingfisher Pond

observation platform

POND LOOP TRAIL

Stony Brook

175

115

dam

Stony Brook Pond

boardwalk

BEECH GROVE TRAIL

SENSORY TRAIL

STONY BROOK WILDLIFE SANCTUARY

175

NORTH ST

visitor center

P

Teal Marsh

BRISTOL BLAKE

STATE RESERVATION

200

© The Countryman Press

ELEVATION PROFILE

230 ft	Visitor Center		Visitor Center
210 ft			
190 ft			
170 ft			
150 ft			
130 ft	0.25	0.5	0.75 mile

THE HIKE

This brief loop begins behind the visitor center, where you'll have to stop inside to pay a $4 entry fee. Head down the gravel path flanked by stone walls—built by a farmer named Enoch Blake to prevent his cows from wandering into his fields—and into the woods. (There are several stops for the Audubon's audio tour along the way, if you choose to participate.) The trail then curves right and leads to a wood-and-aluminum boardwalk over the water. Pause at one of the lookouts here to take note of the different types of wildlife living in this one small section of Teal Marsh. Snapping turtles

sit on the rocks in the water, framed by pond lilies and cattails. Birds feed on the plants floating there. On my trip, I saw a blue heron resting near a nest box in this wetland habitat.

Once you've gotten your fill of creature-watching, continue on to exit into the woods. A short loop called the Beach Grove Trail circles this section of land, offering an observation platform for viewing nearby Kingfisher Pond. Geese and ducks swim here, and during my trip, I saw a beaver swim quietly parallel to the shore, and then a swan preening its feathers. You will head back the way you came to continue this walk, bearing left after crossing the

A DAM AT THE FAR END OF STONY BROOK POND

bridge once more to stay on the Pond Loop Trail. Soon after getting back on the trail, you'll reach a rocky outlook

A NEW ALUMINIUM BOARDWALK

offering another vantage point on King-fisher Pond. Feel free to pause here before continuing to the mill. Walk over a bridge and back into the woods, eventually arriving at a dam at the far end of Stony Brook Pond. A sawmill, gristmill, and cotton mill once operated at this site. You'll see the foundations of the former mill, and you'll be able to get up close and personal with water spilling down the dam. A path bordered by a stone wall leads past the dam to stone steps. Climb them to reach the grassy hill behind the visitor center. There's the option to take a rest in the sanctuary's butterfly garden or rest at a picnic table and watch the Canada geese go about their business. Round the corner of the visitor center to reach the parking lot again.

Wachusett Meadow Wildlife Sanctuary

WHERE: Princeton

ADDRESS: 113 Goodnow Road, Princeton, MA 01541

TOTAL DISTANCE: 5 miles

HIKING TIME: 2 hours 45 minutes

ELEVATION GAIN: 251 feet

DIFFICULTY: Moderate

RESTROOMS: Yes

DOGS ALLOWED: No

WHAT TO EXPECT: A bracing trip through meadows and forests, up hills, and over brooks

There's no place quite like Wachusett Meadow Wildlife Sanctuary to be on an early morning. Step out of your car to see sheep grazing in the fields of Goodnow Farm. Watch the morning light wash over the weathered-shingle barn. Then lace up your boots, because you've got some exploring to do.

Wachusett Meadow Wildlife Sanctuary is a 1,130-acre gem near the base of Mount Wachusett (see Hike #6). The former farmstead was established in the 1780s by Edward and Lois Goodnow, and later, in 1830, their timber-frame house became a tavern. It wasn't until 1956 that the then-owner of the property donated his land, which contained houses, farm buildings, and the three-story gambrel barn that's still standing, to the Massachusetts Audubon Society. Today, the sanctuary doesn't operate as a farm, but it still uses its historical buildings, barns, and pastures for educational programming.

The sanctuary's 12 miles of trails wind through a range of landscapes, from sprawling wet meadows to breezy hilltops. More than 2,000 species of wildlife call the place home. Nesting boxes throughout the property are home to Yellow-rumped Warblers, American Bitterns, and other birds. But the biodiversity here goes far beyond birds—there are meadow-jumping mice, snakes, eastern newts, bullfrogs, and even moose. If you wanted to crunch the numbers, the sanctuary says there are 72 species of dragonflies, 73 species of butterflies, 339 moth species, and more than 50 species of spiders.

The beauty of the sanctuary lies in its transformation. Throughout your hike, you'll be able to see how Mother Nature took over the land, as the farmstead converted back into forest over the years. Plants now grow over centuries-old

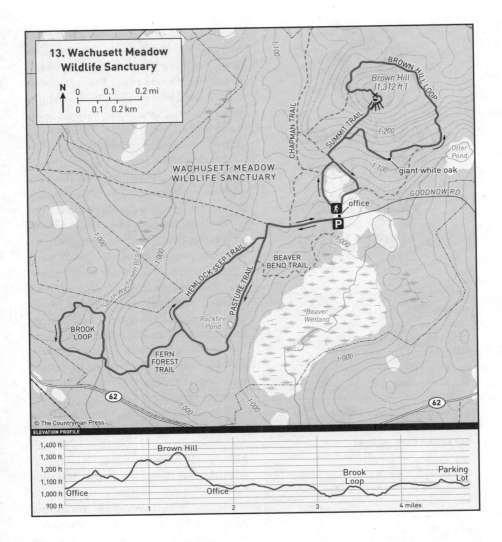

13. Wachusett Meadow
Wildlife Sanctuary

N

| 0 | 0.1 | 0.2 mi |
| 0 | 0.1 | 0.2 km |

BROWN HILL LOOP

Brown Hill
(1,312 ft.)

CHAPMAN TRAIL

SUMMIT TRAIL

1,200

1,100

Otter
Pond

giant white oak

GOODNOW RD

WACHUSETT MEADOW
WILDLIFE SANCTUARY

office

P

1,000

BEAVER
BEND TRAIL

HEMLOCK SEEP TRAIL

PASTURE TRAIL

South Wachusett Brook

1,000

Beaver
Wetland

Rockfire
Pond

BROOK
LOOP

1,000

FERN
FOREST
TRAIL

62

1,000

62

© The Countryman Press

ELEVATION PROFILE

1,400 ft
1,300 ft
1,200 ft
1,100 ft
1,000 ft
900 ft

Office

Brown Hill

Office

Brook
Loop

Parking
Lot

1   2   3   4 miles

stone walls, and trees and shrubs thrive in what once were wide-open spaces. To get the most out of your hike, pick up a map from the information station under the archway at the main office, then pay your $4 admission fee.

GETTING THERE

From MA-140 N., take a left onto MA-62 W. Keep along MA-62, turning right after its intersection with MA-31 in Princeton Center. After 0.6 mile, turn right onto Goodnow Road, and follow it until you reach the sanctuary parking lot on your left.

THE HIKE

This hike comprises two loops: first, one north of the parking lot, then one south of the parking lot. After paying your admission fee in the box under the covered walkway of the Audubon office, pass through it to the other side. The trail in front of you circles the north meadow—head left to follow it briefly before beginning your ascent to the top of Brown Hill. The grassy meadowland you're traveling through is littered with milkweed plants—the only host plant of the Monarch butterfly. As such, the meadow is a haven for Monarchs and other types of insects.

Bypass the Chapman Trail on your left, and continue a short, easy walk to the edges of the woods. Climb a small hill and notice a play zone on your right. You could stop for a moment for some good-old fashioned playtime, then turn left, and quickly right again, to reach the Summit Trail. Turn right once more for the Brown Hill Loop, then figuratively sit back and enjoy the ride (or walk) through shady, cool woods. The trail is overgrown in parts—perhaps suggesting it's the route less traveled for visiting nature lovers—but it's a bracing (and often solitary) walk through the forest. Blue dots will begin to appear on trees. These indicate trails heading away from the main office. Yellow dots, meanwhile, signal you're heading back toward the office. Climb up and down a series of moss-covered rocks to reach the sanctuary's majestic Giant White Oak. You're about a half mile in at this point.

Glimpse mushrooms in red, orange, and yellowish hues flanking the trail, with lush green ferns tenting a protective cover over them. Ahead, bear left to stay on the Brown Hill Loop, then take a moment to marvel at the large population of hickory trees. Keep along the Brown Hill Loop until you reach the second SUMMIT TRAIL sign (there are two). Turn up a set of stone steps to begin your

A LEAFY PART OF THE BROOK LOOP

GOODNOW FARM ABUTS THE PARKING LOT

trek to the summit of 1,312-foot Brown Hill, using your arms and legs to round out the second half of the climb. At the top, southernly treetop views overlook the woods and swamp you just traversed to get here.

Catch your breath on the way down, continuing along the Summit Trail through tall grasses before reaching the woods once again. It's a short shade break until you're spit out at the north meadow again. Turn left to take the opposing path back to the office. It's a welcome change of scenery, especially when you stumble across the small farm pond on the way. See frogs sunbathing

the southern part of the sanctuary by picking up the Chapman Trail. I decided to fill up my water bottle at the office, then I turned right down West Road a bit to reach Beaver Bend Trail. If you went for the latter, continue along the road until you reach a wooden gate. Bypass it, then take the next left onto Beaver Bend Trail. The key here is to take Beaver Bend, but then don't bend. Continue straight to pick up the Pasture Trail. It winds through another grassy meadow of milkweed, where fluttering orange Monarchs put on a brilliant display. Ahead, gaze at Rockfire Pond on your right, then begin a walk through thick, rust-colored pine needles. When you see a sign for the Fern Forest Trail, turn left. Your hike becomes suddenly shaded here, with leafy green ferns festooning the path. The ferns get increasingly taller and thicker as you progress. As you're making your way through them, keep an eye out for granite rocks and boulders among the moss-covered ones. Ahead, turn right onto the Brook Loop, which is even rockier. You'll need to cross a series of stones over a babbling brook to complete the Brook Loop. The circular walk through the forest debuts yellow dots halfway through the loop, signaling your return to the parking lot. It spits you out at the brook once more, inviting you to gaze again upon the dozens of varieties of mushrooms on the ground on your way back. You'll retrace your steps for a bit before picking up the Hemlock Seep Trail. Notice nesting boxes in the distance—they're home to eastern bluebirds and tree swallows. (Don't get so distracted by the boxes that you forget to sidestep the poison ivy along the path.) Head back the same way you came to reach the parking lot.

on lily pads as butterflies and dragonflies flutter over the sparkling waters. There's a bench, if you'd prefer to take a break before embarking on the second half of your hike at Wachusett Meadow.

If you'd like to begin your second loop right away, you could connect to

Walden Pond State Reservation

WHERE: Concord

ADDRESS: 915 Walden Street, (Route 126) Concord, MA 01742

TOTAL DISTANCE: 2.25 miles

HIKING TIME: 1 hour, 30 minutes

ELEVATION GAIN: 108 feet

DIFFICULTY: Easy

RESTROOMS: Yes

DOGS ALLOWED: No

WHAT TO EXPECT: A journey through historic woods, tracing the edges of Walden Pond

Walden Pond just might be the most historic hike in this book. The state reservation is the spot where, in the 1840s, Henry David Thoreau famously spent two years living in a cabin near the shores of the pond. It was an experiment he hoped would bring him closer to nature. The first draft of his most famous work, *Walden*, was written during his time there, and it sings the praises of using nature to forge meaningful connections among the physical and spiritual worlds.

Thoreau was able to build the cabin thanks to his pal Ralph Waldo Emerson, who owned the land around Walden Pond. In 1922, Emerson's family donated this land to the Commonwealth of Massachusetts. According to the National Park Service, the family requested that the land preserve "the Walden of Emerson and Thoreau, its shores and nearby woodlands for the public who wish to enjoy the pond, the woods, and nature, including bathing, boating, fishing and picnicking."

Today, the state reservation and National Historic Landmark stretch to 250 acres. Visitors can walk, hike, swim, picnic, canoe, snowshoe, and more. Don't set out for the pond until you've read at least a few paragraphs of Thoreau's *Walden*—or at least swung by the visitor center for a quick primer. Get there early, though, as the parking lot fills up quickly on summer mornings. Once you're finished competing for a spot, you can get to eschewing the stresses of society in nature.

> I went to the woods because I wished to live deliberately, to front only the essential facts of life, and see if I could not learn what it had to teach, and not,

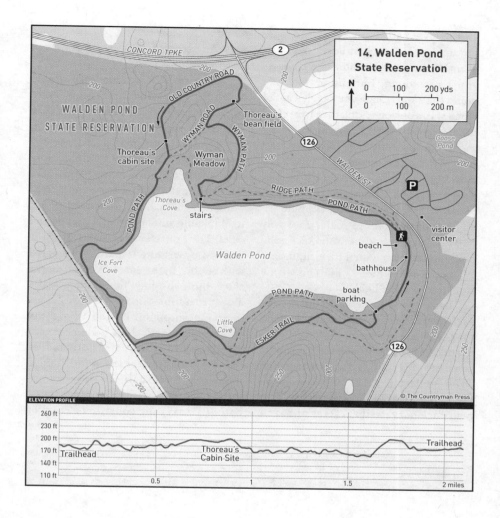

14. Walden Pond State Reservation

N

| 0 | 100 | 200 yds |
| 0 | 100 | 200 m |

WALDEN POND STATE RESERVATION

CONCORD TPKE

OLD COUNTRY ROAD

WYMAN ROAD

WYMAN PATH

Thoreau's bean field

Thoreau's cabin site

Wyman Meadow

Thoreau's Cove

stairs

POND PATH

RIDGE PATH

POND PATH

WALDEN ST.

Goose Pond

P

visitor center

beach

bathhouse

boat parking

POND PATH

ESKER TRAIL

Ice Fort Cove

Little Cove

Walden Pond

© The Countryman Press

ELEVATION PROFILE

260 ft · 230 ft · 200 ft · 170 ft · 140 ft · 110 ft

Trailhead

Thoreau's Cabin Site

Trailhead

0.5 · 1 · 1.5 · 2 miles

when I came to die, discover that I had not lived.
—Henry David Thoreau, *Walden*

GETTING THERE

From I 95-N., take exit 29B to merge onto MA-2 toward Acton and Fitchburg. Follow Route 2 for 4.5 miles, then turn left onto MA-126 S. After less than a quarter mile, you'll see the entrance to Walden Pond State Reservation.

THE HIKE

This hike skirts the edges of Walden Pond, taking a few detours deeper into the woods along the way. To begin, exit the parking lot (where you'll have to fork over an $8 parking fee) and cross the street at the crosswalk. Walk down the ramp-like path to the pond—in summertime, this is where lifeguarded swimming is cordoned off. Turn right and enter the trail at the opening in the woods. This begins your loop around Walden.

The level path, flanked by wire fencing, makes for easy walking. You can glimpse the pond through the trees as you stroll along, imagining Thoreau doing the same. Once you reach a set of stone stairs on your right, turn to ascend them, then turn right again to follow the Ridge Path marked on your trail map. After a few dozen feet, turn right onto Wyman Path, where you'll be met with a view overlooking grassy Wyman Meadow. From here, follow the blue triangle trail markers to make your way to Thoreau's famed bean field. At the next intersection, you'll turn right onto Wyman Road, which is marked with a sign, to reach the field.

These woods are serenely quiet, even as throngs of swimmers set up camp on the pond's shores. But for the only time in the hike, as you approach the bean field, you'll hear the sounds of cars whooshing down Route 126. An engraved stone on the ground marks the spot where Thoreau once harvested 2.5 acres of beans, along with some turnips, peas, and potatoes. An excerpt from *Walden* is carved into the stone.

March on to continue your amble through the woods. Wyman Road curves left as it meets the street to turn into Old County Road. For a few feet, you'll walk along a small part of the Bay Circuit Trail. Continue straight, then stay left at the fork (onto Bean Field Road) to make your way to the site of Thoreau's cabin. Soon, a clearing makes itself visible among the white pines and oaks. The house site, in all its glory, is marked by granite bollards connected with chains. In the center, a stone marks the cabin's chimney foundation, and a sign proclaims one of *Walden*'s most quotable snippets. Beside where the cabin once stood, there's a monumental display of stone cairns created by visitors from all over the world. Take a moment to forest bathe in this environment (Thoreau was the original forest bather, I'd say) and construct a cairn or

A LIFEGUARD CHAIR ON THE POND BEACH

A PONDSIDE TRAIL

two. Appreciate the view of the pond through the trees, and feel the pine needles crunch underfoot. When you're finished, hike toward the pond to continue the rest of your hike.

When you meet the stone marker at the pond, turn right. Meander along the sun-dappled shores until you reach another set of stone stairs at Ice Fort Cove. They lead up to the tracks of the Massachusetts Bay Transit Authority's commuter rail. The one before you is the Fitchburg line, and every hour or so, you'll see and hear a purple MBTA train barrel though.

As the trail bends back toward the aqua-colored waters, you'll see the bathhouse where you started, directly across the pond. At the next fork in the trail, which arrives as you approach Little Cove, turn right onto Esker Trail. This leads up into the woods once more, offering a cool walk back to the parking lot. Keep along the Esker Trail for the rest of your walk—it lets out at the boat parking lot, where you'll have to walk on the side of the road to reach your starting point. Keep left along the fence to return to the trailhead on the pond beach.

In the summertime, there's no question that you should take a dip after your hike. Plopping into the pond is unlike any other swimming experience in Massachusetts. The water is crystal-clear, and the temperature is somehow always just right. Experienced long-distance swimmers often traverse the whole length of the pond, but after hiking a little over 2 miles, the doggy paddle should do.

Willard Brook State Forest

WHERE: Ashby and Townsend

ADDRESS: Hosmer Road, Ashby, MA 01431

TOTAL DISTANCE: 3 miles

HIKING TIME: 1 hour, 45 minutes

ELEVATION GAIN: 297 feet

DIFFICULTY: Moderate

RESTROOMS: Yes

DOGS ALLOWED: Yes

WHAT TO EXPECT: A winding walk through the forest, where the sounds of the rushing brook are never too far away

Cross the boundary into Willard Brook State Forest, and you might think you're in the foothills of the Berkshires. Indeed, the almost 2,600-acre swath of land extending from Ashby to Townsend feels a lot like Western Massachusetts, but it's actually a pocket of wild, untamed beauty in Eastern Central Massachusetts. Its Western vibes mainly emanate from Trap Falls, a picture-perfect cascade just off of Townsend Road. (Definitely visit the falls before or after your hike.)

As in many of the state parks featured in this book, the Civilian Conservation Corps, or the CCC, worked to build walls, bridges, and other recreational features here during the 1930s. While the federal program was not responsible for all of the work done in the forest, the men did create rock walls lining the northern part of Route 119, which winds through the park, as well as the dam and stone bridge to Damon Pond.

A trip to Willard Brook State Forest is perhaps best enjoyed in the fall, when the trees flanking Route 119 erupt in golden yellows and bright oranges. It's also a great spot for seasonal swimming and camping if you'd like to make a weekend of it in warmer months. Read on to discover a short hike through these woods and ways you can glimpse the beauty of Trap Falls.

GETTING THERE

Follow MA-2 W. to Leominster, and then take the Abbott Avenue exit. At the traffic circle, take the fourth exit onto MA-111 N., following Abbott Avenue to John Fitch Highway. At the next traffic circle, take the first exit onto MA-31 N., or Ashby State Road. Turn right onto MA-119 E. after 4.5 miles. Cross the boundary into the park, then turn right onto Hosmer Road. Arrive at the Damon

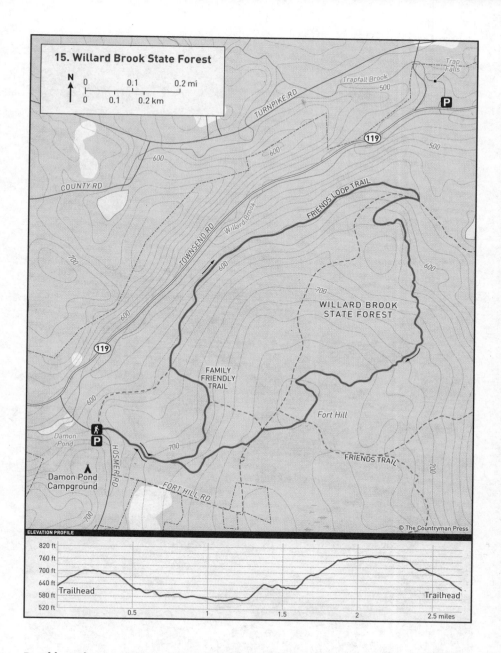

15. Willard Brook State Forest

ELEVATION PROFILE

Pond lot, where you must pay a $5 to $8 parking fee, depending on the season.

THE HIKE

While the Friends Trail is a popular hike in Willard Brook State Forest, it requires two cars to complete. The hike outlined here is called the Friends Loop, and it starts and ends at Damon Pond. It's slightly shorter than the full Friends Trail, which connects to Pearl Hill State Park in Townsend, but it still offers a comprehensive look at the park's landscape.

TRAP FALLS

To kick off your trip around the Friends Loop, cross the street from the Damon Pond parking lot. The trail is marked by orange-reddish blazes on the trees. On my jaunt through Willard Brook State Forest, I took a detour to explore part of the blue Family Friendly trail, which is a shorter option for groups with small children. The hike outlined here veers onto the blue trail for a short while, and then it meets back up with the orange trail.

A stand of shagbark hickory greets you at the trailhead. Pass through the trail's brown gates to arrive at an open, grassy area. To your left, you'll see a pile of old campsite stoves; Willard Brook State Forest also offers tent camping and yurts. Instead of heading toward the stoves, follow the dirt path toward the blazes on the trees, marked in yellow, red, and blue. (The yellow blazes are for the Friends Trail, rather than the Friends Loop described here.) A red pine plantation stands to greet you—this one was planted by the Civilian Conservation Corps sometime between 1933 and 1941. It's one of several plantations throughout the park. The red pine stands were planted to combat "blister rust," a plant disease that had been killing off large populations of white pine. How do you know you're looking at one of the CCC's red pine plantations? The telltale sign is a grouping of trees of similar heights—they'll have red-brown bark and needles in clusters of two.

A greater diversity of trees and plantings lie ahead. Pass by a grove of birches, then a thick, thriving blueberry patch. If you'd like to check out part of the Family Friendly trail like I did, bear left when the trail forks into two paths. Here, you'll spot mountain laurel, a flower not often seen in the woods of Massachusetts, as well as stone walls through the trees. No matter where you are on the trail, the rushing sounds of the brook are never far away. As you approach a runoff of the brook, you'll likely hear its moving waters. I followed the sounds ever so slightly off the trail to discover a natural spring. It's worth it to stop, sit, and listen to the gentle gurgle sounds.

Cross stepping stones over a small brook to discover another diverse patch of plants—witch hazel, viburnum (a member of the honeysuckle family), and Indian cucumber-root grow just beyond the water. As you continue on, you'll notice the remnants of a quarry. Massive block-like stones loom in the woods beyond the trail. Climb them to inspect quarry marks and lines, as well as the still-visible deep drill holes between the rocks.

Your hike continues into a forest populated by mostly oak trees before meeting up with the orange trail, or Friends Loop. Turning right onto the orange loop begins a counterclockwise hike around the loop.

Once off the Family Friendly trail, the path immediately becomes rocky. Large, mossy stones poke up from the ground. Take care not to slip on them as you slightly decrease in elevation. The sounds of the brook meet your ears again, carrying you deeper into the woods. White birch trees grow ahead, and some downed trees crisscross the trail. They appear stunningly white when surrounded by vibrant reds and yellows during fall's peak foliage. Purple and orange mushrooms in the ground, plus the greenest green moss, round out the colorful display. The forest becomes less dense ahead as the trail runs parallel to Townsend Road.

Ahead, a small body of water can

A FALLEN BIRCH ACROSS THE TRAIL

be seen just beyond the trail, and huge boulders beckon you to turn away from the road. It becomes hillier once you do, forcing you to travel up and down rocky inclines and declines. Once you've worked up a sweat, a steady climb begins, leading to an intersection with an unpaved forest road. Turn right to follow the forest road, and keep an eye out for the orange blaze on a tree ahead of you. Once you spot it, hop onto the trail again on your left, continuing your climb of Fort Hill. This kicks off the latter portion of the hike, where all roads lead to Damon Pond. Keep on meandering through the woods until you reach a spooky old shack with a brook running under it. Eventually, the trail meets up with the blue and yellow blazes again as you get even closer to Damon Pond. Follow the path until you reach the rusted camp stoves and the brown gates once again. The parking lot is just beyond them.

After your hike, reward yourself by visiting the ever-picturesque Trap Falls. Head out of the parking lot and back onto Route 119. Turn right, and there should be a small parking area on your left—you passed it on your way in. A leisurely stroll along the brook leads to the falls, where you can stand on a small bridge and snap a few photos. Say cheese!

II

SOUTH OF BOSTON

16

Ames Nowell State Park

WHERE: Abington	
ADDRESS: 739 Linwood Street, Abington	
TOTAL DISTANCE: 2.25 miles	
HIKING TIME: 1 hour, 30 minutes	
ELEVATION GAIN: 122 feet	
DIFFICULTY: Moderate	
RESTROOMS: Yes	
DOGS ALLOWED: Yes	
WHAT TO EXPECT: A refreshing hike through diverse terrain, including over a dam, through a forest, and under huge power lines	

This hike is one of two in this book relating to the 35th Governor of Massachusetts, Oliver Ames. (For the other one, see Borderland State Park in Hike #19.) Ames Nowell, the grandson of Oliver Ames, purchased the land that now makes up Ames Nowell State Park in the 1930s, when the previous owner couldn't afford its property taxes during the Great Depression.

Long before that purchase, however, a sawmill (then a gristmill) operated in the northern portion of the park where Cleveland Pond now sits. In 1903, the mill was razed, and 20 years later, a lawyer named Edwin Holmes transformed the land into hunting grounds and a bird sanctuary. Holmes built a dam near the former mill site to create the human-made body of water known as Cleveland Pond.

Today, the pond is exceedingly popular with boaters and fishermen. Several miles of trails surround the pond in the 700-acre reservation. And besides hiking, visitors can ride horses, go mountain biking, and cross-country ski.

GETTING THERE

From MA-3 S., take exit 17 for Union Street toward Braintree and South Braintree. At the traffic circle, take the third exit onto Union Street. After 0.7 mile, turn right onto Middle Street, and at the next traffic circle, continue straight onto Liberty Street. In 2.8 miles, continue straight through one more traffic circle onto Liberty Street. Continue onto Pine Street, then Sycamore Street, before turning left onto MA-139 E. After 0.9 mile, turn right onto Hancock Street. Continue onto Presidential Drive, then turn right onto Linwood Street.

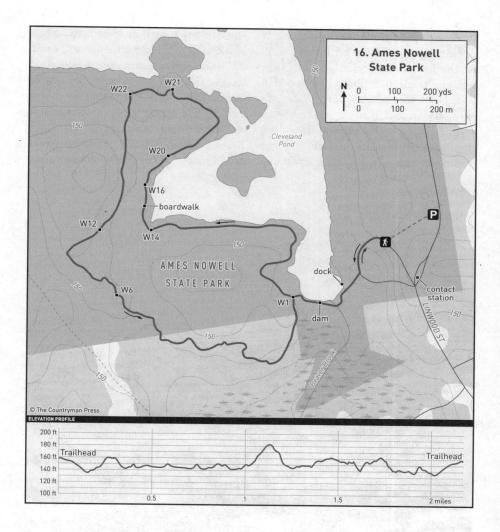

16. Ames Nowell State Park

Cleveland Pond

W22 W21
W20
W16
boardwalk
W12
W14
AMES NOWELL STATE PARK
W6
W1
dock
dam
contact station
LINWOOD ST

© The Countryman Press

ELEVATION PROFILE

Trailhead .... Trailhead

200 ft
180 ft
160 ft
140 ft
120 ft
100 ft

0.5   1   1.5   2 miles

THE HIKE

To kick off your hike, take the path that lies beyond the brown gate off of the parking lot. This leads to a picnic area overlooking Cleveland Pond. Bypass the picnic tables and head towards the pond's dock. Then, bear left to cross the small bridge over the dam. This is where the journey begins.

The trails in Ames Nowell State Park are well-maintained, but they could have clearer markings and blazes. Even the sharpest of eyes might miss signs along the way, because they're covered by branches and brush. So, you might end up moseying down a few trails not outlined here, and that is okay.

After crossing the small bridge, turn up into the woods at marker W1, then turn right. Blue triangles tacked onto the trees vaguely outline hiking trails. Follow the sign here, padding along the grassy trail. The path soon becomes interrupted by rocks and sand, while huckleberry grows on both sides of it. At the first intersection you hit, turn left, and begin to follow a long wooden boardwalk that borders the pond. Lush greenery almost grows over the boardwalk here, and the air smells sweet, thanks to white puffs of clethra. Large boulders and glacial erratics make themselves known up ahead, and a network of pondside paths are exposed. At marker W21, take a left to descend deeper into the oak trees.

An easy walk through the shady, cool woods opens to a grassy meadow at W22. Huge, hulking power lines loom overhead. You'll use these great white structures to guide you for a time

THE DAM AT AMES NOWELL

CLETHRA AND DEW DROPS

as you follow a skinny path alongside them. When the trail opens onto ground covered in rocks and gravel, continue straight. Then, at W12, turn right to complete a small loop in the woods, which acts as a welcome shade break from the wide-open field. The loop spits you back out at the power lines once again, where you'll take an immediate left onto a narrow path. Cut across the grassy expanse to find your way back into the woods. There's an entry point at marker W6. The marker is hard to spot, but a larger sign next to it isn't—when you've reached a brown sign that says NO SNOWMOBILES, ATVS, OR DIRT BIKES, you'll know you've made it.

Ahead, the woods show signs of a recent forest fire. Walk through the charred remnants and leafless trees by hopping from rock to rock. Once you're through the eerily quiet forest, mount the rocky ridge that heads uphill. Keep right at the top of the hill, then turn right again at the next fork. You'll exit the boundaries of the park for a bit to make your way back to the dam. The thick forest trail leads you to a stone wall, where you'll be able to hear the dam water rushing into the river. Bear right to complete the last leg of your walk. Cleveland Pond will come into view up ahead, allowing you to retrace your steps back to the parking lot.

Blue Hills Reservation— Skyline Loop

WHERE: Milton

ADDRESS: 695 Hillside Street, Milton, MA 02186

TOTAL DISTANCE: 3 miles

HIKING TIME: 2.5 to 3 hours

ELEVATION GAIN: 937 feet

DIFFICULTY: Strenuous

RESTROOMS: Yes

DOGS ALLOWED: Yes

WHAT TO EXPECT: A steep scramble up a rocky hillside, topped off with jaw-dropping views of Boston and its harbor

Its boulders aren't made from sapphire, and its trees don't grow cerulean branches, but the Blue Hills are undeniably blue. The reservation's name comes from the observations of early European explorers who glimpsed the peaks from their boats along the Massachusetts coastline. On the exposed hilltops, a type of granite called riebeckite appeared blue from their watery distance.

But in the thousands of years before that, Native Americans roamed the Blue Hills. Referred to as "the people of the Great Hills," they made best use of their resources, tapping the stone to create tools and arrowheads. Later, colonists used the land for logging and farming. The land they cleared to grow crops is still discernible today, thanks to the stone walls that remain on the property.

In 1893, the Commonwealth of Massachusetts purchased the more than 7,000-acre reservation—which spreads to the towns of Milton, Canton, Dedham, and Quincy—to protect it and preserve it for public enjoyment. This was thanks to landscape architect Charles Eliot, who insisted that the land just outside of Boston be maintained as a park. The purchase by the newly formed Metropolitan Parks System was one of the state's first conservation acquisitions.

GETTING THERE

From I-93, take exit 3 for Ponkapoag Trail toward Houghton's Pond. Turn right onto Ponkapoag Trail, then continue onto Blue Hill River Road. Take the next right onto Hillside Road to arrive at the park headquarters. Parking is across the street from the headquarters.

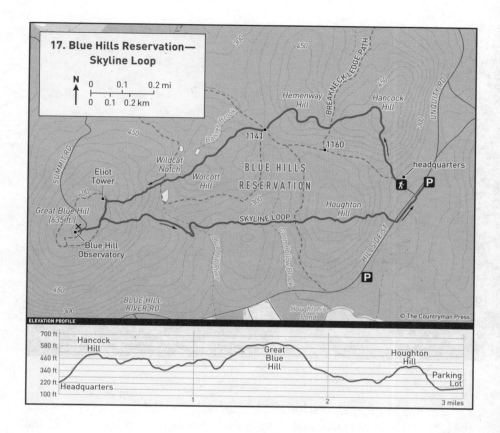

17. Blue Hills Reservation— Skyline Loop

BLUE HILLS RESERVATION

ELEVATION PROFILE

THE HIKE

As one of the Blue Hills Reservation's most popular trails, the Skyline Loop is also one of its most dangerous. This 3.5-mile trek is difficult, and it requires some climbing to reach the top of Great Blue Hill. To begin, head up the path behind the reservation's headquarters. The Skyline Loop is outlined with blue rectangular markers, which you'll immediately spot after a few dozen feet on the trail. At this intersection, head up the set of stone steps fronted by a blue rectangle. The steps will be the first of many steep inclines on your journey.

Once you've climbed the stairs, a more difficult ascent begins immediately. Climb over thick tree roots by

stepping from rock to rock on your way up. It's a good idea to pace yourself here, as you gain more elevation in the first quarter mile of your trip than you do for the rest of the hike. While the climb is tough, the views that instantly pop up behind you make it worth it. Turn around to look over the treetops every once in a while to see the reservation spreading out before you. When the trail begins to level out, you can spot Boston Harbor in the distance. Keep along the blue-blazed trail as you switchback down to blessedly flatter ground.

The trail does indeed become less steep once you're sufficiently out of breath, though it does not become any less rocky. (Read: Watch your footing.) Approach your first short decline soon,

A ROCKY DESCENT

and get used to it. The remainder of the hike—even on your way back down from the top—will be a series of peaks and valleys. Up, down, up, down is your new mantra. You'll need to turn right up another hill at the next intersection, though the clearly marked blue blazes will keep you on track. Veer left at the top of this short hill, spotting a sign for the Skyline Loop. When you're spit out at the next intersection, keep straight for the steady climb to the top.

Your journey will switch from up to down and up to down once again, then it will be broken up by another set of stone steps to give your legs a rest. One final climb and you'll arrive at the 635-foot summit of Great Blue Hill. It's the highest peak on the East Coast, from Boston to Miami. (So, the coast of Maine has it beat.) A rectangular construction called Eliot Tower is there to greet you. You've just scaled the hill, yes, but you'll have to climb one more set of steps to reach the top of Eliot Tower. From there, you can see sweeping views, from the Boston skyline and harbor all the way to Houghton's Pond and Quincy. On a clear day, you can spot Mount Wachusett (see Hike #6) and the Worcester Hills to the west, and the Monadnock region of New Hampshire to the northwest. Pose for a picture as the wind whips your hair at the top of the tower, then explore the base of it.

Below, a stone walkway with a memorial to Charles Eliot—the landscape architect who helped establish the Blue Hills Reservation—leads the way to the Blue Hill Observatory, a weather station with an interesting history. The observatory has been keeping a record of the weather up there since 1885, when the institution was founded. It holds a record for the longest unbroken climate

THE BOSTON SKYLINE FROM ELIOT TOWER

STONE STEPS LEAD DOWN GREAT BLUE HILL

The observatory has a bathroom if you need it, and the staff sometimes offer free fruit and snacks to hikers.

When you're finished exploring, head down the blue-blazed path that sits between the stone bridge and the weather observatory. If you're coming from the tower, it will be on your left. The descent, in a word, is hairy. Your tired legs might find it hard to descend, but you'll get there. Once you've stepped down another set of stone stairs, turn right. Then, at the end of this trail, take a sharp left downward. On my trip, I spotted a remnant of a classic Boston afternoon: a Styrofoam Dunkin' cup. If you're lucky enough to see one, I recommend stuffing it in your backpack to dispose of properly.

Next, pass over a small stream and through a collection of glacial erratics. The boulders feel larger-than-life here, compounded by the effect of walking on a flat of the hill. There are even more of them ahead as you traipse across a mostly flat forest floor under the cover of trees. Cross another stream before beginning a steady climb, the trail carpeted with rust-orange pine needles. Sidestep sharp rocks on your way up and on your way down, keeping right along the blue blazes for the last time. The trail then spits you out at Hillside Street. Look both ways before crossing, then follow the dirt path lining the street back to the parking lot.

record in the country. Tours of the tower are $3 to $4, depending on tour length. Take one to learn more about the meteorologists who made history there. Pro tip:

Blue Hills Reservation— Breakneck Ledge Loop

WHERE: Milton	
ADDRESS: Houghton's Pond Recreation Area, 840 Hillside Street, Milton, MA 02186	
TOTAL DISTANCE: 4.5 miles	
HIKING TIME: 2.5 hours	
ELEVATION GAIN: 560 feet	
DIFFICULTY: Strenuous	
RESTROOMS: Yes	
WHAT TO EXPECT: A long trek traversing woodlands and rocky, rugged hilltops	

Once you've completed the popular Skyline Loop, I recommend you traverse a path less traveled in the Blue Hills. The Breakneck Ledge Loop meanders through the Great Blue Hill section of the reservation. It begins and ends at the Houghton's Pond parking lot, and it should only be followed in one direction: counter-clockwise.

GETTING THERE

From I-93, take exit 3 for Ponkapoag Trail, toward Houghton's Pond. Turn right onto Ponkapoag Trail, then continue onto Blue Hill River Road. Take the next right onto Hillside Road to arrive at the parking lot. I recommend arriving early, because the parking lot fills up quickly. If it's full, there are other spots to park at pull-offs along Hillside Street, as well as across from park headquarters near the State Police Station.

THE HIKE

To start, exit the parking lot and follow the dirt path along the side of the road toward reservation headquarters. Once you reach a trailhead marker with a map on your right, bypass it to cross the road at the nearby crosswalk. Make your way to the reservation headquarters, where there is trail information, posted events, and maps for purchase for $3.

Continue along the path beside the headquarters to enter the woods. The Breakneck Ledge loop is signified with yellow triangular trail markers. The first yellow triangle you see is where the hike truly begins, and it's also where some of the steepest inclines are. A gradual incline leads to a steeper part of the trail. Watch out for rocks and tree roots poking out into the trail.

After scaling the first hill, you'll see

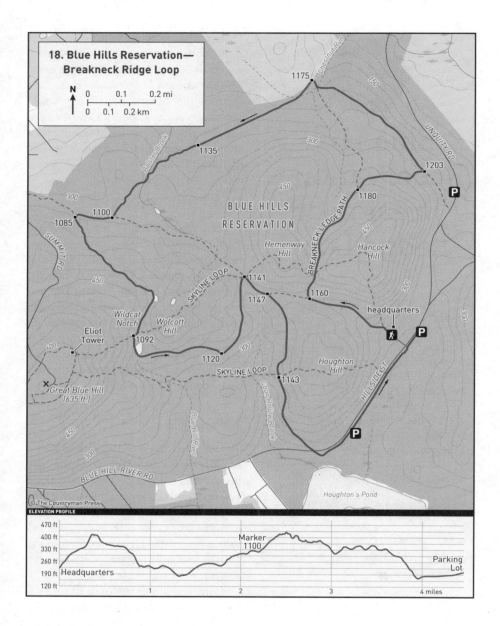

18. Blue Hills Reservation—
Breakneck Ridge Loop

N

| 0 | 0.1 | 0.2 mi |
| 0 | 0.1 | 0.2 km |

1175

Chestnut Rd.

150

BALSTER BROOK

1135

300

UNQUITY RD

1203

300

1180

450

1100

1085

BREAKNECK LEDGE PATH

SUMMIT RD

300

BLUE HILLS
RESERVATION

450

Hemenway
Hill

Hancock
Hill

450

SKYLINE LOOP

1141

1160

300

headquarters

1147

300

P

Wildcat
Notch

Wolcott
Hill

1092

Eliot
Tower

400

1120

300

Houghton
Hill

P

SKYLINE LOOP

1143

HILLSIDE ST

Cook Hollow Brook

X
Great Blue Hill
(635 ft.)

450

300

Blue Hill River

P

BLUE HILL RIVER RD

Houghton's Pond

© The Countryman Press

ELEVATION PROFILE

470 ft
400 ft
330 ft
260 ft
190 ft
120 ft

Marker
1100

Headquarters

Parking
Lot

1   2   3   4 miles

babbling brooks and massive rock formations. The trail then leads downhill, allowing you to catch your breath, and the ground underneath transitions from a rocky, dusty path to a soft dirt padding beneath your feet.

There are myriad trails in the Blue Hills' thousands of acres, so it's important to pay close attention to trail markers. The Breakneck Ledge Loop approaches numerous intersections—many of them three-way—so it's imperative to keep your eyes peeled for yellow triangles for the duration of the trip.

Soon, though, the hike descends into a grove of trees. Notice the towering beech trees to your left. Here, the trail offers good visibility of the route ahead, allowing you to see what lies hundreds of feet ahead of you. As you make your way through this clearing, stop to take in vistas of the hills to your left. The soft whooshing sound of cars will tip you off that you're approaching a road. Here's where the trail gets a little confusing. Once you get to the bottom of the hill, take a sharp left at intersection marker 1203 to continue on the Breakneck Ledge Loop. It's easy to miss this turn—if you end up at one of the two nearby trailheads and parking areas, you will know you've bypassed it. If that happens, just retrace your steps to head back to the intersection you came from, and follow the trees with yellow triangles.

At this point, you'll approach a small stream filled with pebbles. Cross over it, then head left to stay on the correct loop. A stone threshold in the ground seems to divide one part of the forest from the other. Once you cross it, notice how trees transition from deciduous to coniferous, almost as if the stones create a divider between them. Continue until the trail meets with another woodland loop, signified with green dots. There's a five-way intersection here at the 1100 marker. Take a right to follow the yellow triangles, and see the sign marking 1 mile to park headquarters. At the next intersection marker, 1103, it's unclear which way the Breakneck Ledge Loop continues. Head right here, then stretch your legs as you approach the most arduous downhill stretch of the trail. As you round out

A BOULDER JUTS OUT INTO THE TRAIL

A MOSS-FLANKED BROOK

the last mile of your hike, glimpse views of the hills over the treetops. The path curves downward and eventually spits you out at the road. It's a bit unclear where to go from here. You need to cross the street, where there is no crosswalk, and walk along a paved path on the side of the road. Follow it until you reach the parking lot at Houghton's Pond, or swing by the visitor center for a quick lesson about the park's cultural history.

Borderland State Park

WHERE: Easton and Sharon

ADDRESS: 259 Massapoag Ave, North Easton, MA 02356

TOTAL DISTANCE: 6.3 miles

HIKING TIME: 3 hours 25 minutes

ELEVATION GAIN: 345 feet

DIFFICULTY: Moderate

RESTROOMS: Yes

DOGS ALLOWED: Yes

WHAT TO EXPECT: A long walk through a hilly forest, broken up by views of lakes, ponds, a quarry, and a 1910 mansion

Plenty of visitors to Borderland State Park arrive with the intention of playing a few holes of disc golf. Others come to admire the art and architecture of the former estate's 1910 stone mansion. You, I imagine, are here to explore the park's hiking trails, which span 1,772 acres.

Put simply, Borderland is one of a kind. It lies at a border in several senses of the word—it sits literally on the border of Sharon and Easton, it once divided the territory of Native American tribes, and it is home to a border between gentle hills in its northern section and flatter land to the south. The park was once the estate of Harvard botanist Oakes Ames and his wife Blanche. Oakes was one of the country's earliest researchers of orchids, while Blanche was an artist, author, and inventor. Blanche teamed up with Oakes to produce scientifically accurate orchid illustrations for his research, and together they created a body of work that led orchids to become the most-documented plant species—ever.

Both Oakes and Blanche came from wealthy, prominent families. Oakes was the son of Massachusetts Governor Oliver Ames, while Blanche was born into one of the leading families of Lowell, Massachusetts. They started to acquire the land that would become Borderland in 1900. Blanche designed the estate's stone manor herself, which was built with stones that had already existed on the property. The Ames and their children moved into the house just before its official completion in 1912, and they worked to establish their land as a wildlife sanctuary and forest preserve. Foresters helped the family build fire roads on their land, and those roads are now the park's hiking trails.

But even before the Ames made their home on the land, human activity had

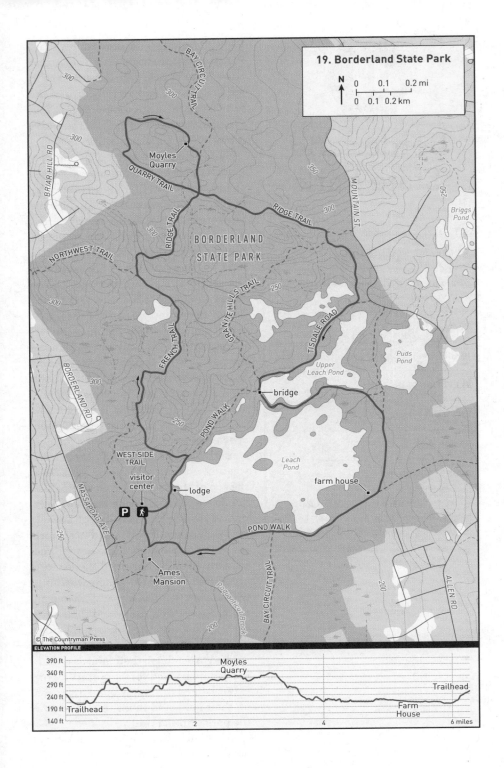

19. Borderland State Park

N

| 0 | 0.1 | 0.2 mi |
| 0 | 0.1 | 0.2 km |

BAY CIRCUIT TRAIL

300

300

Moyles Quarry

QUARRY TRAIL

RIDGE TRAIL

RIDGE TRAIL

350

300

MOUNTAIN ST

250

Briggs Pond

BRIAR HILL RD

300

NORTHWEST TRAIL

300

BORDERLAND STATE PARK

GRANITE HILLS TRAIL

250

FRENCH TRAIL

TISDALE ROAD

Puds Pond

300

Upper Leach Pond

BORDERLAND RD

300

bridge

POND WALK

250

Leach Pond

WEST SIDE TRAIL

visitor center

lodge

farm house

MASSAPOAG AVE

250

P

POND WALK

Ames Mansion

Poquanticut Brook

BAY CIRCUIT TRAIL

200

ALLEN RD

200

© The Countryman Press

ELEVATION PROFILE

390 ft		Moyles Quarry		
340 ft				Trailhead
290 ft				
240 ft			Farm	
190 ft	Trailhead		House	
140 ft		2	4	6 miles

begun to shape it. The Massachusetts and Wampanoag tribes made their home there, hunting and fishing until European settlers came to the scene in the late 1600s. They farmed the land for several centuries, using its streams to power a nail factory and two mills.

Borderland did not become a state park until 1971—two years after the death of Blanche Ames. (Blanche's touches remain, however—her furnishings and paintings are still inside the mansion.) Today, Borderland is home to a range of plant and animal life. Water lilies thrive in the park's six ponds, while deer, rabbits, otters, and other critters make their homes on land.

GETTING THERE

From I-95 S., take exit 10 toward Coney Street. Turn left onto Coney Street, then continue onto Norwood Street. Bear left onto MA-27 S. and continue straight onto Post Office Square. Drive along Massapoag Avenue for 4.7 miles until you reach the park entrance.

THE HIKE

The hike outlined here gives a complete overview of the varied terrain that Borderland State Park offers. It loops beside Leach Pond and up to Moyles Quarry before turning back via the Granite Hills Trail and the Pond Walk. To begin, start down the path behind the visitor center— it's marked with a trail map board. Until you reach Moyles Quarry, you'll follow the Bay Circuit Trail. It's only a few minutes after you've started that you'll reach the lodge at Leach Pond. The stone lodge appears to have been brought here from another era, and it acts as a shelter for folks wanting to build a fire by the pond. The little building was featured in

Martin Scorsese's *Shutter Island*. From the lodge, continue on the Bay Circuit Trail by turning left onto the West Side Trail Loop. This kicks off your first of many uphill climbs today. Gnarly roots grip the soil below you, so watch your footing.

Ahead, turn right onto the French Trail. You'll hike deeper into wetlands interrupted by clusters of glacial erratics. In some areas, it takes scrambling up a rocky incline to reach the next part of the trail. Follow white rectangular markers on the trees here, turning right at a huge monolithic boulder in your path. Cross another large rock in a few hundred feet, keeping left to follow these white rectangles. After a few more minutes of woodsy walking, you'll reach a sign for the Split Rock Trail and Northwest Trail. Turn left for the Northwest Trail. You'll want to stay left again at a large tree hanging over the trail. You'll know you're going the right way if you spot the circular emblems of the Bay Circuit Trail on your walk. There's a short offshoot on the left leading to scenic overlook. Take a detour here for views of a small pond.

The next leg of the journey is flat walking through the forest. It's an excellent opportunity for forest bathing, or mindfully connecting with nature, given that this area of the park is often less crowded than the trails near Leach Pond. On my trip, as I crossed a gently gurgling brook, and a white-tailed deer leaped across the trail ahead of me. After some leisurely walking, a sign for Ridge Trail appears on the right. Another one, for the New England Mountain Bike Association (NEMBA) is on the left. Watch out for mountain bikers who might come whizzing past while you turn right. Another collection of glacial erratics lies ahead. Descend a short yet

A DAM ON THE POND WALK

steep hill to explore, turning away from the NEMBA trail. Bypass a small swamp on the right before glimpsing the first stone wall of the trip. Trace the wall for a bit as you crisscross a huge, flat rock face. The woods become less dense here—you'll need to cross over a boardwalk to make it to the next portion of the hike: the Quarry Trail.

Just past the 2-mile mark, the Quarry Trail invites you to loop around Moyles Quarry, the source for the stone that created the Canton viaduct (a series of stone bridges) for the Boston and Providence Railroad in 1835. It's about a 1-mile trek around the quarry. To shorten your hike, skip the loop and head east on the Ridge Trail. If you've opted to begin the loop, keep left and cross over a series of boardwalks. The majority of this loop is understandably rocky, but still makes for pleasant walking. It's at the end of the loop where you'll finally meet Moyles Quarry. It's underwhelming at first, until you begin to imagine the work it took to convert the stones here into the building blocks of railroad bridges. Stand on a bright green bed of moss overlooking it, or take a seat to enjoy a snack. To get back to the Ridge Trail, take the path that heads away from Moyles Quarry toward the Bay Circuit Trail markers on the trees. You'll end up back at the loop's beginning, where you can turn left onto the Ridge Trail—the opposite of the way you came in.

Here, the eastern portion of the Ridge Trail is less dense and more rocky. Cross over a few open rock faces, then notice the trail becomes wider and easier to walk on. Continue this leisurely stroll past the sign for the Friends Trail, keeping on the Ridge Trail toward Mountain Street. At the next sign along your path, turn right onto the Ridge Trail toward the Granite Hills Trail. You'll know you've made it to the right intersection when you meet a humongous boulder pointing the way. The next sign after that directs you to the left, where you'll descend into a rocky woods once more before spitting you out at a green, grassy expanse. Continue straight along the dirt path before you. At the gate, turn right toward the pond.

This kicks off your journey along the Pond Walk, a wide, flat trail that skirts the shorelines of several of Borderland's ponds. This area gets more crowded than the woodsy trails behind you, so expect to see a lot of casual hikers. Keep right to stay on the Pond Walk on Tisdale Road, crossing a brook to arrive at more flat, easy walking. Through the trees, you'll be able to see the grassy disc golf courses. Upper Leach Pond sparkles before you as you trace its edges.

You'll soon approach a new but rustic-looking bridge and a small dam. If you'd prefer to shorten your hike, do not cross the bridge, and instead keep right along the Pond Walk back to the visitor center. If you'd like to hike the whole 6.5 miles, do indeed walk over this funky little bridge. It frames a view of the dam and the pond, and is worth stopping to see. Ahead, there's a box-like shed that's perfect for bird-watching, if you'd like to take a rest.

Now that you've meandered between the both Leach Pond and Upper Leach

A TINY BOARDWALK LEADS THE WAY

Pond, turn right at the next intersection toward an open field. You'll pass a farm house and a grand, old maple tree. The path is wide and grand here, flanked by centuries-old trees. It transitions to gravel as you approach the Ames' stone mansion and then cuts through disc golf holes. At the end of the trail, turn left to explore the mansion, or head right to go back to the parking lot. There are pamphlets outlining self-guided garden and architectural tours available in the visitor center, if you're game to explore it all.

20

Caratunk Wildlife Refuge

WHERE: Seekonk

ADDRESS: 301 Brown Avenue, Seekonk, MA 02771

TOTAL DISTANCE: 2.6 miles

HIKING TIME: 1 hour 45 minutes

ELEVATION GAIN: 116 feet

DIFFICULTY: Easy

RESTROOMS: No

DOGS ALLOWED: No

WHAT TO EXPECT: A pleasant stroll through an Audubon sanctuary, where you'll spot birds and gurgling brooks aplenty

No, Caratunk Wildlife Refuge is not in Rhode Island. Yes, Caratunk Wildlife Refuge is part of the Audubon Society of Rhode Island. The refuge is a mere 2 miles from the Rhode Island border, and it's part of the Rhode Island chapter (rather than the Massachusetts one) because its land was donated in 1971 by Pawtucket, Rhode Island, resident Charles G. Greenhalgh.

Caratunk spans nearly 200 acres, comprising forests, fields, ponds, and sparkling brooks. It's open year-round, meaning it's suited for birdwatching and hiking in the summer and then snowshoeing in the winter. Some of the property's commonly spotted birds include purple martins, eastern bluebirds, American woodcocks, scarlet tangles, Baltimore orioles, yellow warblers, screech owls, and others. You can learn more about the wildlife that calls Caratunk home in the refuge's newly renovated visitor center. In 2018, the refuge overhauled its parking area, restrooms, and outbuildings, so now the property's historical white barn has an updated backdrop.

GETTING THERE

From I-95 S., take exit 2A for MA-1A-S. toward Newport Avenue. Merge onto Newport Avenue to enter Rhode Island momentarily. After 0.8 mile, turn left after the Monro Muffler & Brake Service building, then after 0.5 mile, turn left onto Central Avenue. In a mile, turn right onto Pine Street, then right onto Brown Avenue. The parking lot will be on your left.

THE HIKE

Caratunk is incredibly easy to navigate. You can pick up a map from the

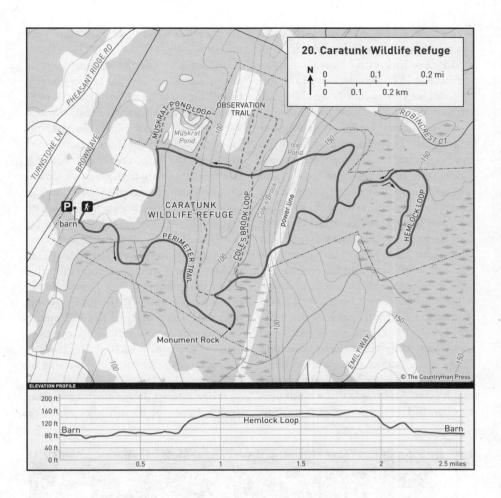

20. Caratunk Wildlife Refuge

N

| 0 | 0.1 | 0.2 mi |
| 0 | 0.1 | 0.2 km |

PHEASANT RIDGE RD

TURNSTONE LN

BROWN AVE

MUSKRAT POND LOOP

OBSERVATION TRAIL

Muskrat Pond

100

Ice Pond

150

ROBINCREST CT

150

P. barn

CARATUNK WILDLIFE REFUGE

PERIMETER TRAIL

COLE'S BROOK LOOP

Cole's Brook

power line

HEMLOCK LOOP

100

100

Monument Rock

100

EMILY WAY

150

150

© The Countryman Press

ELEVATION PROFILE

200 ft
160 ft
120 ft
80 ft
40 ft
0 ft

Barn

Hemlock Loop

Barn

0.5   1   1.5   2   2.5 miles

box toward the end of the parking lot to give you an idea of what your trip will look like, but it's not entirely necessary. Your hike will trace the refuge's Perimeter Trail, plus a trip around Hemlock Loop. Other short loops can be added for a longer stay.

To begin, traipse across the lawn of the white barn, toward the trailhead marker fronting the trees. You'll spot a sign for the Perimeter Trail marked in red. It's an easily visible sign, and one you'll continue to follow throughout your journey. Head down this path, turning right into the woods to follow red blazes.

Then you'll hear it before you see it: a rushing brook up ahead. Gaze at part of this stream before darting between towering sugar maples and oaks. The tree cover doesn't last for long; the trail quickly opens to a field. It's after your trip through the field that you'll stand face-to-face with the strong current of the stream. Cross a narrow footbridge, then step over a stone wall to arrive at a small clearing. You'll spot the rolling green golf course of Ledgemont Country Club in the distance. Turn away from the course, taking care not to trip over thick tree roots gripping the forest floor, to continue. A downed pine fallen across your path will not hinder your hike—a small opening with steps has been carved out of it, allowing you to follow the trail as you normally would (read: without climbing). Charming, indeed.

Cross another bridge, then another boardwalk, keeping right to stay on the Perimeter Trail. Here, you'll begin a scramble through some rocky (and mossy) woods. Keep right again at the next trail intersection to journey farther into the woods, where another stone wall beckons to you from a distance. A huge, aging oak tree then bends over the trail, offering a spot for contemplation, thanks to a small wooden bench. After quick rest, pick up the trail again to spot the first landmark of the hike: Monument Rock. There's no climbing involved to fully appreciate Monument Rock—it's a pair of flat, parallel boulders, one about 8 feet high, and the other half its size. There was unfortunately a bit of graffiti on the pair of rocks during my hike, but it didn't detract from their majesty.

Ahead, another clearly marked sign and a series of red blazes keep you traveling on the Perimeter Trail, parallel to the Cole's Brook Loop, marked with yellow blazes. When the red and yellow trails diverge, take a hard right to stay on the Perimeter Trail, avoiding the straight path that leads to Cole's Brook. A congregation of rocks makes another good spot to stop for a snack or rest. You'll reach another clearing soon, this time for power lines. A momentary steep climb is dotted with hunks of puddingstone, and once you reach the top of the small hill, you'll cross under these power lines. Turn right to duck back into the woods of the Perimeter Trail, rather than following another sign to the powerline cutoff. Heart carvings on trees appear here, remnants of young love.

Enter into wetlands next, clomping over a series of boardwalks to make

BEARS HEAD TOOTH GROWS ON A TREE

A HUGE OAK TREE TOWERS OVER A BENCH

your way to the Hemlock Loop, a pleasant little half-mile stroll at the far end of the refuge. On my trip, I turned right to complete the loop, but you, of course, can head down either direction. More mushrooms poke through the leaves blanketing the ground here. Laid logs on both sides of the trail blaze a runway through nature. Strut your stuff while crossing over stone walls to complete the loop. Follow some mint-green blazes on the trees to arrive at the Perimeter Trail once again.

On my trip to Caratunk, a downed tree and some flooding prevented me from hiking down the Perimeter Trail to where it meets the Hemlock Loop. If this is the case for you, continue back down the way you came and keep your eyes peeled for a narrow trail on your right. This is a short cut-through that avoids the trees and newly formed swamp. It spits you out pretty close to the power lines, which you'll have to cross again to continue your journey. Next, pass over a sturdy stone bridge.

There's the option to explore the Observation Trail loop on your right, which offers flat walking through a similar landscape. A bit farther down, there's also a short 0.3-mile trail that circles Muskrat Pond. Whether you decide to take detours or not, you'll eventually bang a left out of the woods back to the barn. Sidestep beech nuts that litter the ground in the fall. The white barn comes into view soon enough, leading you back to your car.

Copicut Woods

WHERE: Fall River

ADDRESS: Indian Town Road, Fall River, MA 02790

TOTAL DISTANCE: 2.3 miles

HIKING TIME: 1 hour 30 minutes

ELEVATION GAIN: 55 feet

DIFFICULTY: Easy

RESTROOMS: No

DOGS ALLOWED: Yes

WHAT TO EXPECT: An easy trip to an abandoned farm settlement, where you'll see a fairly intact house foundation and cellar

The Trustees-managed Copicut Woods are a part of a larger reservation known as the Southeastern Massachusetts Bioreserve. Spanning a whopping 13,600 acres, the Bioreserve is a vast swath of wetlands and forests that's meant to protect, restore, and enhance the biological diversity and ecological integrity of the region, according to the Southeastern Massachusetts Convention & Visitor Bureau. In addition, the Bioreserve protects public water supplies and cultural resources, as well as providing space for public use, enjoyment, and education.

The Copicut Woods are just one of the many beautiful spots within the Bioreserve. The Woods lie near the Bioreserve's southern border, spreading out to 516 acres. While the Woods only offer about 3 miles of trails, there's a lot to see. From a diversity of landscapes (think cedar swamps, vernal pools, and forests) to a wide range of flora and fauna (hello there, conifers, hardwoods, owls, and hawks), you'll find abundant nature to appreciate. History lives among the trees, too. A hike at Copicut leads to an abandoned farm settlement accessible via a 150-year-old cart path. The best part? You'll be able to envision life on the farm as you stand amidst the overgrown fields and foundations.

GETTING THERE

From I-195, take exit 9 toward Sanford Road, then turn left. The road becomes Old Bedford Road. Take a left onto Blossom Road, and after 1.3 miles, bear right onto Indian Town Road. Follow it for about 1.7 miles to reach the parking lot. A blue sign will mark its entry on your left.

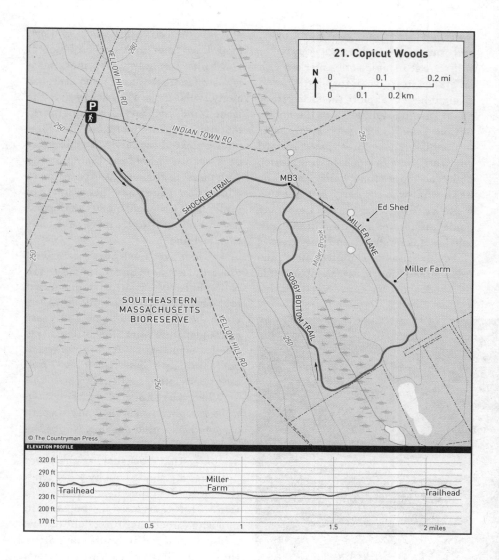

ELEVATION PROFILE

THE HIKE

To begin your journey to the abandoned Miller Farm settlement, exit the parking lot and cross the street to pick up the Shockley Trail. (You can grab a map at an information board in the parking lot, but you probably won't need it.) An important note: Wear bright-colored clothing during hunting season. An informational sign riddled with bullet holes at the beginning of the Shockley Trail should serve as a reminder in case you forget. Pass the sign to kick off an easy jaunt through the forest. Approach a large stand of beech trees on your left before crossing the dirt path that is Yellow Hill Road. Bypass the green gate along the Shockley Trail to see the hallmarks of a New England forest: stone walls, puddingstone, pines and oaks, and crunchy leaves beneath your feet.

Arrive at an intersection marked with an MB3 sign. You can turn left or keep straight here to explore the farm settlement. Turning right leads to the Soggy Bottom Trail, which we'll explore later in the hike. These forest paths reward you with stone bridges, fanning ferns, and even more stone walls. The walls flank what was formerly Miller Lane, a 150-year-old cart path. The scenic boulevard retains an aura of grandness, lined as it is by stones and leafy trees.

You'll soon enter a hunting safety zone (read: no shooting) to find a timber-frame Ed Shed, short for education shed. It's

A CELLAR HOLE FROM THE ABANDONED MILLER FARM SETTLEMENT

a gazebo-like structure where you can plop down to enjoy a packed lunch, if you'd like. Beyond it, even more massive stones are a commanding presence along Miller Lane. They lead you to the Isaac Miller homestead, a former farm that dates back to the 1830s. The Miller family cleared the land with oxen way back when, then bordered their property with massive stone walls. According to a local newspaper, later generations of Miller built a sawmill along the Copicut River, finding it to be more profitable than farming.

Let your eyes wash over the curving vines and weeds to find the homestead's cellar hole. It's a surprisingly intact foundation for its age. Walk down the steps, like Miller did some 190 years ago, and picture what life was like inside this L-shaped abode. A warning: watch out for prickly raspberries—they'll grab onto your clothes for dear life.

When you're finished exploring, continue straight down Miller Lane to a path carpeted with pine needles. Notice the pines surrounding you—their branches are bare. That's because, as the lower branches are shaded out by taller ones, they lose their needles. Arrive at a tree with two arrow signs pointing in opposite directions. Turn right toward a tree with a red blaze to start along the Soggy Bottom trail, which winds through vernal pools. Stone walls slice up huge swaths of land. Immediately you'll notice random piles of stones in the woods beyond the trail. They're not Native American burial markers, as your imagination might lead you to believe, but simply piles of stones likely left over from wall-building.

As you continue to inspect the rock piles, you'll notice the Soggy Bottom trail is overgrown in spots. Rather than making the trek difficult, it makes it

STONE WALLS LINE A FORMER CART PATH

idyllic, as you hop from boardwalk to boardwalk between hanging branches and over vernal pools. This beautiful, moss-covered environment seems like it would be fit for fairies. Keep straight ahead to opt out of the one-way Cedar Swamp trail, keeping on the series of boardwalks. Soon, Soggy Bottom spits you out at Miller Lane once more. Turn left and walk along the former cart path for a few dozen steps, and then turn left again to retrace your steps. This is the Shockley Trail again, leading back to the street where the parking lot is situated.

F. Gilbert Hills State Forest

WHERE: Foxborough and Wrentham	
ADDRESS: 45 Mill Street, Foxborough, MA 02035	
TOTAL DISTANCE: 4 miles	
HIKING TIME: 2 hours 15 minutes	
ELEVATION GAIN: 347 feet	
DIFFICULTY: Moderate	
RESTROOMS: Yes	
DOGS ALLOWED: Yes	
WHAT TO EXPECT: A steady climb through a boulder garden, with a few steep ledges	

Most New Englanders make trips to Foxborough to watch the Patriots win football game after football game at Gillette Stadium. Whether you're in town for a game or not, a trip to F. Gilbert Hills State Forest is equally as exhilarating. The park measures more than 1,000 acres, totaling 23 miles of hiking, biking, and horseback riding trails. It's a foliage-filled wonderland in the fall and a shade-covered haven in the summertime, offering plenty of opportunities for fresh-air fun, no matter what season. The forest is also home to part of the Warner Trail, a 30-mile path that stretches from Sharon, Massachusetts to Diamond Hill State Park in Rhode Island.

Named after a former state forest employee, F. Gilbert Hills State Forest was purchased by Massachusetts in the 1930s for just $5 per acre. But before this swath of forest was ever named, it was inhabited by the Ponkapoag and Wampanoag peoples. The forest is littered with rocks, stones, and larger-than-life boulders, and it's thought that some of the forest's rock formations were created and used by the Native Americans before Foxborough was incorporated as a town in 1778. One such rock formation, called Dolmen Rock, is located in the park's High Rock area. It's a mysterious flat rock perched on three other rocks. Some speculate the Algonquin used it as an altar, others simply call it a result of glacial movement. Whatever it is, its origins—and the origins of many other unusual rocks in the forest—are still disagreed upon by scientists and historians today.

GETTING THERE

From I-95 S., take exit 7B to merge onto MA-140 N. toward Foxboro. Then take a sharp left onto Walnut Street, and after

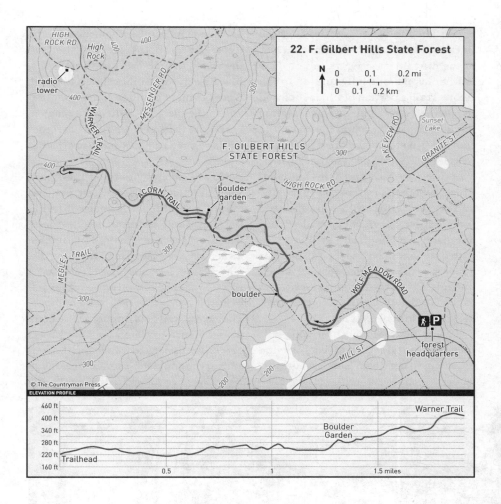

22. F. Gilbert Hills State Forest

ELEVATION PROFILE

0.7 mile, turn left onto South Street. Turn right onto Mill Street, and ahead, take a slight right to stay on it. The parking lot will be on your right.

THE HIKE

This out-and-back hike begins and ends at F. Gilbert Hills State Forest's headquarters. It follows the pink-blazed Acorn Trail to the Warner Trail and then turns back. As you start along the wide bridle trail that leads to the Acorn Trail, you'll likely see a fair amount of pups scampering down the path. This hike is popular with dog owners and in turn is a treat for dogs themselves.

After only a few hundred feet, cross over a small stream that runs beside a huge boulder. Then, when you see a sign pointing toward Wolf Meadow, head that way, passing by another gurgling stream on your right. Ahead, another sign for Wolf Meadow points left. Follow it to approach what's called Water Hole 1, one of 17 water holes carved out by the Civilian Conservation Corps. The water holes, or small ponds, were constructed to serve as water supplies in case of forest fires. Continue on and at the next intersection keep left. This is where you'll officially turn on to the Acorn Trail, a portion of which is closed to bikers. Here, red pines and sassafras flank your path; through the trees, the roofs of private homes are visible. The oak trees here are gilded in the fall, their golden leaves sparkling in the sunlight. This is where the trail becomes rocky—and doesn't let up until you reach the intersection at Warner Trail. You'll approach a huge glacial erratic soon, with a stone wall on its left. The boulder appears to teeter on one small, flat rock under it. Circle the boulder a few times to check out nature's balancing act, then keep right to stay on track.

Pass a body of water on your left, then cross a wider path to reach a ledge overlooking the water. Gentle waves can be seen rippling the pond through the trees. Ahead, another ledge looks out to the water, though this one is quite narrow. Be careful at this point in the trail. Another huge boulder stands to greet you in the distance. When you reach it, keep right to head downhill. Then, cross a bridge over a small swamp to arrive at a maze of rocks.

You've officially entered the Acorn Trail's boulder garden, where you can mount and climb the rocks littering the trail. Some are ultrasmooth stones, while others are covered in lichen. Either way, they make for a stunning display against a woodsy backdrop. Pass a second water hole, then let your eyes roll over the rocks that beg to be climbed. The Acorn Trail cuts through these boulders. Be sure to watch for pink blazes carefully; it's easy to wander off the trail among the boulders. There's some tough

A ROCKY CLIMB IN THE WOODS

ONE OF SEVERAL WATER HOLES

climbing involved here, and it gets even more difficult as you approach the Warner Trail. If you're struggling now, it might be best to turn back at this point. If you do continue climbing, keep right at the grassy path atop the hill, and follow an unpaved gravel road for a bit before climbing uphill again. Once you meet up with the Warner Trail, you can turn around and retrace your steps to the parking lot. Or, if you're feeling up to it, you could continue to the radio tower and the park's High Rock before heading home.

23

Freetown-Fall River State Forest

WHERE: Fall River, Freetown, and Lakeville

ADDRESS: 110 Slab Bridge Road, Freetown, MA 02702

TOTAL DISTANCE: 4.15 miles

HIKING TIME: 2 hours 15 minutes

ELEVATION GAIN: 210 feet

DIFFICULTY: Easy, with one optional strenuous portion

RESTROOMS: Yes

DOGS ALLOWED: Yes

WHAT TO EXPECT: A fun out-and-back through the forest, punctuated by a scramble to the top of a pointed rock

Let's cut to the chase: Freetown-Fall River State Forest (usually just called Freetown State Forest) has a reputation for being haunted. It's part of what's called the Bridgewater Triangle, a 200-square-mile region that's supposedly been home to various bizarre and unexplainable happenings over the years. The 5,000-acre forest is the most "active" part of the triangle, according to mysteriousuniverse.org, which calls it "a veritable wellspring of the weird and bizarre." Among the weird stuff that has been said to happen in Freetown State Forest since Europeans started settling the Wampanoag land in the 1600s? Ghost sightings, UFOs, appearances by Bigfoot, random orbs of light, disappearances, suicides, cattle mutilation, and poltergeist activity are a few examples. Freetown's legends have attracted the likes of Satanist and cultists, coming with their own sets of strange phenomenon.

The spooky stories are countless, and yet their veracity is dubious. Because a Wampanoag reservation abuts Freetown-Fall River State Forest, and because the land was originally settled by Native Americans, it's more likely that centuries of white men have been projecting their fears about the unknown (in this case, the Wampanoag tribe) on the area.

Aside from thrill-seeking teens, Freetown State Forest today attracts hikers, dirt bikers, mountain bikers, horseback riders, and other nature lovers. Of course, the only way to find out if Freetown State Forest is *really* haunted is to visit for yourself. Happy hiking.

GETTING THERE

From I-93 S., take exit 4 for MA-24 S. toward Brockton. Continue on MA-24 S. for 28 miles, then take exit 10 for N. Main

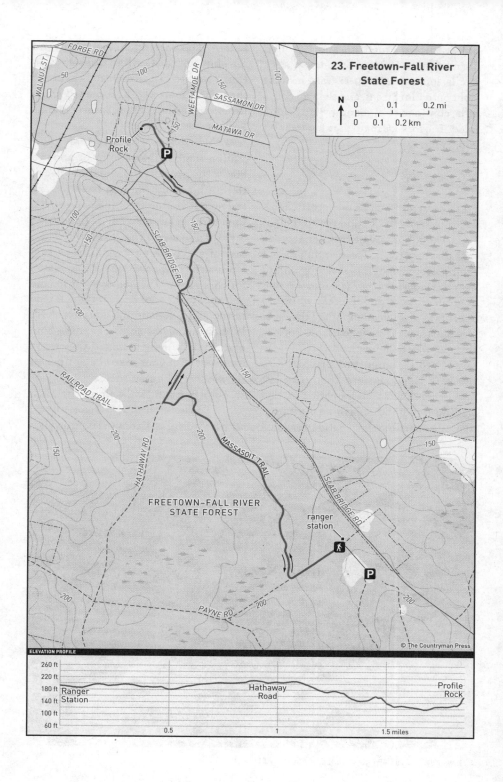

N

| 0 | 0.1 | 0.2 mi |
| 0 | 0.1 | 0.2 km |

FORGE RD.
WALNUT ST.
WEETAMOE DR.
SASSAMON DR.
MATAWA DR.
Profile
Rock
P
SLAB BRIDGE RD.
RAILROAD TRAIL
HATHAWAY RD.
MASSASOIT TRAIL
FREETOWN–FALL RIVER
STATE FOREST
ranger
station
P
SLAB BRIDGE RD.
PAYNE RD.

50
100
150
150
150
100
150
150
200
200
200
200
150
150
150
200
200

© The Countryman Press

ELEVATION PROFILE

260 ft				
220 ft				
180 ft	Ranger	Hathaway		Profile
140 ft	Station	Road		Rock
100 ft				
60 ft				
	0.5	1	1.5 miles	

Street toward Freetown and Assonet. Turn left onto N. Main Street, and after a mile, left onto MA-79-N. Take a slight right onto Elm Street, and then after 0.4 mile, continue straight onto Slab Bridge Road. The forest's main parking lot is on your right.

THE HIKE

Freetown-Fall River State Forest has 25 miles of trails to go along with its legends, though many of them crisscross with dirt bike trails. The piercing roar of their motors is not a pleasant sound to hear during a hike, nor is being worried about having to dodge bikes whizzing by. This is why I've highlighted the bike-free Massasoit Trail up to Profile Rock as the best way to enjoy the forest.

To begin, enter the driveway to the Park Headquarters, then turn left and drive down a short path past the wading pond and splash park—a popular summertime destination for local kiddos. The parking lot is just beyond the statue of the Civilian Conservation Corps worker, installed in 2002 to honor the young men who first blazed trails for Massachusetts State Forests and its Parks system.

Trail maps are available at an information board in the parking lot, and in a box at the nearby ranger station. Reach the trailhead by walking back toward the ranger station from the parking lot, then turning left onto Payne Road. This dirt road leads to the Massasoit Trail, an out-and-back path you'll take to a landmark known as Profile Rock. Watch for cars as you keep an eye out for the entrance to the trail on your right. A blue triangle sign signals that you've made it. While you may be able to hear the hum of dirt bikes in the distance, they won't intersect with your hike at any time—if they follow the rules, that is.

Your pleasant walk along the Massasoit passes a gurgling stream topped with boardwalks. Cross the boardwalks,

A VIEW FROM THE TOP OF PROFILE ROCK, IF YOU DARE CLIMB IT

then use rocks sticking out of the water as stepping stones to make your way across. You'll have to hop over a downed tree ahead. Some parts of the trail are not as well-maintained as others, but there aren't any huge obstructions blocking the path. As for scenery, it's a lot of the same: oak trees, pine trees, fallen leaves, pine needles, stone walls. It's a classically New England walk through the woods, and nothing more. That is the beauty of this walk: It is simple, easy, and refreshing.

Cross another boardwalk before the trail opens to a dirt path called Hathaway Road. Turn right, and walk for about five minutes while watching for a trail opening on your left. A brown stake signals entry to the trail. Immediately, you'll notice, among pines and chestnut trees, an elm tree—a rare sight in these forests, as many elms succumbed to Dutch elm disease in the early 20th century.

Ahead, keep straight to continue your journey to Profile Rock. Cross Slab Bridge Road carefully, and enter into a dense grove of pines. It's shady and cool here, which will recharge you for your Profile Rock climb. Watch the forest floor for hunks of white quartz—the beautiful white stones occasionally rise from the ground on this trail. The journey becomes moderately hilly for a few moments as you climb up a rocky pathway. It then descends into a lower forest. Keep left at the bottom of this hill, then approach another road. This one leads to the parking area for Profile Rock. Take a right to reach the lot, and opt for either entrance to the loop around the rock. It's a short trip to reach a humongous pile of rocks. Trace the base of the mound and you'll see Profile Rock—a 50-foot-high formation that's supposed to resemble

THIS ANGLE SHOWS THE PROFILE OF PROFILE ROCK

the silhouette face of Wampanoag chief Massasoit. If you'd like to catch the profile from a different angle, you can scale the mini mountain, but be warned, the craggy scramble is a dangerous climb. In addition to the climb's difficulty, the rocks you're climbing are often crowded with people. There is broken glass and graffiti tucked into its crevices—unfortunate results of being such a popular landmark. The views from the top, however, are unparalleled. On a clear day, you can see panoramic views of Massachusetts' southern coast.

Your best bet is to climb up the left hand side of the pile, then slowly make your way down under the profile. When you're finished exploring, head back the same way you came. It's about 2 miles back to the parking lot.

Moose Hill Wildlife Sanctuary

WHERE: Sharon	
ADDRESS: 293 Moose Hill Street, Sharon, MA 02067	
TOTAL DISTANCE: 3.2 miles	
HIKING TIME: 2 hours	
ELEVATION GAIN: 331 feet	
DIFFICULTY: Moderate	
RESTROOMS: Yes	
DOGS ALLOWED: No	
WHAT TO EXPECT: An up-and-down climb where you can catch your breath at scenic lookouts	

In 1916, the Massachusetts Audubon Society made a historic purchase: its first-ever wildlife sanctuary. The spot? The nearly 2000 acres of woodlands now making up Moose Hill Wildlife Sanctuary. It was here that Mass Audubon decided that habitat protection could help birds.

In the century since, the many habitats here—which include vernal pools, cedar knolls, ponds, streams, and red maple swamps—have been happy homes for many species. The list includes not just birds, like warblers, bluebirds, and owls, but also turtles, foxes, coyotes, deer, and other animals. The land has been useful to humans, too. Between the trails' rocky ledges and leafy paths, there are stone walls from former farms, a cistern, foundations from long-gone buildings, a fire tower, and an aging barn. There's even a chimney from an old log cabin atop the highlight of the sanctuary: Bluff Overlook.

GETTING THERE

From 1-95, take exit 10 toward Coney Street. Turn left off of the exit and take the first right onto Route 27. Continue for 0.6 mile, then take a left onto Moose Hill Street, a bumpy road off of the main drag. Drive for another 1.3 miles until you reach Moose Hill Parkway. Turn left into the parking lot at the visitor center.

THE HIKE

This hike, which is a link in the Bay Circuit Trail, comprises several connecting trails: the Billings Loop, the Bluff Trail, the Turkey Trail, the Old Pasture Trail, and the Summit Trail. It can be modified for a shorter trip. To do that, you'll need to obtain a trail map from the nature

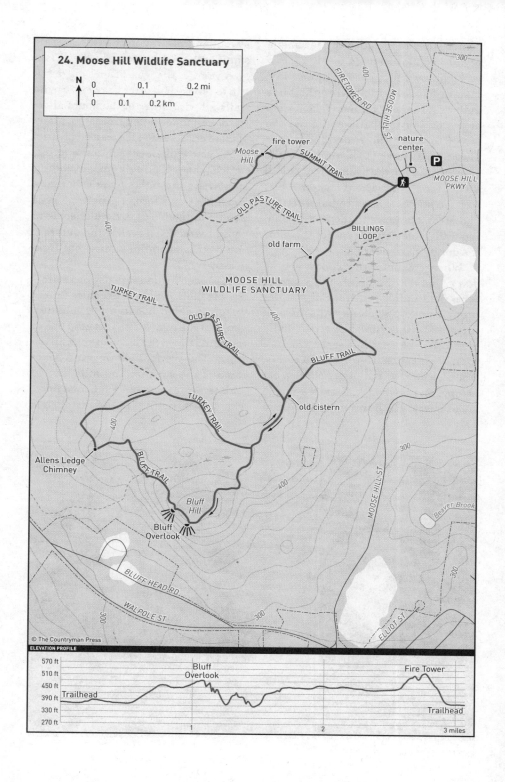

24. Moose Hill Wildlife Sanctuary

N

0   0.1   0.2 mi
0   0.1   0.2 km

fire tower

Moose Hill

SUMMIT TRAIL

FIRETOWER RD

MOOSE HILL ST

nature center

P

MOOSE HILL PKWY

OLD PASTURE TRAIL

old farm

BILLINGS LOOP

MOOSE HILL WILDLIFE SANCTUARY

TURKEY TRAIL

OLD PASTURE TRAIL

BLUFF TRAIL

old cistern

TURKEY TRAIL

Allens Ledge Chimney

BLUFF TRAIL

Bluff Hill

Bluff Overlook

MOOSE HILL ST

Beaver Brook

BLUFF HEAD RD

WALPOLE ST

ELLIOT ST

© The Countryman Press

ELEVATION PROFILE

570 ft
510 ft
450 ft
390 ft
330 ft
270 ft

Bluff Overlook

Fire Tower

Trailhead

Trailhead

1   2   3 miles

center—they're included in the sanctuary's $4 admission price.

Begin by exiting the nature center, map in hand, and following the brick path past the playground. Take a right at the end of the path, and cross the street to reach the two stone pillars ahead. This marks the beginning of the trail. Be warned, the trails at Moose Hill do not have color-coded markers—just wooden stakes in the ground with text and arrows to point to the corresponding trails. Keep an eye out for these for the duration of your hike.

When you enter the woods, just as you round out the first bend, a former farm field unfolds in front of you. Its property-marking stone walls are still intact, and the view has a decidedly old-world feel. Turn left at the juncture for more classical New England sights. Ahead, a storage building houses a bat colony, and beyond it, there's a maple sugar shack. Head through the field to

a wooden walkway in the woods. This signifies the beginning of the Bluff Trail.

A word to the wise? Don't make the trip to Moose Hill after heavy rains; the trails fill with water in the hours afterward. Watch for fallen trees, too. Many of them crisscrossed the trail on my trip.

As you walk deeper into the forest, notice the seemingly never-ending stonewalls throughout the sanctuary. You'll pass by a former cistern on your way up to the lookout. If you decide to pause there, you'll realize the dull roar you hear is not from nature, but from nearby I-95.

A sudden incline signals you're nearing the bluff. The trail becomes immediately rockier, but in a few minutes, you're at the top. Take a rest atop one of the boulders on the ledge to soak up the views. The overlook showcases a panorama of the surrounding hills, dotted with water towers and telephone lines. The large structure in the distance is

BLUFF OVERLOOK IN EARLY SPRING

A CLASSIC NEW ENGLAND LANDSCAPE

the home of the New England Patriots: Gillette Stadium.

Once you've taken at least a few good Instagram photos, begin the descent down the peak. Cross streams and more stone walls, heading up, then down, then up again, to reach Allens Ledge Chimney. The chimney is the only remaining part of a burned-down cabin that once existed at the site. Continue along the trail, then turn right to stay on the Bluff Trail. Turn right again to walk on the Turkey Trail for a few minutes, until you find yourself on the Bluff Trail once again by heading left. Here, you're retracing your steps for a bit until you reach the Old Pasture Trail. Head left. Ignore the signs pointing to the Moose Hill Trail to stay on Old Pasture Trail, which you'll follow until you see a sign for Summit Trail. Begin this route, keeping your eye out for white rectangular trail markers on trees. It's important to follow these markers, as the trail becomes somewhat unclear at points along the Summit Trail. The markers will lead you to the fire tower, which sits at an elevation of 534 feet.

Mind the graffiti and broken beer bottles as you make your way around the tower. There's a road to the left, but don't take it. Instead, continue circling the fire tower until you see the trail in the woods. It's marked by a Bay Circuit Trail icon on the tree. More highway sounds (and the occasional police siren) will remind you you're not far from civilization. Continue walking for 15 more minutes until you're back at the stone pillars.

Myles Standish State Forest

WHERE: Plymouth and Carver	
ADDRESS: Upper College Pond Road, Plymouth, MA 02360	
TOTAL DISTANCE: 3.7 miles	
HIKING TIME: 2 hours	
ELEVATION GAIN: 284 feet	
DIFFICULTY: Moderate	
RESTROOMS: Yes	
DOGS ALLOWED: Yes	
WHAT TO EXPECT: A bracing journey through a scrubby forest near the coast	

At a massive 12,400 acres, Myles Standish State Forest is one of the largest state forests in Massachusetts, and the largest in southeastern Massachusetts. Established in 1916, the park was named after a Mayflower passenger who served as a military leader in Plymouth Colony in the 1600s. Many of the forest's trails and fire roads can be credited to the Civilian Conservation Corps. The 1930s-era federal program improved state parks across Massachusetts, and its workers planted trees and built campsites. In Myles Standish, there's a rare CCC relic: a bathhouse near Fearing Pond is the last-remaining log bathhouse built by the CCC in the Massachusetts State Parks system.

This state forest been a haven for wildlife lovers for over a century, offering up beautiful landscapes and recreational opportunities for notables like Theodore Roosevelt, Woodrow Wilson, William Howard Taft, and Daniel Webster, to name a few. The forest's history goes far beyond when the park was established in 1916, of course. Some 20,000 years ago, this land was covered by a gigantic glacier. As the glacier receded, sand and stone was deposited here, and some chunks of ice became caught in the land's depressions. The chunks eventually melted, creating the forest's 58 kettle hole ponds.

Aside from kettle ponds, Myles Standish is home to a range of habitats and wildlife. Experimental cranberry bogs can be found next to Rocky Pond, for example. It's also known for its "pine barrens," or plant communities made up of pitch pines, scrub oaks, and shrubs. Pine barrens are rare, and they occur when pitch pines form an open canopy on top, while scrub oaks and shrubs (like crowberry, blueberry,

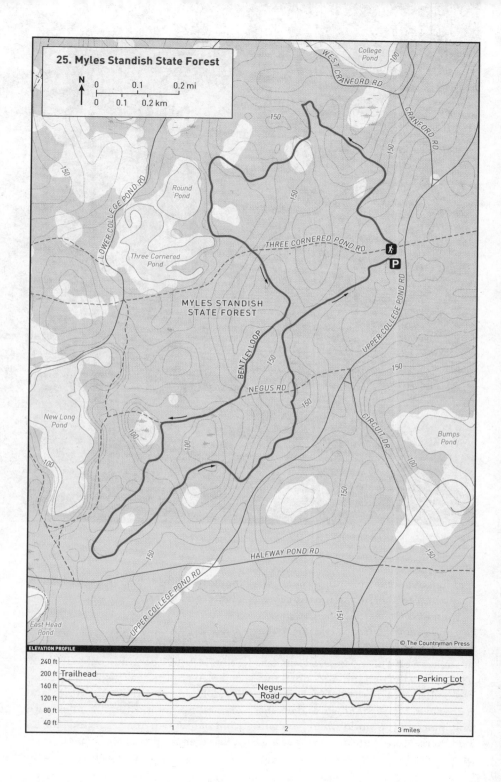

25. Myles Standish State Forest

N

| 0 | 0.1 | 0.2 mi |
| 0 | 0.1 | 0.2 km |

West Cranford Rd

College Pond

Cranford Rd

Lower College Pond Rd

Round Pond

Three Cornered Pond

Three Cornered Pond Rd

MYLES STANDISH STATE FOREST

Bentley Loop

Negus Rd

Upper College Pond Rd

New Long Pond

Circuit Dr

Bumps Pond

Halfway Pond Rd

Upper College Pond Rd

East Head Pond

© The Countryman Press

ELEVATION PROFILE

240 ft
200 ft — Trailhead
160 ft
120 ft
80 ft
40 ft

Negus Road

Parking Lot

1   2   3 miles

TOWERING PINES IN MYLES STANDISH STATE FOREST

and huckleberry) grow underneath it, according to the Department of Recreation and Conservation. The park's dry and sandy landscape is home to the third-largest pine barren in the world, as well as a host of endangered species. The federally endangered northern red-bellied cooter is a turtle that makes its home in Myles Standish, and it's the only place in the world where you can find them. More than 40 other rare and endangered species live in the forest, including birds, butterflies, reptiles, plants, and more.

GETTING THERE

From MA-3 S., continue onto US-44 E. and MA-3 S. Then take exit 5 onto Long Pond Road toward South Street and Plymouth Center. After 3.7 miles, turn right onto Alden Road. Continue for 1.4 miles, then continue onto Upper College Pond Road. Keep left to stay on Upper

College Pond Road. Parking lot #2 will be on your right.

THE HIKE

I recommend driving to the park headquarters on Cranberry Road (parking lot #1) to pick up a trail map and visit the restrooms before hitting the trails. Then, hop in the car again to get to parking lot #2 on Upper College Pond Road, where this hike will begin and end.

To kick off your trip around the Bentley Loop, head to the northern end of the parking lot (or the left side, if you're facing Upper College Pond Road). The narrow trail at the far end of the lot is the one you'll want to hop on. You'll know you're on the right path when you see a small brown BENTLEY LOOP sign in the trees just beyond the parking lot. Follow this sign through the pines and follow the blue blazes for the remainder of your trip.

Things are soft as you get going, in two senses of the word "soft." Not only is the walking flat and easy, but the ground beneath your feet is a cushion of sand and pine needles. You can walk with spring in your step here before the trees open to a grassy field, the first of several wildlife management areas you'll travel through during your hike. Glimpse the gentle hills of the field in the distance as you traverse the clearing. Descend into the forest ahead, then keep left to stay on the Bentley Loop. The woods appear scrubbier here, reminding you that you're not far from the coast. Tree roots hide beneath the orange pine needles underfoot, so watch your step as you begin to climb the first of several hills on this hike. The trail becomes increasingly more narrow at the top of the small hill, winding through the pitch pines that surround you.

Approach a sign pointing toward Torrey Pond. Instead of heading this way, keep left to continue your loop. Scale a sandy hill before making it up to another wide-open field, this one dotted with nesting boxes. Turn right here, and keep right to head back into the woods. Follow a wider, sandier path for a while before entering the third field of the day. You might spot pheasant feathers along the path, and if you pause for a moment, you can detect the ever-fragrant sweet fern growing beside the trail. The plant

A SANDY PORTION OF THE TRAIL

spot blue blazes on the trees. You'll need to cross a wide, unpaved road for a moment before turning onto the narrow trail of the Bentley Loop.

More towering pines stand to greet you here. It's a denser forest than other ones you've seen on this hike—it transitions to a population of white pines as you continue. The trail then spits you out at another unpaved road. Follow this one, called Negas Road, until you see a sign on your left for the Bentley Loop. Turn left, then notice yet another kettle pond on your right. Keep making your way through the sun-dappled woods and continue straight once you reach the next open field. Your path across the field is clearly marked, if you keep an eye out for the blue blazes. A huge pine tree bears a large blue blaze, beckoning you back into the woods from the field. Begin a gradual descent into these woods, then approach one of the last fields of the hike. This one is less clearly marked than the previous one—to make it through, cut straight across the field to a narrow trail opening. (There's a lack of signage here, unfortunately.) You'll then begin a steep climb up a hill, turning left at the top of it. A set of sandy steps leads downward. Cut straight across a sandy pit before picking up a wider trail that offers a slight incline. Walk across one more clearing, and when you see a B6 marker on a tree, continue straight. Then, turn right to return to the parking lot.

If you're visiting during the fall (bonus points during the month of October), it's worth it to drive over to parking lot #7 at Rocky Pond. From there, you can walk along the short Rocky Pond Bog Loop to see crimson cranberry bogs, sprinkled throughout southeastern Massachusetts.

thrives in sandy soil like the kind you're standing on.

Enter into the cover of the forest again, where it becomes shady and cool. Through the trees, you'll be able to spot the sparkling waters of Round Pond, but you won't get close enough to see its shores just yet. The population of pines here creates an almost eerie environment, thanks to an absence of needles or greenery on lower branches. Another pond, Three Cornered Pond, appears through the trees ahead of you. You'll get a closer look as you walk beside the water on your right. Instead of turning toward the water, turn left where you

26

Nasketucket Bay State Reservation

WHERE: Mattapoisett

ADDRESS: 94 Brandt Island Road, Mattapoisett, MA 02739

TOTAL DISTANCE: 2.5 miles

HIKING TIME: 1.5 hours

ELEVATION GAIN: 50 feet

DIFFICULTY: Easy

RESTROOMS: No

DOGS ALLOWED: Yes

WHAT TO EXPECT: A low-key walk through meadows and woodlands, leading to the clean, sparkling waters of Buzzards Bay

Nasketucket Bay State Reservation has it all: eelgrass meadows, coastal forests, salt marshes, shellfish beds, and a breezy bay. Made up of almost 400 acres along Buzzard's Bay, the property is popular with hikers, horseback riders, and in wintertime, cross-country skiers.

The reservation's six trails flaunt a range of trees, including beech, birch, pine, oak, and holly. According to the Buzzards Bay Coalition, they provide a sheltered environment for birds, reptiles, and plenty of woodland mammals. Keep an eye out for salamanders and frogs in the woods' three vernal pools, and at the beach, look for oyster, clam, and whelk shells. The shells, says the coalition, signal a robust shellfish population in the healthy waters.

No matter which route you take here, every leafy trail leads to the sparkling shores of Nasketucket Bay. Who says a lofty mountaintop is a hike's greatest reward?

GETTING THERE

From I-93 S., use the left two lanes to take exit 4 for MA-24 S. toward Brockton. Continue on MA-24 S. for 23 miles, then take exit 12 for MA-140 toward New Bedford/Taunton. Turn right at the exit, and then after 18 miles, take exit 2A to merge onto I-195 E. toward Cape Cod. Take exit 18 for MA-240 S. toward Fairhaven. Follow US-6 E. until you reach Brandt Island Road on your right.

THE HIKE

This lollipop hike beings with Nasketucket Bay State Reservation's Bridle Trail. It connects to the Salt Marsh Trail, then the Holly Trail, to complete a loop, before turning back onto the Bridle Trail once more. To begin, pick up the

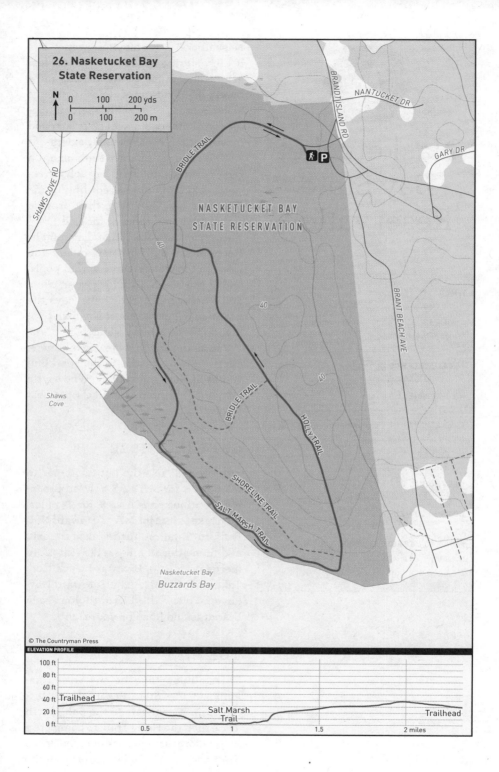

26. Nasketucket Bay
State Reservation

N
0   100   200 yds
0   100   200 m

BRANDT ISLAND RD
NANTUCKET DR
GARY DR

SHAWS COVE RD

NASKETUCKET BAY
STATE RESERVATION

BRIDLE TRAIL

40

40

40

BRANT BEACH AVE

BRIDLE TRAIL

HOLLY TRAIL

Shaws
Cove

SHORELINE TRAIL

SALT MARSH TRAIL

Nasketucket Bay
Buzzards Bay

© The Countryman Press

ELEVATION PROFILE

100 ft
80 ft
60 ft
40 ft Trailhead
20 ft
0 ft

Salt Marsh
Trail

Trailhead

0.5   1   1.5   2 miles

LOOK FOR SEA SNAILS AMONG THE SALTY STONES

Bridle Trail from the (free) parking lot, skirting around a set of green gates. The wide, grassy trail makes for flat and easy walking. The grass, however, grows tall in some sections, and the trail is flanked by thick woods—this is the perfect recipe for acquiring a pattern of mosquito bites, so be sure to pack bug spray.

When you see a sign marking the Meadow Trail that reads 0.8 MILE TO THE COAST, bypass it and continue straight on the Bridle Trail. Soon, the walk opens to a lush meadow with tall grasses and black-eyed susans. Ahead, keep right to veer onto the Salt Marsh Trail, which will lead you to the blue waters of Buzzards Bay. Upon entering the woods of the Salt Marsh Trail, you'll immediately smell the salty brine of the sea. Blue blazes—and the scent of the ocean—will lead you out of the woods and onto the beach.

Though there are patches of sand, this beach isn't the place to stake an umbrella in the ground and sprawl out on a blanket. The rocky coastline is best suited not to sunbathers, but to nature-lovers. Approach the shore, where gentle waves wash over the rocks, to find common periwinkles, or sea snails, latching onto the salty stones. Look up to catch glimpses of West Island, a land formation jutting off Fairhaven, Massachusetts, as well as sailboats dotting the waters. On a hot day, hikers are invited to go for a swim.

After a proper visit with the sea, continue along the coastline. A sandy stretch flanked by sea grasses forms an aisle for you to walk down. Follow it, and feel the breeze in your hair, as dried seaweed crunches underfoot. In the distance, two trees growing toward the ocean beckon you closer. Approach them and round this bend to complete

THE TRAIL TRACES THE SHORELINE

your coastal walk. A hefty boulder with an arrow painted on it marks the entrance back into the woods—and the connection to the Holly Trail. Head left to duck back into the forest, and immediately notice the ferns and holly plants festooning the path. This cooler, shaded walk offers respite from the sunny beach and meadow. At the next trail intersection, continue straight to stay on the Holly Trail. Then you'll meet up at the Bridle Trail once more, where you'll turn right to emerge from the forest. This part of the Bridle Trail—where you started—is familiar. Follow it to reach the parking lot.

Whitney and Thayer Woods

WHERE: Cohasset and Hingham

ADDRESS: Howes Lane, Cohasset, MA 02025

TOTAL DISTANCE: 3.5 miles

HIKING TIME: 2 hours

ELEVATION GAIN: 172 feet

DIFFICULTY: Moderate

RESTROOMS: No

DOGS ALLOWED: Yes

WHAT TO EXPECT: A restorative jaunt through a forest dotted with flowers, brooks, and streams

A wild azalea garden, a hermit's cave, old carriage roads—the Whitney and Thayer Woods, a South Shore jewel, are teeming with unique sights and sounds. Before they became a place to enjoy nature, however, the woods were very much a place for work. In the 17th century, it wasn't the sea of bright-pink flowers that brought folks to the woods, but utilitarian fields for farming and logging. Known as the Common Lands of the Hingham Planters, the land was sliced up into parcels, and stone walls were put in place as dividers. Over the years, the amount of trees dwindled as settlers continued to cut them for firewood.

By the early 1900s, many of the trees had repopulated as agriculture in New England waned. The woods took on new use as a location for sporting grounds, thanks to a man named Henry Whitney. An equestrian, Whitney sought to create a private retreat for horseback riding, complete with bridle trails and carriage roads for buggies. Later, the land was turned over to a horseback-riding group called the Whitney Woods Association. The group donated the land to the Trustees of Reservations in the 1930s. About 10 years after it was acquired, the Trustees named the reservation the Whitney and Thayer Woods. Thayer was tacked onto the name in honor of the wife of a former dean of Harvard Law School, Mrs. Ezra Ripley Thayer. Born as Ethel Randolph Clark, she donated land west of the original plot to the Trustees. Donating to the Trustees became a bit of a family affair, as Thayer's daughter, artist Polly Thayer Starr, turned over Weir River Farm to the organization in 1999.

The Whitney and Thayer Woods' current 824 acres include 10 miles of trails. There are plenty of offshoots to explore away from the main path, allowing you

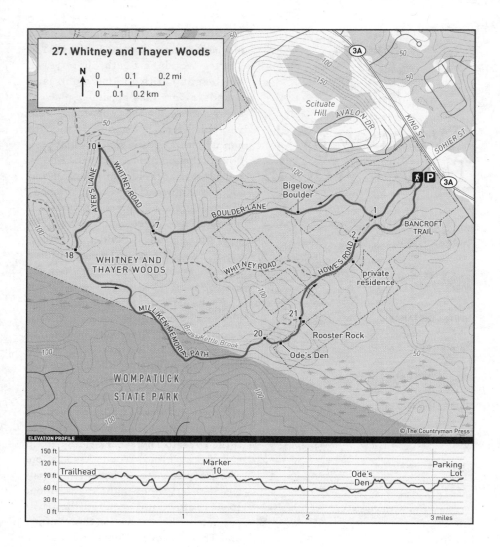

27. Whitney and Thayer Woods

N
0   0.1   0.2 mi
0   0.1   0.2 km

Scituate Hill

Bigelow Boulder

BOULDER LANE

AYER'S LANE

WHITNEY ROAD

WHITNEY AND THAYER WOODS

WHITNEY ROAD

HOWE'S ROAD

private residence

BANCROFT TRAIL

MILLIKEN MEMORIAL PATH

Bassketttle Brook

Rooster Rock

Ode's Den

WOMPATUCK STATE PARK

AVALON DR

KING ST

SOHIER ST

© The Countryman Press

ELEVATION PROFILE

150 ft
120 ft
90 ft
60 ft
30 ft
0 ft

Trailhead

Marker 10

Ode's Den

Parking Lot

1   2   3 miles

to examine a rock formation called Ode's Den, a grove of American holly, and more.

GETTING THERE

From Route 3, take exit 15 for Derby Street toward Hingham/Weymouth. Keep right at the fork, then merge onto Derby Street, or Route 53. After 1.5 miles, turn left onto Cushing Street, then after a mile, turn right to stay on Cushing Street. Turn right onto Route 3A, and follow it for 2 miles. Once you see a Mobil station on the left, look right. Do not turn right onto Howes Lane, where your GPS may have led you. Instead, take the road just after it—this is the parking lot.

THE HIKE

You can begin this loop, which combines the blue and yellow trails, on either end of the parking lot. I chose to start the hike on the right side near the trail map sign. Throughout the hike, you'll see a range of colorful plant life, including holly, azaleas, and rhododendrons.

At the first juncture in the trail, keep right to stay on Boulder Lane, and head past the green set of gates. You'll soon understand how this path got its name. To your right, admire stone walls and huge rock formations, then continue on until you reach the hike's first landmark: Bigelow Boulder. It was named for E. Victor Bigelow, the first author to write a narrative history of Cohasset. Bypass the offshoots onto the white-marked trails, instead staying straight for blue. You'll continue to be surrounded by larger-than-life boulders for much of the trail. Soon, the trail transitions into a wide gravel path. Take a sharp right onto Ayer's Lane, which straddles both the red and yellow trails.

Take a left to turn onto the Milliken Memorial Path, named for Mabel Minott Milliken, who planted a garden along the trail in the 1920s. (Notice a boulder with a plaque dedicated to her on your left.) To enjoy this path to its fullest, visit during late spring, so you can see the rhododendrons, azaleas, and other vivid flowering shrubs lining it. The rhododendrons are particularly beautiful—a grove of them forms an arch over the trail at one point, creating a pink and purple tunnel for you to walk under. Here the trail levels out, and the flat forest floor makes for a leisurely walk. If you do end up needing a rest, the Milliken Memorial Path is dotted with wooden benches. One bench in particular, on the left hand side of the path, overlooks a glacial depression. This is a good spot to catch your breath before embarking on the last leg of the trip.

From here, the walk becomes greener, and more rhododendrons are visible. Cross a stream via a short wooden foot

BIGELOW BOULDER

A REST AREA

bridge, and take care to sidestep some toppled trees. Many of them are quite old and, in their supine position, put their massive roots on display. Once you reach Brass Kettle Brook, you'll notice the rocks at the bottom of the stream look like they've been covered with a golden amber filter.

Toward the end of the yellow Milliken Memorial Path, I suggest taking a detour at markers 21 and 22 to see two landmarks. The first is Ode's Den, a group of glacial erratics you can climb up and down into. The rocky hideaway is named for Theodore "Ode" Pritchard, who, according to the Trustees, lost his home in 1830 and decided to make a new shelter beneath the rocks. Inspect the many crevices here. Can you picture him relaxing in the underbelly of the formation? Once you're out of the den, ascend a hill covered in tree roots, noticing the moss- and lichen-covered stones on the way back down. Ahead, the second landmark, Rooster Rock, looms in

the distance. This formation is made of a massive boulder balancing atop a flatter one, with a single small rock holding it all in place. It resembles a sitting hen and also makes for a good photo opp.

Here, the detour lets out back onto the yellow trail, which soon meets back at the blue trail, dubbed Howe's Road. At trail marker 22, you must enter a small stretch of private property. Don't be deterred by the gates and the abundance of signs. Simply walk past them and onto a driveway-like path. You'll see the private residence—a charming grey Cape house—on your right. Continue on to reach the main trail once again. You'll know you've made it when you see trail marker number 2. Turn right out of the driveway and back into the woods.

Cross a wooden footbridge over a stream, and notice how the hike becomes somewhat hillier as you near its end. Take whiffs of a few more rhody blossoms before you arrive back at the parking lot.

28

Wompatuck State Park

WHERE: Hingham	
ADDRESS: 204 Union Street, Hingham, MA 02043	
TOTAL DISTANCE: 4.8 miles	
HIKING TIME: 2.5 hours	
ELEVATION GAIN: 321 feet	
DIFFICULTY: Moderate	
RESTROOMS: Yes	
DOGS ALLOWED: Yes	
WHAT TO EXPECT: A long ramble through the woods broken up by a journey to the summit of Prospect Hill	

Wompatuck State Park, lovingly called Wompy by locals, stretches to almost 3,600 acres, covering a large swath of Hingham, as well as parts of Cohasset, Norwell, and Scituate. The land was originally owned by a Native American chief known as Josiah Wompatuck, but it's what happened at the spot in the mid-1900s that put the area on the map.

In 1941, the US Navy acquired the once-private land that makes up Wompatuck State Park to expand its Hingham Naval Ammunitions Depot, also known as the Cohasset Annex. To house more munitions, the Navy built cement bunkers and other storage units. It turned out that building these bunkers was a good idea, as the munitions depot became the main supply of ammunitions for North Atlantic naval forces during World War II. The bunkers were deactivated at the conclusion of the war, then they were reactivated at the start of the Korean War. According to the Friends of Wompatuck, these bunkers stored explosives like TNT, bombs, fuses, and projectiles. Cartridges were produced and stored, missile parts were tested, and rocket fuels underwent experimentation—all on-site.

By 1962, the Cohasset Annex was deactivated for good, and four years later, in 1966, the Commonwealth of Massachusetts possessed the property. The land was purchased to be transformed into a public park in 1967, and eventually opened for limited outdoor recreational use in 1969. The Friends of Wompatuck cite the year of the land's dedication as Wompatuck State Park as 1973.

In the years after the park's opening, visitors could waltz into these former storage bunkers to find, as the *Boston Globe* called it, "rusting barrels of toxic materials." The Army Corps of Engineers worked for decades to patch up the

28. Wompatuck State Park

N

0   0.1   0.2 mi
0   0.1   0.2 km

FREE ST

UNION ST

visitor center

P

NW2

NW7

LAZELL ST

Woodpecker Pond

Bunker N-9

Accord Brook

NW8

NW5

NW10

S PLEASANT ST

UNION ST

W1

WOMPATUCK STATE PARK

Fulling Mill Brook

LAZELL ST

S PLEASANT ST

W2

W3

CHARLES ST

MARYKNOLL DR

W4

W6

SAW MILL POND RD

S1

MAST HILL RD

S2

Accord Brook

Holly Pond

PROSPECT ST

Prospect Hill

S7

S9

S5

Aaron River

© The Countryman Press

ELEVATION PROFILE

300 ft
240 ft
180 ft
120 ft
60 ft
0 ft

Trailhead

Prospect Hill

Trailhead

1   2   3   4 miles

various contamination problems that stemmed from the land's military history. A spot where the Navy destroyed the annex's unused munitions, dubbed the "burning ground," is still fenced off from the rest of the park. It continues to be monitored for water and soil contamination by the state Department of Environmental Protection.

The park is, of course, totally safe for all kinds of outdoor recreation. Today, visitors to Wompatuck State Park hike, camp, and bottle water at the famed Mt. Blue Spring. A favorite activity for locals? Stepping inside the restored N-9 bunker. It was renovated by three Eagle scouts in 2008 and is a stop on this hike.

GETTING THERE

From MA-3 S., take exit 15 for Derby Street toward Hingham/Weymouth. Keep right for MA-53 and merge onto Derby Street. After a half mile, bear left onto Cushing Street. Follow it for just over 2 miles, then turn left onto MA-228 N. After 0.8 mile, turn right onto Free Street. After another 0.8 mile, continue onto Lazell Street. Turn right onto Union Street, and the park will be on your left in just under 2 miles.

THE HIKE

Begin your hike at the NW1 junction marker. The opening to the trail is just behind the visitor center, toward the side of the parking lot that extends around and back to Union Street. On the Friends of Wompatuck map, which can be obtained from the visitor center, you'll see that this loop follows the NW markers until they become W markers, then S markers, and W and NW markers once more.

Your long walk through the woods starts off easy and stays that way for

A GURGLING BROOK

most of the trip. Dirt paths littered with stones lead to a footbridge over a brook. At the NW7 marker, turn left, and you'll notice the trail becomes more well-defined. It's only a few minutes later that Woodpecker Pond comes into view on your left. There's a seat at an overlook spot where you can survey the lily pad-sprinkled waters.

Continue on, meandering through the woods until you reach a boardwalk. Take a right at the end of it, noticing huge boulders left by glaciers just up the hill. This part of the trail follows the western edge of Wompatuck State Park, which becomes evident as you're invited to walk parallel to a worn, rusted fence that acts as a dividing line. When you approach the park's Pleasant Street entrance, continue past the gurgling steam on your right, and at market W1, turn right. Here, the trail widens, and at W2, becomes more of a gravel pathway lined with telephone poles.

THE ART-COVERED BUNKER

Turn right at marker W3, and enter a shady, sun-dappled forest where youngsters have carved their initials into beech trees. It's here you should start being vigilant about passing mountain bikers. Like you, they'll be heading up and down Prospect Hill very soon. After crossing a short bridge, continue straight after marker S1 to reach S2. This kicks off your ascent to the summit of Prospect Hill, the highest point in the town of Hingham. Turn left to begin a short, switchback trail to the top, noticing stone walls leading the way. There are several routes to get to the top, so when you reach an intersection in the trail, just make sure to head upward.

When you reach the top of the hill, there's a podium with a map on it, but not much else. Trees obstruct any views you might have had. This spot was once called Mount Ararat and had a fire tower atop it. The tower was constructed in 1916, and was actively used by the military until 1955. See if you can find the first three steps of the tower foundation.

When you're ready to head back down, follow the S5 marker, noticing the cairn on your left. As you approach S7, you'll see more stone walls lining the trail. Keep an eye out for S9, as it's easy to miss this left turn. Rocky outcroppings can be seen on both sides of the trail, and the terrain becomes a bit rockier. You'll soon be spit out at Wompatuck's campground— take your next left on the paved road here to pick up W6. You'll pass by a few more campsites before ambling down another grassy path. It leads to the beginning of the W3 route you took to Prospect Hill not too long ago.

Continue on, making your way through another meadow. At marker NW10, you'll see a paved path with graffitied propane tanks, but don't take it. Instead, go straight, and you'll head toward a former bunker. Called bunker N-9, it's one of the remnants of a time when the land that makes up Wompatuck State Park was the Cohasset Naval Annex. A handmade sign encourages visitors not to post pictures of the spot online, presumably because its walls are splashed with vibrant graffiti in all hues. When you're done exploring, keep along the path. There are not too many markers toward the end here, but you'll bear left to head back to the visitor center.

World's End

WHERE: Hingham

ADDRESS: Martins Lane, Hingham, MA 02043

TOTAL DISTANCE: 3.2 miles

HIKING TIME: 2 hours

ELEVATION GAIN: 310 feet

DIFFICULTY: Easy

RESTROOMS: Yes

DOGS ALLOWED: Yes

WHAT TO EXPECT: A picturesque stroll atop four harborside drumlins, where a grand estate was planned but never built

World's End is an extremely unique—and stunningly beautiful—property owned by the Trustees. Its four drumlins once formed an island at high tide, but in the 1600s, colonial farmers dammed the salt marsh there to grow hay, then cleared out the trees to grow crops. Two centuries later, in the 1880s, a wealthy Bostonian named John Brewer planned a farming estate on the land. He enlisted renowned landscape architect Frederick Law Olmsted to design a sprawling subdivision of 163 homes. Fortunately, the houses were never built, but the 4 miles of carriage paths that Olmsted laid out are still maintained today. (Walking along the grand allees feels like being transported back to the 19th century.)

This gem on Hingham's coast was almost wiped out—several times. After the housing subdivision plans were thwarted, the property again was put in jeopardy. In 1945, it was considered for the site of the United Nations headquarters, which eventually were established in New York City. Two decades later, there was talk of installing a nuclear power plant there, but plans never materialized. In 1967, the Trustees swooped in to the rescue, buying and preserving the land with help from locals and fundraisers.

This unequaled property offers incredible views of Boston Harbor, its islands, and the city skyline. In one visit, you'll glimpse a wide variety of landscapes, including meadows, salt marshes, woodlands, and granite ledges. Prepare to spot blueberry thickets underfoot, to look up at towering red cedars, and to feel compelled to buy a World's End t-shirt in the extremely tiny gift shop.

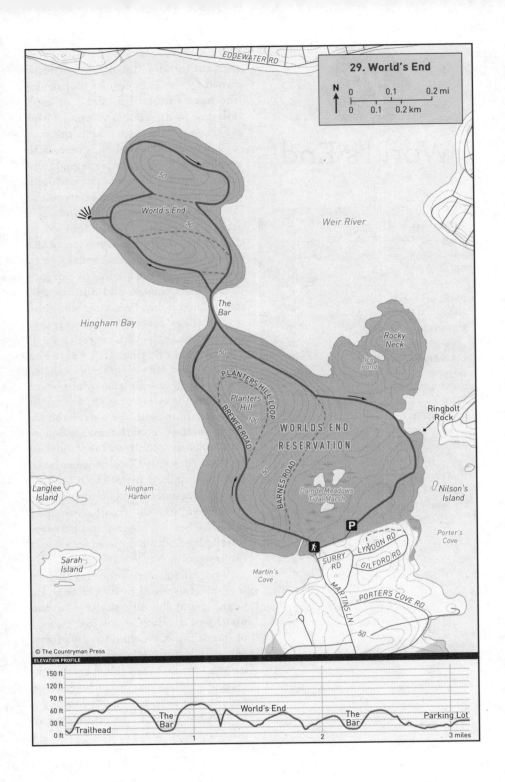

29. World's End

N

| 0 | 0.1 | 0.2 mi |
| 0 | 0.1 | 0.2 km |

EDGEWATER RD

World's End

Weir River

Hingham Bay

The Bar

Rocky Neck

Ice Pond

PLANTERS HILL LOOP

Planters Hill

BREWER ROAD

Ringbolt Rock

WORLDS' END RESERVATION

BARNES ROAD

Langlee Island

Hingham Harbor

Damde Meadows Tidal Marsh

Nilson's Island

P

Porter's Cove

LYNDON RD

SURRY RD

GILFORD RD

Sarah Island

Martin's Cove

MARTINS LN

PORTERS COVE RD

© The Countryman Press

ELEVATION PROFILE

150 ft				
120 ft				
90 ft				
60 ft		World's End		Parking Lot
30 ft	The Bar		The Bar	
0 ft	Trailhead			
		1	2	3 miles

THE BOSTON SKYLINE SEEN FROM WORLD'S END'S SHORES

GETTING THERE

From MA-3A S., enter the traffic circle at Quincy Point. Take the third exit to stay on MA-3A-S., or Washington Street. Follow MA-3A-S. for 5 miles, then follow Summer Street to Martins Lane. The parking area is behind the visitor center shed.

THE HIKE

Once you've taken care of the $8 entry fee at the beginning of the trail, cross the bridge over Damde Meadows tidal marsh. The hike outlined here will loop around this one-of-a-kind land formation, heading up a hill, over a sandbar, and to what feels like the end of the earth.

Immediately the path commands a grand presence. Grassy, bucolic meadows can be seen on either side of the trail, while aging towering trees, like lindens and maples, guide you along. These impressive allees were meant to be carriage paths for the housing subdivision that never was.

At the first fork in the trail, bear left onto Brewer Road. Tall grasses sway in the wind here, and as you admire them dancing in the sunlight, a view of the Boston skyline will sneak up on you. The city skyscrapers are partially obscured by Peddocks Island (see Hike #49), a popular Boston Harbor Island, as well as Bumpkin Island and parts of the nearby town of Hull. You'll notice deposits of Roxbury puddingstone along the trail as you round the base of Planters Hill.

Then "the bar" makes itself known.

This short, sandy spit looks out to the harbor on one side, and to boats docked along the Weir River on the other. A small beach invites you to take a load off before continuing on. Once you cross the spit, keep left to climb a short but steep hill. Poison ivy is abundant here. It flanks most of the paths, so take care not to wander off trail. You'll meet a gravel path with a bench, which is an excellent spot to get a complete view of the bar. As you trot along, look for a small spur trail on your left. Take it into the grasses to get a complete view of the city. This, like much of the reservation, is an ideal spot for Instagramming.

Pick the trail back up again to descend into a shady grove of trees. Upon emerging from them, you can watch planes fly in and out of Logan Airport across the waters in East Boston. You'll probably also experience a bit of coastal home envy, as the houses across the waters in Hingham and Hull appear all the more inviting in warm summer sunlight. Here, at the part of the peninsula dubbed World's End, it truly feels like the end of the earth. Grassy expanses overlook a deep blue harbor, and when there aren't other hikers around, the environment is almost dreamlike.

Continue your stroll around the perimeter of World's End, sticking left at each turn. Once you've made the rounds, you'll end up at the bar once again. This time, after crossing it, bear left to explore the eastern side of the reservation. The stroll stretches east, displaying occasional rock outcroppings. There's the option to head up and around Rocky Neck on your left, but this hike does not incorporate that additional loop. Keep along Weir River Road to be greeted by Ringbolt Rock on the coastal edges of the trail. From here, it's about 0.3 mile to the entrance to the park.

THE FAMED SPOT KNOWN AS "THE BAR"

III

NORTH OF BOSTON

Boxford State Forest

WHERE: Boxford

ADDRESS: 208 Middleton Road, Boxford, MA 01921

TOTAL DISTANCE: 4.25 miles

HIKING TIME: 2 hours 30 minutes

ELEVATION GAIN: 285 feet

DIFFICULTY: Moderate

RESTROOMS: No

DOGS ALLOWED: Yes

WHAT TO EXPECT: A thorough exploration of a lush forest, interrupted by glacial erratics, wildflowers, and a pond

Like many forests across New England, Boxford State Forest's farming history is still visible today in the form of extant stone walls. The land that makes up the forest was originally home to almost 200 members of the Agawam tribe, but when European settlers arrived in the mid-1600s, they cut down its trees to create farmland. By the 1800s, after farming in the rocky soil was abandoned, the land reverted to forest once again. The trees were logged until the 1920s and '30s, when the property was acquired by the Commonwealth of Massachusetts.

The nonprofit Friends of North Andover Trails (FONAT) summarizes the history of Boxford State Forest best: "The area is a patchwork of properties that have been conserved gradually over the course of a century." About 300 acres of the forest was donated as a bird sanctuary in the 1920s, and then in 1933, a naturalist sold about 460 abutting acres to the state. More and more land was donated from former family estates, and by the 1960s, an area called Bald Hill was added as state forest land. Today, the all-encompassing area known as Boxford State Forest stretches to some 1,000 acres. Its trails are maintained by a host of organizations, including the Department of Conservation and Recreation, the Essex County Greenbelt Association, and the Boxford Trails Association/Boxford Open Land Trust. The "patchwork" of properties FONAT refers to is visible on a park map, as various types of shading and marking denote different sections of the forest. Today, visitors can easily visit the various parts of the forest in one trip; the property's extensive trail system connects each section with the other.

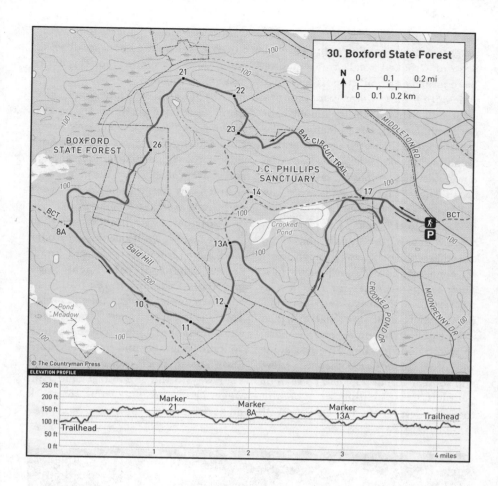

BOXFORD STATE FOREST

J.C. PHILLIPS SANCTUARY

Bald Hill

Pond Meadow

Crooked Pond

BAY CIRCUIT TRAIL

MIDDLETON RD.

CROOKED POND DR.

MOONPENNY DR.

© The Countryman Press

ELEVATION PROFILE

250 ft
200 ft
150 ft
100 ft
50 ft
0 ft

Trailhead

Marker 21

Marker 8A

Marker 13A

Trailhead

1 2 3 4 miles

GETTING THERE

From US-1 N., use the right two lanes to hop on I-95 N. toward New Hampshire and Maine. From I-95 N., take exit 51 toward Topsfield and Middleton. Turn left onto Endicott Road, then take a sharp right onto Middleton Road. Continue 1.5 miles. A small parking lot will be on your left.

THE HIKE

Print out a map from the DCR website or pull one up on your phone before embarking on your Boxford State Forest hike. At the time of writing this book, the trailhead sign did not have maps or information for hikers. But don't let that deter you—this hike is a hidden gem north of the city. That's probably because Boxford has almost no commercial development, and conservation land abounds here.

This journey begins by tracing part of the Bay Circuit Trail in the Boxford Wildlife Sanctuary. A wide, easy dirt path littered with leaves opens up just beyond the parking lot's gate. Follow it until you reach Crooked Pond, a body of water that's actually two ponds connected by a stream. The pond is often used by state and federal agencies for water testing. According to the Town of Boxford, Crooked Pond's water quality "is regarded as a gold standard against which other state water resources are measured." This makes it a unique habitat for unusual flora and fauna. Unlike other more acidic wetlands, this area is home to dogwoods, wild roses, marsh marigolds, maidenhair ferns, and spice brush. These plants attract rare owl and hawk species—a treat for birders.

Bear right at Crooked Pond and cross a board over a gurgling stream. Along the edge of the pond, you'll spot a colorful concentration of cardinal flowers. Their red petals make for a stark contrast from lush green surroundings. Begin a short climb up a small hill, then bear right. It becomes rockier here, so watch your footing. The first stone wall of the hike then comes into view, and soon, a vernal pool can be seen on your left. Cross another set of boards, then stay left for the Bay Circuit Trail.

Continue to follow signs for the Bay Circuit Trail, designated by a small white-and-green tree marker, for the entire first half of the hike.

Large swaths of bright green moss begin to appear on the path, as well as thick tree roots and sharper rocks. Notice the huge glacial erratics on both sides of the trail. Pause for long enough and you'll probably have the pleasure of seeing a tiny tree frog hop across your path. Turn right at trail marker 23.

Take a left at trail marker 22, then another left at 21. It becomes grassier (and even greener) here, and you'll notice clumps of wild huckleberry growing. At the fork in the trail, bear left, then descend into a thicker forest. This, and the appearance of trail marker 26, signals that you've exited Boxford Wildlife Sanctuary and entered Boxford State Forest. You'll now begin making your way to the summit of Bald Hill, weaving in and out of tall shagbark hickory trees.

A STONE WALL DEEP IN THE WOODS

A DRAGONFLY SITS ATOP A CARDINAL FLOWER

Ferns grow on both sides of the trail, creating a jungle-like atmosphere. A trail marker in the ground for 8A will soon make itself known—this is where your trip along the Bay Circuit trail ends, and a less-traveled journey through wilder forests begins. Turn left at 8A to complete the loop back to the parking area. Immediately the trail is grassier than before, and wild roses poke out from the greenery. Take care to not be pricked by their thorns as you head toward a wide-open field. The trail is not as meticulously maintained here, so you'll be walking through the tall grasses of this meadow for some time. The blades will cease tickling your legs soon enough, and you'll spot the remnants of an old chimney up ahead. Turn right here, at marker 13A, and begin to approach the other side of Crooked Pond's smaller section. When you see two arrows posted to a tree, you have a choice. Bear left to take the shortest route back to the parking lot, or walk straight to complete one more loop through the forest before finishing off your hike. I continued straight, ducking into a forest dominated by pines. Climb up and down rocks along this path until you reach the southern shores of Crooked Pond. You'll trace the edge of the pond once more. This leads back to where you started, just before those red cardinal flowers. Turn right to retrace your steps back to the parking area.

Breakheart Reservation

WHERE: Saugus and Wakefield

ADDRESS: 177 Forest Street, Saugus, MA 01906

TOTAL DISTANCE: 4.25 miles

HIKING TIME: 4 hours

ELEVATION GAIN: 614 feet

DIFFICULTY: Moderate

RESTROOMS: Yes

DOGS ALLOWED: Yes

WHAT TO EXPECT: A good workout on your way up to rocky hilltops and through cool, damp forests

Legend says Breakheart Reservation got its name during the Civil War, when troops training there felt the place was remote and lonely, and in keeping with this feeling, broke their hearts. One historian argues the land was named after Breakheart Hill in Gloucestershire, England, the original home of an early Saugus settler. Whatever its origins are, one thing is clear: Breakheart is rich in wildlife and history.

Native Americans originally lived at the spot, quarrying a red buff stone called Saugus Jasper to create pointed tools. When European settlers arrived, an attempt at farming the land was made, but it was better suited for logging. Later, in the 1800s, a group of wealthy businessmen from Boston bought the land to create a hunting retreat. All was well until 1900, when the "crime of the decade," occurred, according to local papers. In 1897, one of the businessmen had hired a man named George E. Bailey to be the caretaker of the land's farm and forest. Then Bailey hired another man named John Best to help with work on the farm. But in October 1900, the two men got into a fight about money—and Best's drinking habits. This led to Best's shooting of Bailey in the back, according to a Breakheart Reservation history book from the Images of America series. Best allegedly chopped up Bailey's body with an axe, put the dismembered pieces into burlap bags, and tossed them into Lynn's Floating Bridge Pond. One newspaper headline at the time read, "Ghastly Find. Headless Body of a Man Found in Floating Bridge Pond." The story dominated the news throughout Best's trial. He was eventually found guilty and sentenced to death.

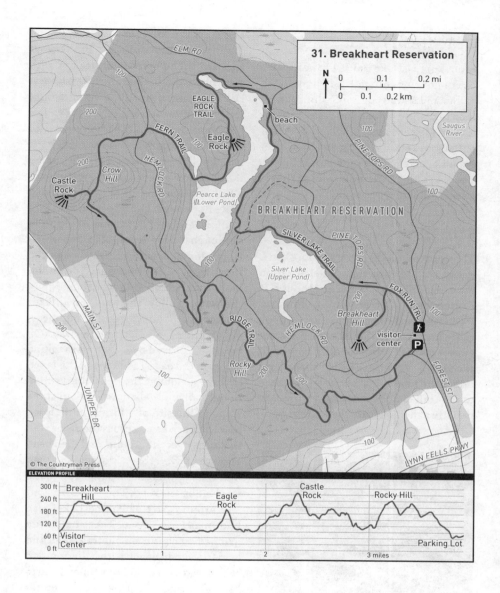

ELEVATION PROFILE

Somehow, the hubbub eventually died down, and life at Breakheart returned to normal.

In the 1930s, the land once again changed hands, this time to the state's Metropolitan District Commission. Landscape architect Arthur Shurcliff helped shape the property for public enjoyment, and the Civilian Conservation Corps got to work on building his vision.

Today, visitors can hike, swim, cross-country ski, and picnic in the park. Its 700 acres of pine-oak forest boast views of the Boston skyline from rocky hills and ledges, while freshwater ponds offer refreshing spots to cool off in the summertime.

GETTING THERE

From 1-93 N., take exit 27 toward US-1 N. For just under 10 miles, delight in the sights and sounds of Route 1 in Saugus, then take the exit for Lynn Fells Parkway toward Melrose and Stoneham. Turn left onto Lynn Fells Parkway, and then after 0.2 mile, take a right onto Forest Street. You'll see the DCR sign to Breakheart Reservation on your right.

THE HIKE

This loop connects several short trails listed on the Breakheart Reservation map available at the Christopher P. Dunne Visitor Center. You'll need a map to successfully complete the loop, as there are parts of this hike that are not clearly marked. With a map in hand, exit the visitor center, then turn left to pass under the nearby gazebo. The entrance to the trail is just beyond it, with a sign denoting the Fox Run Trail. Enter here,

A REFLECTIVE POND BESIDE THE TRAIL

and start a steep ascent almost immediately, turning onto the Breakheart Hill Trail. The journey starts out with a steady climb to the top of Breakheart Hill, the first of five hills you'll mount today. You'll reach the top in just a few minutes, to be rewarded with views of the Boston skyline. Linger here for a moment before either continuing along the trail you entered on or locating the cut-through at the back of Breakheart Hill. Both lead back to the Fox Run Trail, where you'll continue walking to approach Silver Lake, also known as Upper Pond. From here, cross a paved road, then turn right onto the Silver Lake trail, which skirts of the edge of the water. Follow the blue trail blazes around the pond, trotting along a carpet of pine needles leading the way. (On my hike, I passed by a yoga class taking place on the eastern shores of the lake.)

Take a right at the next intersection in the trail and walk down a set of stone steps to the site of a former mill. Keep good balance as you cross the stone wall that runs over the stream, and then head up to the paved road. Cross it, and then find the continuation to the trail just a few feet up the road. This kicks off your trip around part of Pearce Lake, also known as Lower Pond. These banks are gripped by centuries-old tree roots and lead to a sandy beach with a lifeguarded swimming area in summertime. If you're hiking during warm weather, laughter and children's squeals of delight will signal you're almost there. The Pearce Lake beach has restrooms, too, in case a mid-hike pit stop is needed.

After taking a breather beside the clear waters of the pond, continue along the shoreline, over to where a wooden dock overlooks the lake. You'll start following blue blazes again until red ones appear. When they do, follow those,

EAGLE ROCK OVERLOOKING PEARCE LAKE

and begin the scramble to your second hilltop of the hike: Eagle Rock. This 206-foot-tall land formation is a treat to summit, offering views over Pearce Lake and back over to the city skyline.

There are significantly fewer blazes on the way down from Eagle Rock. But, once you make it to the bottom, you'll switch from the Eagle Rock Trail (red) to the Breakheart Hill Link Trail (blue). Cross a footbridge and take a right at the next intersection, following yellow blazes through a cool, damp forest. This is the Fern Trail, and it leads to a paved road once again. Cross the road, turn left, and continue on a few steps until you see a trail entry on the right. Here, follow the light pink blazes on the Spruce Path Trail for just a few hundred feet. Bypass the sign for the Ridge Trail, and instead, turn left up ahead onto the other side of the Ridge Trail. This part, which leads to Castle Rock, is marked by orange blazes, then red.

As you make your way to Castle Rock, you'll see a huge rock formation on your left. This is Crow Hill. While there's no set path to reach the summit, you can explore it if you're feeling energetic. If not, the spur trail to the top of Castle Rock is just up on the right. This is the highest peak on the hike, at 286 feet tall. Mind the broken glass once you reach the top, peering out at power lines, Wakefield, Saugus, and, once again, the city skyline. After descending Castle Hill, you'll reach an intersection and a tree with an arrow sign. Turn left to follow this arrow, which marks the last leg of your hike.

The remainder of the trip traverses rocky terrain, heading up and down, then up and down again, over a series of short hills. In summer months, wild blueberries grow between the rocks. Pick a few and you will be surprised by how sweet they are. This last part of the Ridge Trail is straightforward, marked by red blazes. Follow it up Rocky Hill, then Ash Hill, both of which don't offer the panoramic views of the first few hills, until you reach the end. The trail lets out of the other side of the visitor center, right up to a beautiful post-hike sight: the water fountain.

32

Charles W. Ward Reservation

WHERE: Andover and North Andover

ADDRESS: Prospect Road, Andover, MA 01810

TOTAL DISTANCE: 4 miles

HIKING TIME: 2.5 hours

ELEVATION GAIN: 618 feet

DIFFICULTY: Moderate

RESTROOMS: No

DOGS ALLOWED: Yes

WHAT TO EXPECT: Meadows, woodlands, and hilltops with energizing inclines and gradual descents

Settled in the mid-1600s by an early Andover resident named Nicholas Holt, the land where the Ward Reservation now exists was farmed for about 200 years before it was scooped up by Charles W. Ward in 1917. It wasn't until seven years after Ward's death in 1940, however, that the land was preserved in his name. That's thanks to his wife, Mabel Ward, who paid tribute to her husband by donating 153 acres of their land to the Trustees of Reservations. Over the years, the Ward family continued to donate land to the organization. Their donation now comprises a whopping 704 acres.

Today, visitors enjoy the Ward Reservation's 14 miles of trails. These trails connect three hills: Shrub, Boston, and Holt. Holt Hill claims the title as the highest point in all of Essex County, and it has a one-of-a-kind landmark atop it to boot. Read on to learn more about Holt Hill's Solstice Stones.

The Ward Reservation is also a part of the Bay Circuit Trail. To enjoy the reservation's varied landscapes, you'll have to pay $5 to park in a medium-sized parking lot on Prospect Road. Trustees members, however, can park for free.

GETTING THERE

From I-93, take exit 41 toward Andover/North Andover. Stay on Route 125 N. for 5 miles, then turn right onto Prospect Road. Follow Prospect Road for 0.3 mile and you'll see the blue Trustees sign marking entry to the parking lot on your right.

THE HIKE

Embark on your journey through Ward Reservation by picking up the trail at the eastern end of the parking lot near

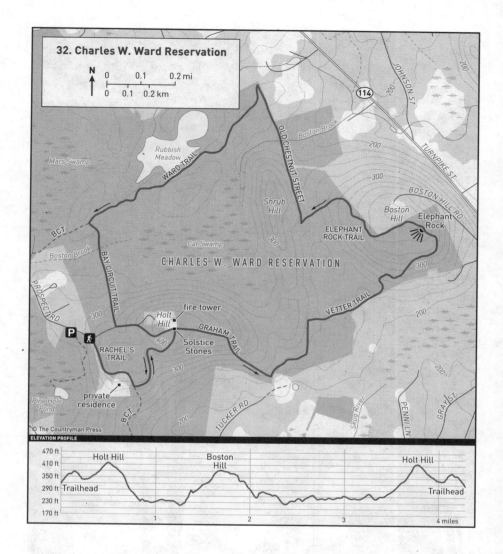

32. Charles W. Ward Reservation

N

| 0 | 0.1 | 0.2 mi |
| 0 | 0.1 | 0.2 km |

114

JOHNSON ST

TURNPIKE ST

Boston Brook

BOSTON HILL RD

Rubbish Meadow

WARD TRAIL

Mars Swamp

200

300

Shrub Hill

Boston Hill

Elephant Rock

OLD CHESTNUT STREET

BCT

Boston Brook

BAY CIRCUIT TRAIL

PROSPECT RD

ELEPHANT ROCK TRAIL

Cat Swamp

CHARLES W. WARD RESERVATION

300

VETTER TRAIL

200

300

300

P

Holt Hill

fire tower

GRAHAM TRAIL

RACHEL'S TRAIL

Solstice Stones

400

300

200

Pine Hole Pond

private residence

BCT

TUCKER RD

Skug River

PENNI LN

GRAY ST

© The Countryman Press

ELEVATION PROFILE

| 470 ft | Holt Hill | Boston Hill | | Holt Hill |
| 410 ft |
| 350 ft |
| 290 ft | Trailhead | | | | Trailhead |
| 230 ft |
| 170 ft | | 1 | 2 | 3 | 4 miles |

the trailhead sign. This hike connects the reservation's red, yellow, and blue trails. Grab a map and begin by following the wide dirt path of the red and yellow trails, which run parallel to each other for a short time. Turn left to climb your first steep hill of the hike, then cross the road at its crest, turning right to follow the red blazes. Here, the red and yellow paths form Rachel's Trail. You'll follow the edge of a grassy

meadow before skirting by a private residence called Holt Farm. The house envy becomes real when you see this property's rolling hills and orchard. Follow the yellow trail from here on out, climbing a rocky path that cuts through a thick forest of trees. Keep right to stay on the yellow trail, which briefly forms part of the Bay Circuit Trail, and your walk opens onto a wide meadow. In a few moments, you'll glimpse the fire tower

A LEAFY SPOT NEAR ELEPHANT ROCK

THE SOLSTICE STONES, WITH THE BOSTON SKYLINE IN THE DISTANCE

atop Holt Hill, and almost immediately, the Solstice Stones appear before you.

Ah, the Solstice Stones. They're an unusual-looking group of rocks for sure. The compass-like installation was dreamed up by Mabel Ward to honor her husband. A rounded central stone is surrounded by four rectangular ones to mark the cardinal points on a compass. More oblong stones represent the summer, winter, spring, and autumnal equinoxes. From here, you can clearly see the Boston skyline and the Blue Hills in the distance. It's said that during the Revolutionary War, Andover residents scaled Holt Hill to watch the burning of Charlestown following the Battle of Bunker Hill. Later additions to the hill, which you can still see today, are a fire tower and a capped water reservoir.

Using the directionals of the Solstice Stones to guide you, pick up the easternmost path. It's the one with a blue blaze painted onto an informational sign. The sign has several QR codes that link to audio tours. They're worth a listen. From here, you'll glide downhill into another grassy meadow, and then into the forest. Keep right at the next intersection, following the trail as it winds in and out of a valley and then turns up into a ridge covered with pine trees. New England's ubiquitous stone walls make an appearance here, guiding you down an old road marked as the Vetter Trail on your map. Wind through maples and oaks, and then a grove of pitch pines, to reach the summit of Boston Hill. In summertime, the hill will announce its arrival with clusters of wild blueberries. Knock back a few of the small, sweet berries before inspecting the odd shape of Elephant Rock, one of Boston Hill's most-recognized glacial erratics. From this granite boulder, you can see Holt Hill, which you just climbed, and the buildings of Boston in the distance. The view, admittedly, is not as lovely as Holt Hill's. The landscape, though, is quite interesting. According to the Trustees, the top of Boston Hill is considered a "barrens habitat," which is rare for the

A VIEW FROM BOSTON HILL

region. It was created from a combination of fire, land clearing, and grazing, and it is home to uncommon species of insects, birds, animals, and wildflowers. Trees continue to fight their way onto the land, but the Trustees keep them at bay by clearing, mowing, and hosting controlled fires at the spot to preserve the unique habitat.

Pick up the trail again at the right of Elephant Rock, then drop down into another grove of trees. Take care to stay to the right up ahead as you turn onto Old Chestnut Street, or the red trail. This former road is wide and makes for easy walking. Ahead, you'll see a sign for the Judy Family Trail. If you'd like to get in a workout, take this trail to climb up and down a few more hills. If not, keep along the red trail until it reaches the northern border of the Ward

Reservation. Take a sharp left here onto the Ward Trail. Clearly marked signs tacked onto the trees will help you navigate. Keep left on this trail, which offers glimpses of Rubbish Meadow on your right, until you reach the next intersection. Turn left again as the red trail meets part of the Bay Circuit Trail. Ferns festoon the path here. Follow the path until your walk meets up with the yellow trail. Turn right for a short walk to the parking lot.

If you have enough stamina, it's worth taking the short walk along the boardwalked Bog Trail to Pine Hole Pond. This one-of-a-kind body of water is known as a quaking bog. Inside, concentric rings of floating vegetation thrive in their respective growing conditions. You'll see orchids, insect-eating pitcher plants, and other funky greenery.

33

Dogtown Woods

WHERE: Gloucester

ADDRESS: 65–75 Cherry Street, Gloucester, MA 01930

TOTAL DISTANCE: 2.5 miles

HIKING TIME: 1 hour 30 minutes

ELEVATION GAIN: 118 feet

DIFFICULTY: Easy

RESTROOMS: No

DOGS ALLOWED: Yes

WHAT TO EXPECT: A mysterious, and at times confusing, walk through a peculiar patch of woods

Frankly, the Dogtown Woods are downright bizarre. Settled in the mid-1600s, the secluded area offered protection from enemies of all kinds—including pirates coming from the sea and native peoples inching inland. For a time, the safeguarded community thrived, but once the American Revolution reared its head, things went downhill. Men left home to fight in the war while their wives maintained their homes in Gloucester. Some say the settlement got its name from the dogs the women in the settlement owned for protection, while others claim a pack of wild dogs took over the land once humans left it. When the war ended and settlers gradually moved closer to the harbor to make a living fishing, Dogtown's dissipation became imminent. By 1830, the settlement had been completely abandoned, and it's been eerily empty since then.

A century later, in the 1930s, wealthy philanthropist and Gloucester native Roger Babson devised an idea for Dogtown. To give unemployed skilled workers jobs during the Great Depression, he purchased part of the land that makes up Dogtown. Then, he commissioned stonecutters to carve sayings into more than 20 impressive boulders scattered around Dogtown Commons, the settlement's former town center. Babson, who founded Babson College in Wellesley, had some words of advice carved into the stones: KEEP OUT OF DEBT and BE ON TIME are just a few nuggets of his wisdom.

These days, the Dogtown Woods make up 3,600 acres of the Essex National Heritage Area. The inspirational boulders are still there, as are dozens of cellar holes where colonial homes once stood. A trip to the woods will prove to be curious experience. Explore the woods' winding trails and

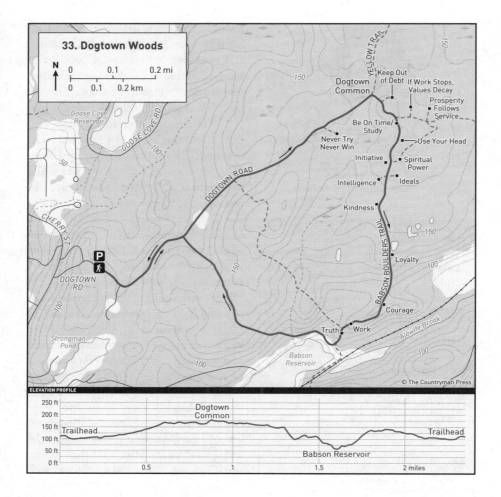

33. Dogtown Woods

experience their air of mystery. And whatever you do, try not to get lost.

GETTING THERE

From Route 127 N., turn left onto Centennial Avenue, then after 0.6 mile, turn left onto Washington Street. At the traffic circle, stay straight on Washington Street. After 0.2 miles, turn right onto Poplar Street, and after 0.7 mile, turn left onto Cherry Street. Dogtown is marked by a brownish ESSEX NATIONAL HERITAGE

AREA sign. Take a quick right to arrive at the small parking area for Dogtown.

THE HIKE

From the Cherry Street parking area, make a stop at the information board near the beginning of the trail. Sometimes there are maps available, and sometimes there are not. Your best bet is to print one online, or to pick one up at the Gloucester Office of Tourism at 9 Dale Avenue. It'd be unwise to venture into the forest without a map, as the trails are not only confusing but poorly marked. Your trip will start along the Blue Trail, leading to the Babson Boulders. You could veer onto the lollipop Yellow Trail to peek at a broken boulder known as Whale's Jaw, but the hike outlined here circles around to the Red Trail along Dogtown Road to form a loop.

On any given visit, you may hear shots ringing out from the nearby Cape Ann Sportsman's Club. While they add to the woods' strange atmosphere, you can pay them no mind as you pass through a gate on your left. Walk until you arrive at a gravel pit, and continue straight on the dirt path flagged with blue circular markers on the trees. Cellar holes peek through the forest on your left—see if you can find them. After about 30 minutes of walking, you'll reach Dogtown Commons, which kicks off your exploration of the Babson Boulders. It's easy to get lost here, but my

best advice is to not try to follow a set route. Don't bury your nose in this (or any) book while walking. Instead, pay close attention to your surroundings, and always retrace your steps if you become confused. That said, don't get so absorbed in the strangeness of the atmosphere that you forget to sidestep the copious poison ivy. Additionally, while there are several signposts with information and QR codes placed by an organization called Digital Dogtown, many of them have been blurred by the elements. It's just you, your map, a compass, and (hopefully) a hiking buddy out there.

Dozens of spur trails off of the Dogtown Common path lead to each Babson Boulder. Some boulders are visible from the main trail, while others wait to be discovered. Pennies tucked into the nooks and crannies in the KEEP OUT OF DEBT boulder glisten from a distance. When the sun is shining, the sparkling

SOME WORDS OF WISDOM

coins almost appear to be small candle flames, until you draw closer and see how your eyes have tricked you. Put a penny of your own into the mix if you wish, and continue on. Along the way, you'll probably spot the boulders with sayings such as STUDY, BE ON TIME, and IF WORK STOPS, VALUES DECAY.

You may not see every boulder on this trip, and that's OK. You'll probably need to return several times to check off every boulder and every cellar hole. It's wise to visit Dogtown in the fall or winter, when leaves and tall grasses can't obscure your route. When your eyes are sufficiently tuckered out from searching for boulders, follow the trail marked with red circular signs on the trees to head back to the parking lot. And good luck.

34

Great Brook Farm State Park

WHERE: Carlisle	

ADDRESS: 1018 Lowell Road, Carlisle, MA 01741

TOTAL DISTANCE: 2.7 miles

HIKING TIME: 1 hour 30 minutes

ELEVATION GAIN: 177 feet

DIFFICULTY: Easy

RESTROOMS: Yes

DOGS ALLOWED: Yes

WHAT TO EXPECT: A leisurely, family-friendly trip through forests, fields, and wetlands

This hike is the only one in this book to take place at a working dairy farm. Nestled in Carlisle, Great Brook Farm State Park's sprawling 900 acres are a sight to behold. They're home to cows, sheep, pigs, chickens, and other barnyard animals, some of which you can pet or feed, if you're so inclined. Free tours of the farm are given on weekends. There's also a seasonal ice cream stand near where the animals dwell, with more than 60 flavors. A scoop is a hard-earned reward after exploring the park's more than 20 miles of trails on foot or horseback. Step inside the ice cream stand to watch educational videos about the farm and dive headfirst into a sundae. The park also includes the Great Brook Ski Touring Center, which rents out skis for cross-country skiing in wintertime.

While Great Brook Farm State Park was established in the 1970s, its history dates back farther than that. Centuries ago, Native Americans created sacred sites on portions of the land. Later, European settlers took up residence here—you can spot their cellar holes beside some of the park's trails—and they worked in mills that once stood on the land.

The state of Massachusetts bought what was formerly called the Farnham W. Smith Farm in 1974, paving the way for the park to become what it is today. The Farnham Smith cabin still stands by the former millpond and its canoe launch, and it is used for public programming.

GETTING THERE

From I-95 S., take exit 32 A-B for US 3-N. toward Lowell. Continue on Route 3 for almost 7 miles, then take exit 28 toward N. Billerica and Carlisle. Continue on Treble Cove Road for 1.4 miles, then

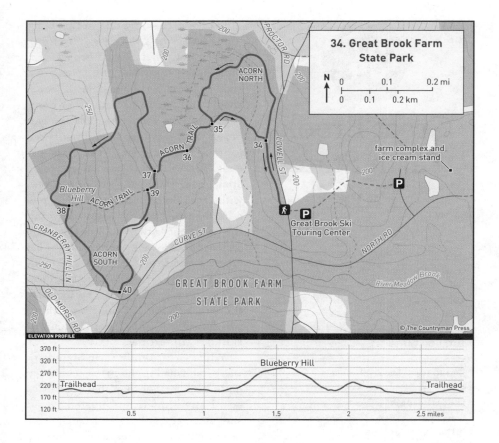

ELEVATION PROFILE

370 ft
320 ft
270 ft   Blueberry Hill
220 ft Trailhead   Trailhead
170 ft
120 ft   0.5   1   1.5   2   2.5 miles

turn right onto West Street. After 0.3 mile, continue onto North Road, passing by the barns and fields of Great Brook Farm. Turn right onto Lowell Street, and the parking lot will be on your right.

THE HIKE

Park at Great Brook Ski Touring Center, listed on some maps as the Hart Barn & Ski Center, for easiest access to the Acorn Trail. (You may also park in the lot closer to the farm complex and ice cream stand. Parking passes are $3 from May through October.) Great Brook Farm's Acorn Trail is a hike much loved by families, nature enthusiasts, and avid hikers alike. Its easy terrain offers plenty of places to stop and admire the landscape. It's also separated into three sections: Acorn Trail, Acorn South, and Acorn North. Here, we'll trace the outskirts of each section, but the option to shorten your hike and skip a section is there if needed.

Begin by walking to the end of the parking lot and crossing Lowell Road. There, just across the street, lies the entrance to the Acorn Trail. It's marked by a small sign and bridge. The trail starts out flat, and for the most part, stays this way. For the duration of your journey, follow the red blazes on the trees. It'll be tough to lose your way, as the trails are quite well-marked. The beginning of the hike, which crosses a portion

A FERN PATCH IN AUTUMN

THE VERY BEGINNING OF THE TRAIL

of a field, remains parallel to the road for a few hundred feet before intersecting with Acorn North. Keep straight here, at trail marker 34, to trace the perimeter of Acorn North. You soon duck into your first cover of trees, and the walk becomes slightly hilly. The soft ground is littered with rocks and bright-green patches of moss, leading to a narrow esker, or ridge, flanked by oak trees. You'll spot the trail's namesake, acorns, here, as you cross over the esker. Cross over a gas pipeline that runs through the park and continue on to a series of wooden bridges. Head past a small swamp, and sidestep rocks jutting out from the ground to turn right at trail marker 35.

The trail opens onto a sprawling corn field, where you'll want to keep right at marker 36 and turn right again at 37. Descend into the woods again and you will immediately stumble upon one of New England's ubiquitous stone walls. Keep right at a blue arrow tacked onto a tree up ahead (some of the blue arrows have acorn designs, while others display acorns that have almost faded away completely) to head toward Blueberry Hill.

Take a left out onto the bucolic expanse of grass again, and then take another quick left to reenter the woods. Glimpse private homes through the trees as you approach the base of Blueberry Hill. You'll notice blueberry bushes on both sides of the trail, which counts for one part of its name, but a steep hill it is not. It offers a slight incline, and that's all.

To begin the third portion of your hike, turn right at marker 38 for Acorn South. Here, you'll meander through the woods and cross several boardwalks. Glacial erratics greet you from the woods just beyond the dirt trail. More stone walls and vibrant patches of ferns await you ahead. Cross an almost-too-narrow footbridge before turning right at trail marker 39.

Here, the trail picks up where you started, traversing the charmingly pastoral field once more. Keep straight at marker 38 to head toward the road. Cross another boardwalk over a brook, and retrace your steps to arrive back at the trailhead. Time to check out the farm animals, and maybe devour a scoop or two of ice cream.

35

Halibut Point State Park

WHERE: Rockport

ADDRESS: Gott Avenue, Rockport, MA 01966

TOTAL DISTANCE: 1.5 miles

HIKING TIME: 1.5 hours

ELEVATION GAIN: 100 feet

DIFFICULTY: Easy

RESTROOMS: Yes

DOGS ALLOWED: Yes

WHAT TO EXPECT: A one-of-a-kind loop tracing the outer rim of a former quarry, plus the opportunity to explore a rocky coastline

The iconic granite cliffs that Halibut Point is known for are a whopping 440 million years old. The sheets of rock, which drop off along the coastline, proved to be invaluable to the peninsula's range of residents over the years. The Pawtucket tribe were some of the first people to live at the spot, making good use of its fishing and hunting opportunities. According to the Massachusetts Department of Environmental Management, settlers took up residence in the 17th century, using the land for farming and cattle.

It wasn't until 1702 when a man named Samuel Gott built a home in the area. His house still stands today along Gott Avenue, but it is privately owned and thus not open to the public. Around this time, Halibut Point was referred to as Haul About Point by sailors, as they needed to tack at this spot to successfully navigate around Cape Ann. It's thought this is how the land formation got its name, rather than from a population of fish.

Halibut Point is best remembered for its booming granite quarry. Workers began quarrying in the 1840s, and the industry picked up when a company called the Rockport Granite Company bought the Babson Farm quarry there and expanded its footprint. However, the granite industry took a turn as the Great Depression loomed, collapsing in 1929. The quarry closed that year, putting the Rockport Granite Company out of business. The property changed hands several times in the decades following, from hosting MIT researchers to serving as a private park. Some 56 acres of Halibut Point were acquired by the state in 1981. Another part of the peninsula is managed by the Trustees of Reservations. But today, rather than the 20th-century-era sounds of stone cutting and steam engines, visitors can

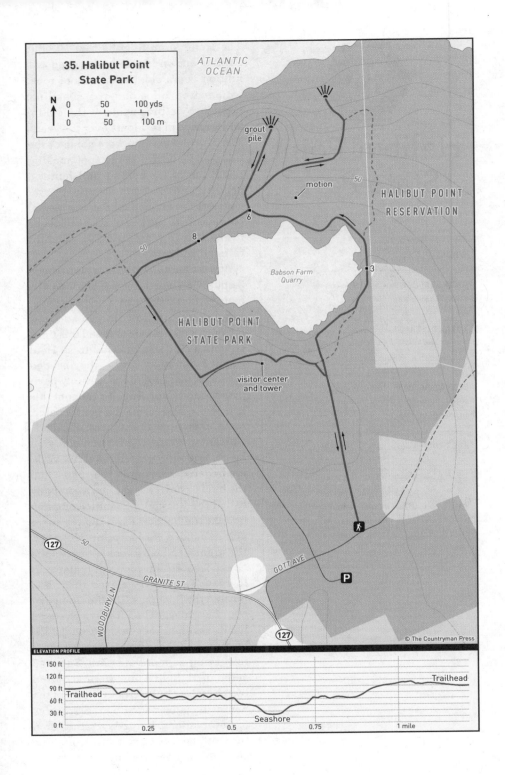

35. Halibut Point State Park

ATLANTIC OCEAN

N

| 0 | 50 | 100 yds |
| 0 | 50 | 100 m |

grout pile

motion

HALIBUT POINT RESERVATION

8

6

Babson Farm Quarry

3

HALIBUT POINT STATE PARK

50

visitor center and tower

50

127

GRANITE ST

GOTT AVE

WOODBURY LN

P

127

© The Countryman Press

ELEVATION PROFILE

150 ft
120 ft
90 ft
60 ft
30 ft
0 ft

Trailhead

Trailhead

Seashore

0.25   0.5   0.75   1 mile

enjoy listening to crashing waves and cawing gulls.

GETTING THERE

From I-95 N., keep left at exit 45 to continue onto MA-128. After about 19 miles, at the traffic circle, take the third exit onto Washington Street. The street eventually becomes Andrews Street, then Langsford Street. Continue on to follow MA-127, then, after just under a mile, take a left onto Gott Avenue. The entrance to the parking lot is on your right. For Massachusetts residents, parking is $5. You'll have to buy a ticket at the kiosk in the lot.

THE HIKE

The entrance to the trail is opposite the parking lot. Before crossing Gott Lane to get there, grab a guided map from the information board in the lot. Then take a quick look at the trailhead sign before starting down the dirt path.

Your walk starts out in a leisurely way. The flat trail is surrounded by mature hickories and cedars, leading you to the main event: the Babson Farm Quarry. Turn left at the first intersection, or away from the sign pointing toward the restrooms. In a few moments, a jaw-dropping vista unfolds in front of you: the gaping hole left by the former seaside quarry. It's been filling with rainwater since the quarry was abandoned in 1929, after Cape Ann's granite industry faltered. Now, with its almost turquoise tint, the water makes a stunning backdrop for a few trail photos.

Traces of the working quarry can be seen throughout this trail. From dog holes, or rows of depressions that allowed workers to split the granite, to dead men, or large iron staples that held

THE ROCKY COASTLINE

cables, see if you can spot all of the man-made additions to this landscape. You'll enjoy the history more with help from the park's guided trail map, available in the parking lot. It identifies points of interest along the hike, including holes from steam-powered drills and several granite bollards, with information on how they came to be.

As you explore the edges of the quarry, steer clear of poison ivy. At trail marker 3, a fork in the path leads to another park on Halibut Point, this one owned by the Trustees. For the purposes of this hike, we're going to stay within the confines of the state park. Keep right, taking the time to peek out at every overlook along the edge of the quarry. On your right, you'll see another small body of water. This is a motion, or a small quarry. According to the Halibut

THE QUARRY

THE TOWERING GROUT PILE

Point Association, they were usually operated by two men. They cut granite blocks here that would help pave streets. At trail marker 6, take a left to mount a ginormous grout pile. It's a deposit of discarded granite pieces that was dumped at the spot for decades.

The views from the top of the pile are fantastic, stretching from Crane Beach and Castle Hill in Ipswich all the way to Mt. Agamenticus in Southern Maine. On a clear day, you can see the Isles of Shoals off the coast of New Hampshire and Maine and the Seabrook nuclear power plant in Seabrook, New Hampshire. Much closer than those landmarks, though, is a brilliant display of buoys. The colorful instruments dot the waters below the grout pile, bobbing up and down before the vast, open ocean.

After drinking in all the views, head back down the grout pile path to hook around to the ocean and back. On the trail below the pile, you can see the massive rocks you were just standing on—a monumental structure jutting out toward the sea. At the bottom of this path, you'll happen upon a cairn colony constructed from chunks of grout. Continue on to climb up and down the rocky shore, taking care not to slip on the wet rocks. It's a treat to take a rest on one of the gigantic rocks, listening to the waves gently break on them.

Several skinny paths to the right of the rocks lead back to the quarry. Some lead to trail marker 6, while others backtrack to marker 3. Once you've made it back to where you started, you'll want to keep along the edge of the quarry until you reach marker 8. Just beyond it, you can extend your hike by turning right to explore the coastal Bayview Trail. Or, you could keep along the trail you're on, which loops back to the quarry entrance.

Whatever you decide, you'll eventually end up at a strange-looking building. It's a World War II-era fire tower, renovated for present-day enjoyment. When it's not closed for maintenance, the 60-foot tower and park visitor center offers impressive views on a clear day, similar to those atop the grout pile. The trail curves around the rear of the fire tower before leading back to the entrance.

36
Harold Parker State Forest

WHERE: Andover, North Andover	
ADDRESS: 90 Harold Parker Road, Andover, MA 01810	
TOTAL DISTANCE: 3.5 miles	
HIKING TIME: 2 hours	
ELEVATION GAIN: 181 feet	
DIFFICULTY: Moderate	
RESTROOMS: Yes	
DOGS ALLOWED: Yes	
WHAT TO EXPECT: A smooth tour through the woods and around a pond	

More than 3,000 acres of woodland, this forest spans from Andover to North Andover, and edges into nearby North Reading and Middleton. The land was originally used for farming and was also the site of a gristmill, sawmill, and later, a soapstone quarry. The owner of the soapstone quarry, a man named William Jenkins, was a well-known abolitionist in the 1850s. His house, which is located near the park on Douglass Lane, along with other houses in the area, was a stop on the Underground Railroad. Secret compartments and hideouts were built into the home to accommodate escaped slaves, and notable abolitionists like Frederick Douglass and Harriet Beecher Stowe were known to frequent the area.

Yet when the plains of the Midwest became more popular for growing crops, the land was reclaimed and reforested by the Commonwealth of Massachusetts. The state purchased the majority of the forest between 1915 and 1938 and transformed it into a state park with help from the Civilian Conservation Corps, a federal work project that employed young men during the Great Depression. The workers dammed streams and carved small ponds into the landscape.

The state forest's namesake, Harold Parker, was a civil engineer born in Lancaster, Massachusetts. The Harvard graduate served as a State Representative and the State Highway Commissioner before becoming the Chairman of the Forestry Commission.

Today, the vast forest comprises 56 miles of trails, dotted with 11 ponds. It attracts hikers, mountain bikers, equestrians, swimmers, fishermen, hunters and other outdoor recreationalists. Two things to note before you go: be cognizant of hunting season in the park, and

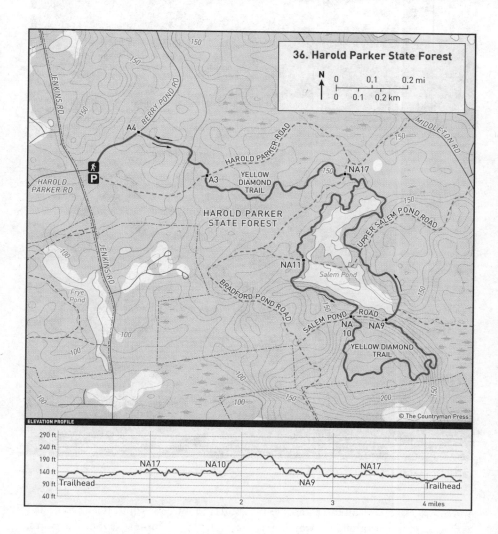

© The Countryman Press

do not head into the woods without first applying bug spray.

There are no trail maps available at the parking area I've noted here. I strongly recommend stopping by the park headquarters to grab a map before parking near the trailhead to begin your hike. The park headquarters can be found at 269 Middleton Road in North Andover.

GETTING THERE

From 1-93 N., take exit 41 toward Andover North/North Andover. Merge onto Route 125 N., and follow it for about 2.6 miles. Turn right onto Gould Road, then keep straight onto Harold Parker Road. In 1.5 miles, Harold Parker Road meets with Jenkins Road. Continue straight to find the parking lot along Berry Pond Road to your right.

THE HIKE

This hike follows Harold Parker State Forest's yellow diamond trail, a lolli-pop route that heads down and around Salem Pond. It's a popular trail for hikers

A DELICATE LADY SLIPPER

and mountain bikers alike, so keep your ears open for bikers along the way. You'll also want to pay close attention to the yellow blazes and numbered trail markers. Check your map frequently to make sure you're on track; it's especially easy to make a wrong turn in this dense forest crisscrossed by numerous trails.

With a map in hand, make your way to the gates at the beginning of Berry Pond Road. Pass by them, and continue on this paved road until you see the beginning of the yellow diamond trail on your right. It's marked with an A4 sign, which can also be seen on the map.

Stroll past a corrugated steel out-building on your right. It's been pelted by plenty of bullets over the years, serving as a reminder that hunting is allowed in Harold Parker State Forest. While park officials recommend wearing bright clothing during hunting season, I recommend hiking on a Sunday. Why? Because hunting is not allowed in the park on Sundays.

Continue on, crossing a footbridge over a stream. When you come to an intersection with the Harold Parker Road trail, stop before you cross it. In springtime and early summer, there's a good reason to take a break here, as a few delicate lady slippers can be seen in the grasses on either side of the trail. After you make an orchid sighting, cross the Harold Parker Road trail and bear right to stay on the yellow diamond trail. The continuation is marked with an A3 sign. You'll notice the trail becomes quite manageable and mostly flat. It switches between a carpet of rust-colored pine needles on the forest floor and rockier terrain. You'll also undoubtedly hear gunshots ringing out from the nearby Andover Sportsmen's Club no matter the day of the week.

As you creep deeper into the woods, it gets increasingly buggier, thanks to small swamps and other pockets of standing water. A reapplication of bug spray might be in order before you reach the shores of Salem Pond.

The NA17 marker signals the beginning of the loop around the pond. I turned right to start my journey around the water (just before the trail bends sharply left), but of course, either way

makes for a pleasant stroll. As you approach the pond, the terrain becomes hillier. Listen for bullfrogs bellowing below, and glimpse the blue waters through the trees at every turn. There is a small causeway that cuts across Salem Pond, marked by an NA11 sign. You could take this trail to condense your trip, in the event that the mosquitoes are eating you alive.

Staying on track will lead you to the western portion of the pond. In springtime, you can admire flowering dogwood trees among the maples and other hardwoods. The trail eventually cuts away from the pond at its southern edge, and crosses into the town of North Reading momentarily before leading back to the banks of the pond. You'll follow the length of the body of water until you return to the point where the loop began. Here, you'll head back toward the parking lot by the same way you came in.

A RUSTED OUTBUILDING

37

Hellcat Interpretive Trail

WHERE: Newbury

ADDRESS: Parker River National Wildlife Refuge, Refuge Road, Newbury, MA 01951

TOTAL DISTANCE: 1.5 miles

HIKING TIME: 1 hour

ELEVATION GAIN: 50 feet

DIFFICULTY: Easy

RESTROOMS: Yes

DOGS ALLOWED: No

WHAT TO EXPECT: A breezy stroll along a boardwalk with a lot of stairs, boasting views of salt marshes and the ocean

Parker River National Wildlife Refuge is easily one of the most breathtaking spots along the Massachusetts coast. It takes up three-quarters of the southern part of Newbury's ever-lovely Plum Island, and the Hellcat Interpretive Trail offers wonderful views of both the ocean and the salt marshes on either side of it.

The refuge is a home to many species of migratory birds and other types of wildlife. Established in 1941, the park is an important stopover for waterfowl, songbirds, and shorebirds making their way down south. More than 4,700 acres of land make up the refuge, ranging from swamps to dunes and beaches to mud flats. You can learn about all of the forms of life that thrive in the refuge by visiting the headquarters and visitor center at 9 Plum Island Turnpike. The center contains numerous exhibitions about the park, and it is worth a stop before heading out on a hike.

The park's unspoiled beauty is truly a welcome change of pace from the cottages and multicolored beach blankets dotting Plum Island's northern shores. There are a plethora of trails (and vistas) to explore, though I cover only two in this book. The first of those is Hellcat Interpretive Trail. For the second, see Hike #43.

GETTING THERE

From I-95 N., take exit 56 to merge onto Scotland Road toward Newbury and West Newbury. Continue along the road, driving east. Turn onto Highfield Road, then Middle Road, then Hanover Street. Continue onto Rolfe's Lane and Ocean Avenue, then turn right onto Walter Street, which becomes the Plum Island Turnpike. I advise stopping at the Refuge Headquarters and Visitor Center first, located at 6 Plum Island Turnpike (across from Mass Audubon's Joppa

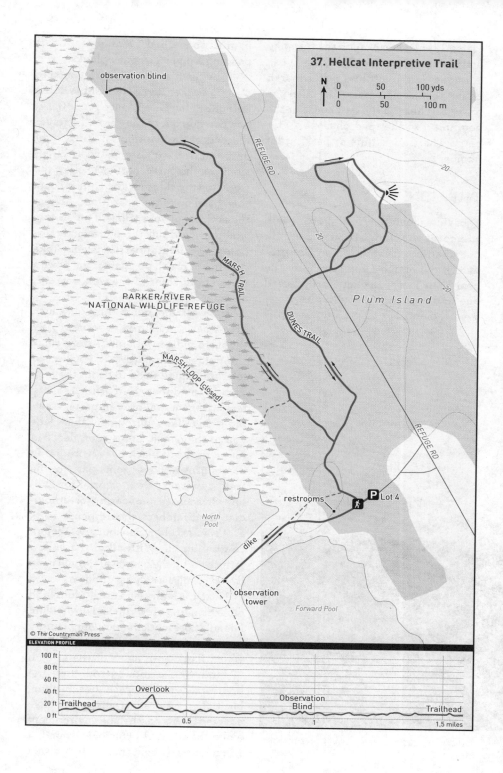

37. Hellcat Interpretive Trail

N
0   50   100 yds
0   50   100 m

observation blind

REFUGE RD

MARSH TRAIL

PARKER RIVER
NATIONAL WILDLIFE REFUGE

MARSH LOOP (closed)

Plum Island

DUNES TRAIL

REFUGE RD

restrooms

P Lot 4

North
Pool

dike

observation
tower

Forward Pool

© The Countryman Press

ELEVATION PROFILE

100 ft
80 ft
60 ft
40 ft   Overlook
20 ft Trailhead   Observation   Trailhead
0 ft   Blind
                      0.5   1   1.5 miles

Flats). Then, get back onto the turnpike and turn right onto Refuge Road—it has cottages on the left and a salt marsh on its right. A sign marks the entrance to the refuge, and the gatehouse at the beginning of the road charges $5 for entry. The trail begins at parking lot number 4.

THE HIKE

Your hike along the Hellcat boardwalk will cover the Dunes Loop and a walk out to an observation point. Unfortunately, the Marsh Loop section of the boardwalk has been temporarily closed due to deteriorating conditions. However, the entirety of the Dune Loop is

HELLCAT'S EXTENSIVE BOARDWALK NETWORK THROUGH THE DUNES

in great shape, and it awaits your boots padding along its wooden planks.

To begin this walk, park at lot number 4 along Parker River National Wildlife Refuge's Refuge Road. Once you're there, you can hop out of the car and stroll to the end of the parking lot. Turn right onto the trail. (It's the pathway opposite from the port-a-potties.) Follow the signs to stay right for the Dunes Loop, then head up to the boardwalk. Almost the entirety of your trip will follow this winding boardwalk through a sandy section of the natural barrier island. Take care not to brush up against the poison ivy on both sides of the walkway—it's abundant here.

The walk meanders through a lush green oasis, nurtured to vibrancy by the surrounding wetlands. After a short jaunt along the boardwalk, you'll need to cross Refuge Road to begin the loop around the dunes. Here, the greenery tents over the walkway in parts, creating a cave-like environment that leads you to the ocean. Steps soon descend into a grove of black oaks, with hardy plants growing over some parts of the trail. You'll reach a memorial for Ludlow Griscom, a pioneering ornithologist. Birdwatchers should pause here, as it's an excellent lookout spot, before continuing on. With all of the yellow stripes lining the boardwalk, you'll luckily never miss a step up or down.

Next, the stairs lead to a 50-foot-high dune boasting views up and down Plum Island. It presents the rare opportunity to see both marshes and the Atlantic, which flank both sides of the stretch of land. The plants surrounding the boardwalk—sea grasses, beach plum, black cherry, and some poison ivy—have adapted to this harsh dune environment along the coast. As you look around, it will become evident that the boardwalk

THE VIEW FROM THE OBSERVATION TOWER

is serving an important purpose—to allow visitors to float over the dunes, preventing them from interfering with the living landscape.

When you're finished admiring the views and filling your lungs with salt air, continue down a maze-like series of steps. They zig-zag back into a forest-like setting with crooked black cherry trees, and the boardwalk snakes around another dune covered in beach heather. Soon, you'll finish the loop and need to cross the street again to head back to where you started. Upon your arrival at marker 1, turn right as if you'd be starting along the Marsh Loop. Here, you'll only be tracing the hike's walk out to an observation point, rather than completing the loop. (You'll see signs on your left marking the loop and noting its deteriorating boardwalk conditions.)

Your walk out to the point is much like the previous boardwalk, with salt mist roses infusing the jaunt with a sweet scent. After just over a quarter of a mile, you'll arrive at the observation blind: it has a bench that invites you to enjoy the scenery. Look out to the runoffs of Plum Island Sound, and see if you can glimpse any of the refuge's many winged residents. Stop to listen and you'll hear a cacophony of bird calls and songs.

To round out your walk, head back to the original starting point once again. This time, exit and head right toward the restrooms. Pass them to begin a short walk to an observation tower, where you'll be rewarded with views of North Pool. Bang a sharp right onto a dike path to reach the tower. A warning: It's windy up there, so hold onto your hat. If you're exploring during July and August, you'll also want to watch out for greenheads—their bites can sour a pleasant summer afternoon. After you're finished scoping out North Pool, return to the parking lot to conclude the excursion.

Ipswich River Wildlife Sanctuary

WHERE: Topsfield

ADDRESS: 87 Perkins Row, Topsfield, MA 01983

TOTAL DISTANCE: 3.5 miles

HIKING TIME: 2 hours

ELEVATION GAIN: 240 feet

DIFFICULTY: Easy

RESTROOMS: Yes

DOGS ALLOWED: No

WHAT TO EXPECT: A scenic journey through meadows, marshes, and woodlands, all home to a diverse range of wildlife

Before wildlife enthusiasts glimpsed birds through binoculars from the Ipswich River Wildlife Sanctuary's 12 miles of trails, the Agawam people lived off of the land here. Later, it belonged to Simon Bradstreet, the last governor of the Massachusetts Bay Colony. Bradstreet's grandson built the surviving home on the farm, known as the Bradstreet House, in 1763. This building is now home to the visitor center and offices for the sanctuary.

By the 20th century, a man named Thomas Proctor purchased the Bradstreet property and used it to plant a lush arboretum. He sourced specimen trees from Asia and Europe, built stone bridges, and created carriage paths on the land. Perhaps his most interesting addition to the landscape is the rockery, a rock garden composed of glacial boulders and designed by a Japanese landscape architect.

Much of Proctor's improvements to the land can still be seen today, while the former farm and farmhouse maintain their bucolic charm. Mass Audubon purchased the property in the mid-1900s, transforming it into the wildlife haven it is today. The landscape, which makes up one of Mass Audubon's largest properties, is refreshingly varied, with almost 2,500 acres of meadows, woodlands, ponds, and marshes sliced up by the winding Ipswich River.

Before hitting the trails, you'll have to dole out $6 at the visitor center if you're not a member of the Audubon Society. (There are canoe rentals available here if interested.) Be sure to pick up a free trail map.

GETTING THERE

From Route 1 N., take the ramp to I-95 N. Then, take exit 50 to merge back onto

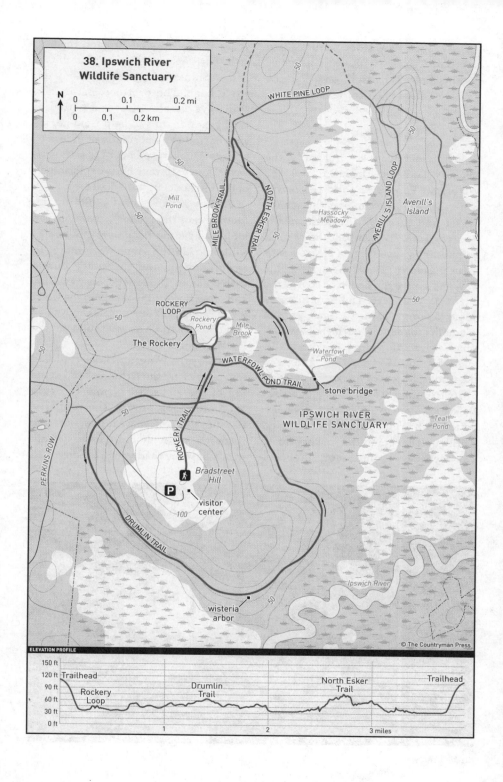

38. Ipswich River Wildlife Sanctuary

N

| 0 | | 0.1 | | 0.2 mi |
| 0 | 0.1 | | 0.2 km | |

WHITE PINE LOOP

Mill Pond

MILE BROOK TRAIL

NORTH ESKER TRAIL

Hassocky Meadow

AVERILL'S ISLAND LOOP

Averill's Island

50

ROCKERY LOOP

Rockery Pond

Mile Brook

The Rockery

WATERFOWL POND TRAIL

Waterfowl Pond

stone bridge

IPSWICH RIVER WILDLIFE SANCTUARY

Teal Pond

ROCKERY TRAIL

50

Bradstreet Hill

PERKINS ROW

P

visitor center

100

DRUMLIN TRAIL

Ipswich River

wisteria arbor

50

© The Countryman Press

ELEVATION PROFILE

150 ft	Trailhead					Trailhead
120 ft						
90 ft			Drumlin Trail		North Esker Trail	
60 ft	Rockery Loop					
30 ft						
0 ft		1		2	3 miles	

Route 1, and follow it for 3 miles. Turn right onto Central Street, which becomes Perkins Row. Turn right onto Perkins Row once more to enter the sanctuary.

THE HIKE

This hike connects several trails: the Rockery Trail, the Drumlin Trail, the Waterfowl Pond Trail, and the North Esker Trail. To begin, exit the visitor center and turn right to pick up the Rockery Trail. It's just past the two red outbuildings—you'll see a cleared path in the meadows beyond them. Head this way, and notice the dozen or so nesting boxes to your left. The sanctuary is home to dozens of bird species, as well as smaller mammals like meadow voles, which serve as food for hawks and owls.

As you descend a series of steps in the woods, a view of Rockery Pond will begin to unfold in front of you. A boardwalk allows you to glide over the water—dotted with bright green lily pads—and a bridge connects to the rockery itself. The rockery was built more than 100

years ago by Thomas Proctor. In 1901, he hired a Japanese landscape architect named Shintare Anamete to design the stone heap. The grottoes, paths, and stairways were built over a period of nine years, thanks to help from horses who carted the enormous boulders to the site. Duck in and out of the tunnels, caves, and pathways here, exploring all of the offshoots in this small area.

After you've finished exploring the footpaths of the rockery, complete the loop by heading back over the boardwalk and up the steps once more. In early summer, the sanctuary bursts with color, as rhododendrons, azaleas, and other flowers bloom along the walkways. Bright pink and purple rhodys will tent over the trails as you round out the Rockery Loop.

Pass by the Waterfowl Pond trail, and instead pick up the Drumlin Trail at the top of the steps. Turn right to begin a 1.3-mile loop around the property. Because this trail was a former carriage road, it's relatively flat. The easy walk winds past the road you drove in on, so

THE ROCKERY

RHODODENDRONS IN SPRINGTIME

look both ways before you cross Perkins Row. In an effort to remove diseased trees—some in danger of falling—from the property, Mass Audubon is clearing a few acres of non-native conifer trees. You might see their logs stacked along the trail. Eventually, they'll be carted away to make more room for fields. The fields will serve as habitats for birds like Tree Swallows, Eastern Bluebirds, and American Woodcock.

Trees arch over parts of the Drumlin Trail, which circles a drumlin, or a raised landscape sculpted by the movement of glacial ice sheets. As you make your way around the drumlin and through the property's Bunker Meadows, you'll pass by a century-old wisteria arbor as well as plantings from Proctor's former arboretum. Frogs, deer, and other wildlife will likely cross your path as you complete the Drumlin Trail loop. When you reach the intersection with the Rockery Trail once again, walk down the steps to reach the Waterfowl Pond Trail. This,

naturally, leads to Waterfowl Pond and its picturesque stone bridge. From here, you can view the cattail-filled marsh at Hassocky Meadow. Aside from several species of birds, you might also be able to glimpse beavers or river otters from the bridge.

Once you cross over the bridge, meander along the path until it meets up with the North Esker Trail, which rises above the surrounding swamps. It has steep drops on both sides, and according to the sanctuary, it follows the remains of sand and gravel deposits from a river that ran through a glacier at the spot about 15,000 years ago. Step over tree roots and rocks on this raised trail until you reach the Mile Brook Trail, which connects to the other side of the stone bridge. Turn right to pick up the Waterfowl Pond Trail once again, retracing your steps through the marsh. (I saw a great egret standing in the meadow here.) Ascend the steps one more time to reach the visitor center.

Lynn Woods

WHERE: Lynn

ADDRESS: 106 Pennybrook Road, Lynn, MA 01905

TOTAL DISTANCE: 3.75 miles

HIKING TIME: 2 hours

ELEVATION GAIN: 363 feet

DIFFICULTY: Easy

RESTROOMS: No

DOGS ALLOWED: Yes

WHAT TO EXPECT: An easy walk through the woods boasting views of the city from a stone tower, plus some pirate lore

If you were to guess which town claims the largest municipal park in New England, Lynn might not be the first place that comes to mind. But it's true—this lesser-known spot is also one of the largest city parks in the entire United States. At 2,200 acres, it's more than twice the size of Central Park in New York City.

Though it can't compare to Central Park in size, the Lynn Woods shares something else in common with New York's famed park: its designer. Renowned landscape architect Frederick Law Olmsted, who dreamed up Central Park, Boston's Emerald Necklace, and other landmark green spaces around the country, consulted with the chairman of the Lynn Park Commission, Phillip Chase, after the park was founded in 1881. After touring the woods, Olmsted recommended to Chase that the Lynn Woods were far better than a public park or garden. Rather, the place was a "real forest," and should remain unspoiled, "supplying a place of refreshing and restful relief," according to researchers at North Shore Community College. This was in line with Olmsted's outlook on city parks in general. As the country's first professional landscape architect, Olmsted believed city parks should be sanctuaries from the noise and grit of urban life, providing peaceful settings and picturesque views as a contrast to their industrial surroundings.

The Woods do just that—they feel worlds away from the blinking signs and honking horns on nearby Route 1. The park acts as a sanctuary of sorts, leading urban and suburban dwellers through thick woodlands and up to scenic outlooks. It also has its share of local legends and pirate lore, so read ahead

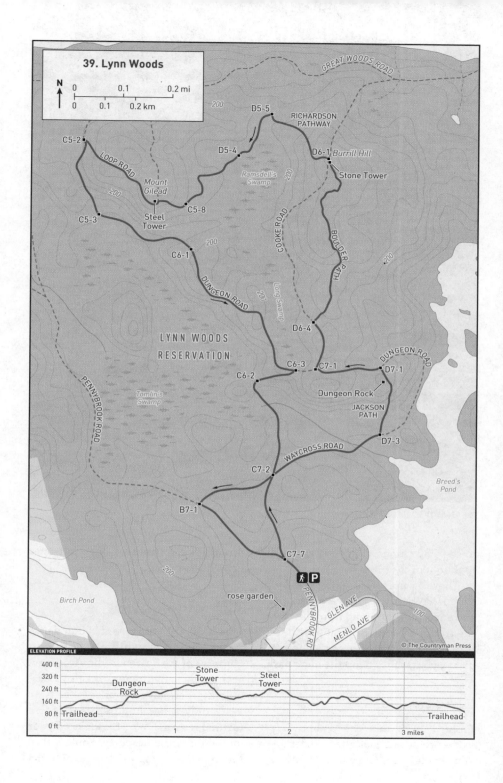

39. Lynn Woods

N

0   0.1   0.2 mi
0   0.1   0.2 km

GREAT WOODS ROAD

RICHARDSON PATHWAY

D5-5

D5-4

C5-2

LOOP ROAD

Mount Gilead

Ramsdell's Swamp

D6-1 Burrill Hill

Stone Tower

COOKE ROAD

BOULDER PATH

C5-8

Steel Tower

C5-3

C6-1

DUNGEON ROAD

Long Swamp

D6-4

LYNN WOODS RESERVATION

Tomlin's Swamp

C6-2   C6-3   C7-1   DUNGEON ROAD   D7-1

Dungeon Rock

JACKSON PATH

PENNYBROOK ROAD

WAYCROSS ROAD

D7-3

C7-2

Breed's Pond

B7-1

C7-7

Birch Pond

rose garden

PENNYBROOK RD

GLEN AVE

MENLO AVE

100

© The Countryman Press

ELEVATION PROFILE

400 ft
320 ft
240 ft
160 ft
80 ft
0 ft

Trailhead   Dungeon Rock   Stone Tower   Steel Tower   Trailhead

1   2   3 miles

THE STEPS TO DUNGEON ROCK

to see why Dungeon Rock is easily the highlight of the hike.

There is no fee to enjoy the Lynn Woods. When you arrive at the park entrance, pick up a map from the box at the trailhead. This grid map with Cartesian coordinates is essential to navigating your way around the huge park.

GETTING THERE

From US-1 N., take the Walnut Street exit on the right, just after Trader Joe's and Applebee's. Continue on Walnut Street for 2 miles, then turn left onto Pennybrook Road.

THE HIKE

This leisurely walk cuts through dense forest and rocky hilltops, offering glimpses of the Boston skyline from several perches. Begin your hike by passing the green gated entrance to the trail. Walk only a few hundred feet before turning right at C7-7. This kicks off your loop around the property. You'll follow green blazes here, which designate the reservation's "nature trails." Orange blazes mark fire roads, red ones overlook trails, and blue ones all other trails.

A short jaunt leads you to Needham's Clearing, an open green space that appears as an oasis in the thick woods. Turn right at C7-2 to follow a wide, unpaved path called Waycross Road. It leads to Dungeon Rock—one of the highlights of the hike. Take a left onto Jackson Path, then head up the stairs to Dungeon Rock, a boulder with a curious history.

Legend says during the late 1600s, pirates traveled up the Saugus River to trade silver for shackles, presumably made at nearby Saugus Ironworks. These pirates were said to have buried treasure in a cave at Dungeon Rock, but unfortunately, during an earthquake, one of the pirates was sealed into the cave with the treasure, never to be seen again. This pirate, Thomas Veal, was thought to have been crushed by the cave, or trapped there until his death. For years, the idea of treasure concealed in a Lynn cave piqued the curiosity of many. A man named Hiram Marble of Charlton, Massachusetts, was probably the most intrigued of all. In 1852, Marble claimed he received a message from the ghost of Thomas Veal. Veal told him to dig at Dungeon Rock if he wanted to become a rich man. Marble became so obsessed with finding this treasure that he purchased the 5 acres surrounding the rock and started his search. He built a home at the spot, and you can still see remains of its cellar hole and flower garden today. Marble and his son, Edwin, worked tirelessly to dig and blast through the rock with explosives, and yet they never found the bounty. After Hiram passed away in 1868, Edwin kept up the digging—that is, until he eventually died in 1880. His dying wish was to be buried at Dungeon Rock. According to the Friends of Lynn Woods, the pink stone at the top of the stairs marks the grave of Edwin Marble.

Confirm there's no treasure lying out in the open, and continue down the trail past the rock. You'll meet another wide unpaved road. Turn left here, and then, after a few steps, right onto Cooke Boulder Path at D6-4. This winding trail gifts hikers with wild blueberries in summertime. To those distracted by the blueberries, Lynn Woods' stone tower seems to appear out of nowhere at the crest of the 285-foot Burrill Hill. Built in 1936 by the Works Progress Administration for fire observation, the building offers sweeping views of Lynn's waterfront, Boston, and beyond. It's open for climbing certain days of the week—check the park's website, flw.org, for up-to-date visiting hours.

WILD BLUEBERRIES GROW ALONG COOKE BOULDER PATH

THE STONE TOWER ATOP BURRILL HILL

To continue your loop, find the D6-1 marker to turn onto Richardson Pathway. It's a rocky descent to the bottom of the hill, so ensure firm footing with each step. By now, at the hike's halfway mark, you're probably marveling at the fact that Lynn Woods is a city park. It feels very much like a state-owned reservation, which is part of its charm.

Keep an eye out for glacial erratics along the trails before turning left at D5-5. Continue straight onto a trail called Tyler's Mom's Way to reach the next landmark: a steel tower atop Mount Gilead. Like the stone tower, this fire tower comes into view abruptly. From a rocky ledge near the tower, you can see impressive views over the treetops, all the way from the Blue Hills to the south and New Hampshire to the north. Perhaps the best view is, once again, the city skyline. Peep at Boston Harbor and its islands to the left of the buildings.

When you're ready to keep going, take the path that continues past the tower—almost in a straight line jutting from the trail you entered from. Take a left at the bottom of this hill, and continue past marker number 3. Then turn right at marker 2 for one more rocky descent. From here on, the trail levels out, making for leisurely walking in these leafy woodlands. Part of this last leg of the hike feels almost like walking through a jungle. Huge swaths of ferns fringe the trail, creating a rainforest-like atmosphere. You'll emerge from the jungle to turn onto a fire road once more. Follow Pennybrook Road on your left all the way back to the Woods' Pennybrook Road entrance. Take a spin through the reservation's Rose Garden before hitting the road.

Maudslay State Park

WHERE: Newburyport	

ADDRESS: 74 Curzon Mill Road, Newburyport, MA 01950

TOTAL DISTANCE: 2.6 miles

HIKING TIME: 1 hour 15 minutes

ELEVATION GAIN: 163 feet

DIFFICULTY: Easy

RESTROOMS: Yes

DOGS ALLOWED: Yes

WHAT TO EXPECT: A pleasant cruise through a former estate along the Merrimack River

It wasn't long ago that Maudslay State Park was, rather than a rambling park traversed by hikers, bikers, and horseback riders, a magnificent riverside estate. In 1893, a horticulture-loving bunch known as the Moseley family transformed the land into a sprawling country home called Maudsleigh. Named after their home in England, the estate was laid out by a top-notch group of landscape architects: William Rantoul; Charles Sprague Sargent, the then-director of Boston's Arnold Arboretum; and Martha Brookes Hutcheson, one of the first females in the field. The architects expanded an existing cottage on the property into a 40-room retreat, complete with a greenhouse, a swimming pool, a tennis court, formal gardens, and more. There were once a total of 30 structures on the land in addition to a working farm.

Years before the Moseleys built their estate, a horticulturalist named William Ashby held "laurel parties" on the property to celebrate the beauty of a flourishing stand of native mountain laurel along the banks of the Merrimack River. Notables such as William Lloyd Garrison and Ralph Waldo Emerson attended these parties and likely sniffed the same mountain laurel you'll see during your hike. Today, this flower patch is one of the largest naturally occurring stands of mountain laurel in all of Massachusetts.

It's not just mountain laurel that's worth stopping for—the 480-acre park boasts an impressive diversity of plantings. Azaleas and rhododendrons put on a brilliant display that bursts with pink and purple hues in early summertime and should not be missed.

Maudsleigh's Main House was demolished in 1955, after the deaths of Frederick and Helen Moseley. Another structure, known as The Hedges, was

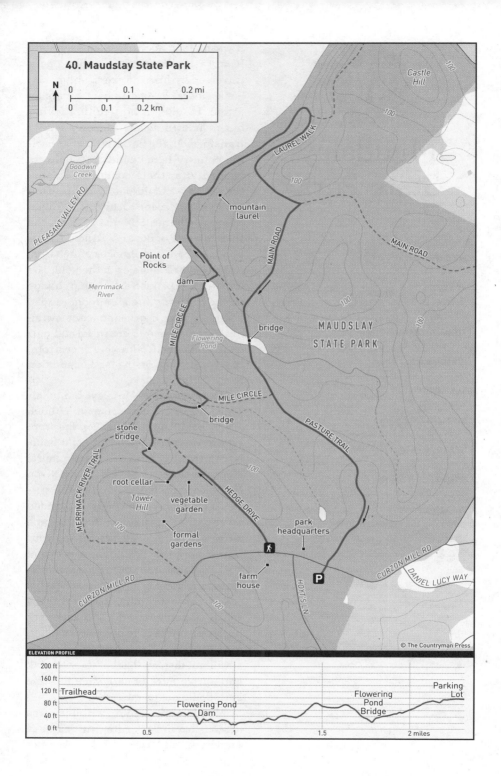

40. Maudslay State Park

N

| 0 | 0.1 | 0.2 mi |
| 0 | 0.1 | 0.2 km |

Goodwin Creek

PLEASANT VALLEY RD

LAUREL WALK

Castle Hill

100

100

MAIN ROAD

MAIN ROAD

mountain laurel

Point of Rocks

dam

Merrimack River

MILE CIRCLE

Flowering Pond

bridge

100

MAUDSLAY STATE PARK

100

100

MILE CIRCLE

bridge

stone bridge

PASTURE TRAIL

MERRIMACK RIVER TRAIL

root cellar

vegetable garden

Tower Hill

100

formal gardens

HEDGE DRIVE

100

park headquarters

farm house

P

CURZON MILL RD

CURZON MILL RD

HOYT'S LN

DANIEL LUCY WAY

© The Countryman Press

ELEVATION PROFILE

200 ft	
160 ft	
120 ft	Trailhead
80 ft	
40 ft	
0 ft	

Flowering Pond Dam

Flowering Pond Bridge

Parking Lot

0.5   1   1.5   2 miles

THE MERRIMACK RIVER THROUGH THE TREES

lost to a fire in 1979. The land was purchased by the state in 1985. Today, 480 acres of Maudslay State Park are yours to explore, from the former estate's greenhouse ruins and ornamental plantings to its mansion foundations and network of carriage paths.

GETTING THERE

From 1-95 N., take exit 57 for Route 113 toward W. Newbury/Newburyport. After exiting the highway, take a sharp left to get on Route 113. Then turn right onto Daniel Lucy Way, a short residential street. At the stop sign at the end of the street, turn left onto Curzon Mill Road. The parking lot, which is visible in the distance, will be on your right.

THE HIKE

Stop by the information board toward the front of the parking lot to grab a map. Then head down the stairs behind the board, and cross the street toward the park headquarters. Walk along the road until the stone wall lets out into an opening. This is the start of Hedge Drive, where you'll begin your hike.

Much of the walk will take place on a gravel path like the one you've started out on. This easy trip along Hedge Drive will eventually meet up with Mile Circle, and then the Pasture Trail. There is much to see on this jaunt around the former estate, so rather than follow this 2.6-mile loop to a T, I encourage you to poke around the property, and to explore its many small, winding paths. The magic of this park lies not in its rigorous trails, but its land use history. There are ruins of past lives to be discovered around every corner.

To keep along the general loop I've outlined, continue straight after passing an outbuilding on your left. After walking through a grand allee of pines, you'll see a vegetable garden to your left. Turn left to duck into a bunker-like structure circa 1929. It's a root cellar, used to preserve the vegetables grown in the garden you just passed.

Once you're finished admiring the graffiti adorning the walls of the cool, damp cellar, continue along the path, and turn right to pass over a small stone bridge. You'll get your first glimpse of the Merrimack River through the trees, and you'll likely hear boats whizzing past. As you approach the river, imagine what it was like for the Moseleys to take this same stroll down to the water. Could they have imagined their carriage paths would eventually be traversed by thousands of hikers each year?

At your next intersection, turn left over another bridge to begin walking on the Mile Circle Trail, which traces the riverbanks. Take a left once you reach the dam of Flowering Pond, and prepare for a treat. The gem of the hike lies just ahead: the largest naturally occurring stand of mountain laurel in Massachusetts. Admire the delicate white blossoms before continuing your leisurely stroll along the water. As you mosey around the property, you'll notice the trail markers are slim to none, and if there are some, they are somewhat vague. It's difficult to get truly lost in this park, and as mentioned before, it's best enjoyed via unscripted exploring.

Turn right at the next intersection, which keeps along the Mile Circle rather than turning onto the Castle Hill trail. Turn left at the top of the next small hill and then right to pass over another stone bridge on the opposite side of Flowering Pond. Pause to see dozens of turtles slowly gliding through the water. After the bridge, you'll veer left, then right, then left again for the Pasture Trail, which cuts across the open field adjacent from the park headquarters. It lets out at the stone wall across from the parking lot, concluding the loop.

MOUNTAIN LAUREL GALORE

Middlesex Fells Reservation

WHERE: Medford, Stoneham, Malden, Melrose, and Winchester

ADDRESS: South Border Road Parking Lot, S. Border Road, Medford, MA 02155

TOTAL DISTANCE: 7.5 miles

HIKING TIME: 4.5 hours

ELEVATION GAIN: 311 feet

DIFFICULTY: Strenuous

RESTROOMS: No

DOGS ALLOWED: Yes

WHAT TO EXPECT: A long trek through rocky hills, with a picture-perfect view of the Boston skyline as a reward

As a welcome respite from urban life for many Bostonians, Middlesex Fells Reservation is a highly trafficked outdoor recreation area just minutes from city limits. Its rugged beauty has attracted outdoor-loving visitors for years, though these days, it's more likely they're artfully capturing Instagrams during their visits. Hikers, horseback riders, mountain bikers, cross-country skiers, and casual picnickers make use of the reservation in all seasons. Its 2,575 acres stretch across Malden, Medford, Winchester, Stoneham, and Melrose.

The area was dubbed The Fells after a Saxon word that translates to "rocky, hilly tracts of land," per the DCR. History enthusiasts will appreciate the significance of the spot: it was first explored by Governor John Winthrop in the winter of 1632. In his private papers, Winthrop describes happening upon a pond with his men—this particular pond had rocks standing up in it, so, naturally, he called it Spot Pond. Spot Pond went on to become the heart of the Middlesex Fells Reservation, being a favorite place of contemplation by a man named Elizur Wright. In the late 1800s, Wright suggested creating a park with the land surrounding Spot Pond. While Wright is credited with the idea of creating the Fells, it was the Trustees of Reservations founder Charles Eliot who put a plan in motion. He proposed a nonprofit entity that could manage the land for public enjoyment. Thus, the Trustees was created, and land was donated to begin the creation of borders for the Fells.

Thanks to Eliot's vocal support for creating a parks commission, the Massachusetts state legislature established the Metropolitan Parks Commission in 1892. Two years later, in 1894, the Commission acquired one of its first parks: Middlesex Fells. This put it under the

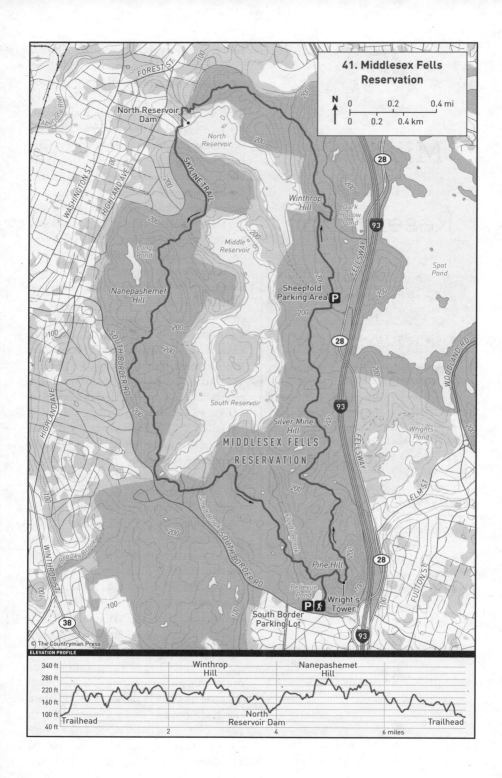

41. Middlesex Fells Reservation

FOREST ST.

North Reservoir Dam

North Reservoir

SKYLINE TRAIL

Winthrop Hill

Dark Hollow Pond

Spot Pond

Middle Reservoir

Long Pond

Nanepashemet Hill

Sheepfold Parking Area 🅿

South Reservoir

Silver Mine Hill

MIDDLESEX FELLS RESERVATION

Wrights Pond

WASHINGTON ST.

HIGHLAND AVE.

SOUTH BORDER RD.

HIGHLAND AVE.

FELLSWAY

WOODLAND RD.

ELM ST.

FULTON ST.

Smelt Brook

Floyds Brook

Brooks Brook

SOUTH BORDER RD.

WINTHROP ST.

Pine Hill

Bellevue Pond

Wright's Tower

🅿 South Border Parking Lot

© The Countryman Press

28

93

28

93

28

93

38

ELEVATION PROFILE

340 ft
280 ft
220 ft
160 ft
100 ft
40 ft

Trailhead

Winthrop Hill

North Reservoir Dam

Nanepashemet Hill

Trailhead

2   4   6 miles

supervision of the Commission, rather than the Trustees. Today, the historical Metropolitan Parks Commission is a division of the DCR.

Even as you revel in the nature that surrounds you—the Fells is a popular spot for "forest bathers," or fully clothed folks who set out to connect with the natural environment—there are many reminders that you're not far from the city. Aside from the spectacular view awaiting you on this hike, you'll hear the highway at times and see houses and other buildings in the distance. Somehow, none of it detracts from the unique beauty radiating from Middlesex Fells.

GETTING THERE

This hike takes place on the western side of the Fells. The Skyline Trail can be accessed from any number of points in the reservation but here, I chose the South Border Parking Lot. To get there, you could take the T to Wellington Station on the Orange Line, then the 134 bus toward north Woburn. Get off at Main Street and Chestnut Street, and walk about a mile along Chestnut Street and Leslie Road to the parking lot.

By car, take exit 33 from I-95 N. Merge onto Route 28, and at the traffic circle, take the second exit toward Somerville/Boston. Continue onto South Border Road until you see the parking lot on your right.

THE HIKE

You can't make the trip to Middlesex Fells without drinking in its magnificent views of the Boston skyline. This makes the reservation's Skyline Trail an obvious choice, even among the dozens of trail options. But be warned: this path only offers one real chance to see the skyline. The rest of it is a journey up and down rocky hills without a skyscraper in sight.

To begin, grab a map from the

THE VIEW FROM WRIGHT'S TOWER

WRIGHT'S TOWER

BELLEVUE POND TRAILHEAD sign just beyond the South Border Street parking area. Give it a once-over—if just to understand the sheer length of the trail you'll be tackling today—and walk about to where the Skyline loop will begin, passing Bellevue Pond and a stone picnic area on your left. A brown wooden sign with the words SKYLINE TRAIL marks the beginning of the loop. Turn right here. (Note: turning left will leave your visit to Wright's Tower until the very end of the hike. If you prefer to be rewarded when your hike is finished, consider turning left instead of right.) Amble up the hill—sidestepping the broken glass—toward one of the Middlesex Fells' most recognizable landmarks: Wright's Tower. Built in 1937 by the Works Progress Administration under the New Deal, the stone structure was named after Elizur Wright, the man who advocated for the creation of the Fells. The tower is open for climbing seasonally. If you're able to follow the short set of steps to the top, definitely do so. The views are unmatched, offering panoramic vistas from the shining waters of the harbor in the east to the outline of the Blue Hills (see Hikes #17 and #18) in the south.

Once you've taken three to five Instagrams and maybe one Boomerang, exit the tower and return to the trail. As you make your way through this relatively open wooded area, you'll see and hear cars barreling down I-93. The sounds of the highway, which are a bit jarring in this natural environment, won't fade away until you make it to the western side of the North Reservoir. Continue up and down the rock faces of Pine Hill, crossing several other forest paths in the process. Watch for mountain bikes when you do cross other trails; bikers whip around the hills at a good clip.

Then descend back into the forest, passing by small ponds. From here on out, pay close attention to the white rectangular trail signs on trees and white painted markers on the rocks. (The trail is well marked, though somewhat confusing at points.) You'll need to cross a paved road and walk through the Sheepfold Parking Area to continue on the Skyline Trail. The path transitions to pavement for a bit here, and if you veer off the trail for just a minute, you can see the reservation's dog park atop the crest of the hill on your left. The spot next to the meadow was once an old soap box derby track, where small motorless cars raced down a hill, using gravity as their source of speed.

Eventually the trail becomes dirt once again. It's at this point that I saw the first of two garter snakes. In case you were wondering, garter snakes are mostly harmless. They're not poisonous, but if you're bitten, make sure to clean the wound thoroughly and completely.

Once you're back under the cover of pine trees, the sun-dappled forest floor will lead you to the North Reservoir. Pay no attention to the large industrial building on your right; it will only distract you from your nature walk.

This is about the halfway point of the trip, and a good time to stop for lunch or a snack. The reservoir is used for drinking water, and as such, the town of Winchester prevents swimming or recreation of any kind along its shores. After a break along the reservoir, follow the trail to a residential road in Winchester. Houses—from charming Victorians to postwar ranches—will be visible from the trail going forward. They serve as a reminder that you're only a short distance from town and 6 miles from the largest city in New England. You'll see a tennis court across the street, but

ONE OF THE TRAIL'S MANY ROCKY HILLSIDES

be sure to stay on the left side of the road to get back on the trail. The terrain becomes flatter for a few hundred feet, until several steep ledges approach.

This is one of the most difficult stretches of the trail, because once you descend one rocky ledge, another one appears in front of you. Take extra care with your footing here, depending on how fatigued you're feeling. Again, you'll enter and exit pine forests, clearings, and ponds surrounded by woods. The varying landscapes offer a refreshing mix of shade and sun. You'll notice a blue water tower looming in the distance, and soon, you'll glimpse a few ranch houses through the trees. This is

where the Skyline Trail mixes with the Reservoir Trail and the Mountain Bike loop on the west side of the Fells. You'll know you're in the home stretch when tree trail markers begin to resemble Irish flags, with their green, white, and orange designations.

The end of the hike is signaled by a change in landscape—a rocky, woodsy one that resembles the part of the trail you traversed just after Wright's Tower. There's less shade here, which might mandate a reapplication of sunscreen. Descend a few more rocky, root-gripped ledges until you reach the beginning of the loop. Turn right to head back toward the parking lot.

42

Ravenswood Park

WHERE: Gloucester

ADDRESS: Ravenswood Park Main Gate, 481 Western Avenue, Gloucester, MA 01930

TOTAL DISTANCE: 4.5 miles

HIKING TIME: 2.5 hours

ELEVATION GAIN: 410 feet

DIFFICULTY: Moderate

RESTROOMS: No

DOGS ALLOWED: Yes

WHAT TO EXPECT: A bracing ramble through the woods, plus a bonus view of a lighthouse

In 1889, a wealthy businessman named Samuel E. Sawyer realized he wanted to share the beauty of his summer residence with others. The seasonal Gloucester dweller created Ravenswood Park that year to preserve the land for the public. According to the Trustees, who began managing the property in 1993, Sawyer sought to make it "laid out handsomely with drive-ways and pleasant rural walks."

The place is just that—all 600 acres along Cape Ann's Essex Coastal Scenic Byway are a journey to a simpler time. In fact, simple times defined the experience of Mason Walton, a hermit who built himself a log cabin in the woods here in the 1880s. The property's interesting history does not stop there, however. Ravenswood's Great Magnolia Swamp, which is the largest and northernmost stand of magnolia in Massachusetts, also has a claim to fame. It's the namesake for the nearby village of Magnolia.

GETTING THERE

From US. 1 N., take the I-95 N., MA-128 N. ramp toward Gloucester. Follow MA-128 N. to School Street in Manchester-by-the-Sea, then take exit 15 toward Essex/Manchester. Follow MA-127 N. to Gloucester. The entrance to the park is along Route 127, or Western Avenue, on the right. There are a limited number of spots in the lot, and parking along the street may be necessary.

THE HIKE

Once you're armed with a Trustees-issued map, you'll recognize that this hike traces the outer rim of Ravenswood Park. The 4.5-mile loop goes from the Ledge Hill Trail (orange) to the

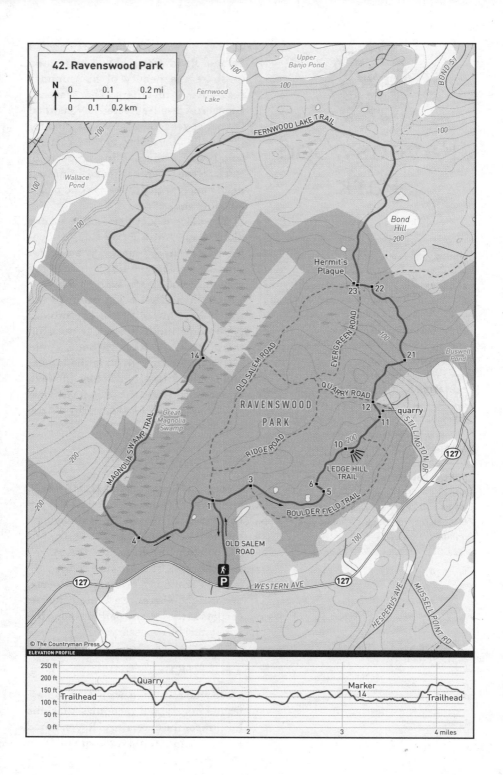

42. Ravenswood Park

N

| 0 | 0.1 | 0.2 mi |
| 0 | 0.1 | 0.2 km |

Upper Banjo Pond

Fernwood Lake

FERNWOOD LAKE TRAIL

Wallace Pond

Bond Hill

Hermit's Plaque

23 22

Buswell Pond

14

OLD SALEM ROAD

EVERGREEN ROAD

21

QUARRY ROAD

12

11 quarry

STILLINGTON DR

127

Great Magnolia Swamp

MAGNOLIA SWAMP TRAIL

RAVENSWOOD PARK

RIDGE ROAD

10

LEDGE HILL TRAIL

3

6

5

BOULDER FIELD TRAIL

1

4

OLD SALEM ROAD

P

WESTERN AVE

127 127

HESPERUS AVE

MUSSELL POINT RD

© The Countryman Press

ELEVATION PROFILE

250 ft				
200 ft	Quarry		Marker 14	
150 ft				
100 ft	Trailhead			Trailhead
50 ft				
0 ft	1	2	3	4 miles

Fernwood Lake Trail (blue) to the Magnolia Swamp trail (yellow).

Kick off the trip by passing the trailhead marker at the end of the parking lot. A wide dirt path leads to two signs—one pointing toward the Magnolia Swamp Trail and one toward Ledge Hill. Take a right to start along the Ledge Hill Trail, which becomes edged by rocks and boulders. Along this route, marked by orange blazes, you'll glimpse vernal pools, abundant moss-covered landscapes, and other bright green features. If you wanted to extend your trip by about 0.6 mile, you could opt to take the Boulder Field Trail (marked in red on the map) at trail marker 3. If not, keep left there, and then again at markers 5 and 6. Along the way, you can explore the massive crevices between boulders, which can be found on both sides of the trail.

The trail becomes rockier as you approach a quarry. But before you get there, stop for a moment at the scenic overlook at trail marker 10. It's a quaint New England scene: a rocky coast interrupted by a clean, white lighthouse. This one is called Eastern Point Light and was first lit on January 1, 1832. It signals the entrance to Gloucester Harbor.

As you continue on, you'll spot former cellar holes, traces of Native American burial mounds, and the remnants of a former quarry. It now abuts a private residence but once was a source of the region's highly coveted Cape Ann granite. Make sure not to turn onto Quarry Road here, instead keeping on the Ledge Hill Trail. A boardwalk protects you from the muck of a small swamp, and then a steep hill leads up to a massive display of boulders. (They're worth climbing.) You'll then descend into a grassy area, where you can look for a plaque honoring a hermit who once

A BOULDER ENCROACHES ON YOUR PERSONAL SPACE

ROCKS LEAD THE WAY

dwelled in these woods. Indeed, in the 1880s, a man named Mason Walton built a log cabin on the land, avoiding human contact and instead penning books on the local flora and fauna. His work *A*

Hermit's Wild Friends, which details his 18 years in the woods, is available for free on Google Books.

At the next clearing, bang a left to start along the blue Fernwood Lake Trail, which only briefly passes by Fernwood Lake. This trail is within the city of Gloucester's Watershed Lands and is maintained by the town. It's less neatly marked than Trustees trails but is just as enjoyable. For the next two miles, the trail becomes grassier, and in parts, muckier. It skirts a stone wall before putting on a healthy display of mountain laurel.

A green sign marks the Trustees' reservation boundary. Pass by it and take a sharp right at trail marker 14 to begin your walk along the Magnolia Swamp Trail. It's here you'll find Massachusetts' endangered flower: sweetbay magnolia. This stand—in the Great Magnolia Swamp—is the northernmost grouping in the state. It's also the largest one. A black plastic fence guards some of this treasure, with the most impressive blooms marked by wooden posts.

An impressively long boardwalk leads over much of the swamp before arriving at a cluster of glacial erratics. When you see a large boulder looming in the distance, you'll know you're almost finished. Approach it and turn right, following the trail a few more hundred feet to the parking lot.

43

Stage Island Trail

WHERE: Ipswich

ADDRESS: Parker River National Wildlife Refuge, Refuge Road, Newbury, MA 01951

TOTAL DISTANCE: 1.6 miles

HIKING TIME: 1 hour

ELEVATION GAIN: 38 feet

DIFFICULTY: Easy

RESTROOMS: No

DOGS ALLOWED: No

WHAT TO EXPECT: A coastal walk featuring wildflowers and sea breezes

The Stage Island Trail in three words? Short, sweet, and scenic. Though it's more of a nature walk, this second highlighted trail in Parker River National Wildlife Refuge is an hour well-spent. It's also a new addition to the refuge, offering a 0.75-mile walk to the tip of Stage Island, and then the same distance back.

You could enjoy this hike either before or after a trip to the Hellcat Interpretive Trail (see Hike #37), but be warned: parking is limited here. Stage Island Trail hikers must park at lot number 6, and there are only a few spots. As the saying goes for most of the places to visit on Plum Island, get there early.

GETTING THERE

Follow the same directions for the Hellcat Interpretive Trail, but instead of parking in lot number 4, continue to parking lot number 6 along Refuge Road.

THE HIKE

Cross the street to start your trip out to the very tip of Stage Island, also known as Ipswich Bluffs. Pass by the closed gate marking the entrance to this lollipop trail, and follow the wide dirt path. Though it's only about 0.75 mile to the bluffs, there's a lot to appreciate along the way. You'll want to sniff the salt air—that is, until you reach the wildflowers flanking the trail. Then you'll want to smell those.

The pink, purple, and yellow petals create contrast among the bright green shrubs in summertime. Let your eyes sweep from left to right, noticing salt mise roses, vetch, wild grapes, mullein, and milkweed, a favorite for butterflies. By now, you may have realized this

DON'T SLEEP ON SNIFFING THE SALT MIST ROSES

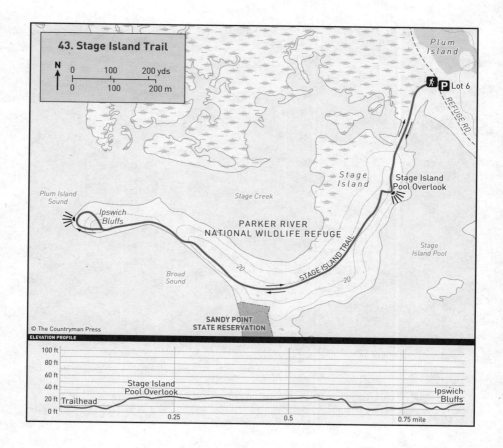

N

| 0 | 100 | 200 yds |
| 0 | 100 | 200 m |

Plum
Island

Lot 6

REFUGE RD.

Plum Island
Sound

Stage
Island

Stage Creek

Ipswich
Bluffs

Stage Island
Pool Overlook

PARKER RIVER
NATIONAL WILDLIFE REFUGE

Stage
Island Pool

-20

STAGE ISLAND TRAIL

-20

Broad
Sound

© The Countryman Press

SANDY POINT
STATE RESERVATION

ELEVATION PROFILE

| 100 ft |
| 80 ft |
| 60 ft |
40 ft	Stage Island			Ipswich
20 ft	Trailhead	Pool Overlook		Bluffs
0 ft		0.25	0.5	0.75 mile

hike is less about breaking a sweat than about savoring the coastal beauty of the landscape.

Trees in the distance mark the beginning of the loop around Stage Island. Stick to the left up here to start your circuit and you'll be greeted by a rocky beach. Here, dozens of boats bob in the water off the opposite coast, and you may even see folks digging for clams. The charming scene across Plum Island Sound is Ipswich's Great Neck neighborhood. If you reach out, it feels like you can almost touch it.

Feel free to linger on this beach, listening to the birds and watching the water sparkle. When you decide to continue on, you'll reach a bench at the end of Stage Island's grassy knoll. There are more vistas of town to be enjoyed on your way to this bench, just beyond a wooden fence lining the trail. Sit down and drink in the view—it's almost like looking at a painting of boats and moorings. Confirm that it is indeed real life, and return to the lush grasses of the trail. You'll exit the same way you walked in, along the wildflower-packed path.

IV

CAPE COD AND BOSTON HARBOR

Atlantic Cedar Swamp Trail

WHERE: Wellfleet	

ADDRESS: 195 Marconi Station Road, Wellfleet, MA 02667

TOTAL DISTANCE: 1.25 miles

HIKING TIME: 40 minutes

ELEVATION GAIN: 74 feet

DIFFICULTY: Easy

RESTROOMS: Yes

DOGS ALLOWED: No

WHAT TO EXPECT: An easy trip to a boardwalk that winds through a cedar grove in Cape Cod National Seashore lands

European settlers decimated the land you're about to stroll through after years of overforesting. When they arrived on Cape Cod in the 1600s, they saw infinite uses for Atlantic white cedar trees. As the Cape Cod National Seashore Park Service explains, the wood was perfect for almost every aspect of colonial life. It was light enough for cutting down en masse, easy to mold and shape, and fairly resistant to decay. It became the top-choice material for building houses and barns—the frames, joists, floorboards, and doors were all crafted from cedar, and outside, cedar was shaped into fences, window boxes, and just about every other built structure you can imagine. Later, during the Revolutionary War, the tree's charcoal was even used to produce gunpowder. To say the wood was invaluable to the settlers would be an understatement.

Fast forward a century to the 1850s, and this Atlantic white cedar swamp stood barren. The colonists logged each and every tree, leaving none from the original stand surviving. For years after that, however, the land lay untouched, allowing pine, oak, and cedar trees to rise again. The Park Service notes that Atlantic white cedar naturally grows in the Cape's wetlands, so no matter the type of land disturbance—whether it be human destruction, gypsy moth takeovers, storms, or another factor—the cedars will always come back. If disturbances don't come, then other species, like tupelo and red maples, will squeeze their way in. The makeup of the swamp is a delicate balance of trees and plants competing for resources, sunlight, and shade. Its continued evolution will be a show worth watching.

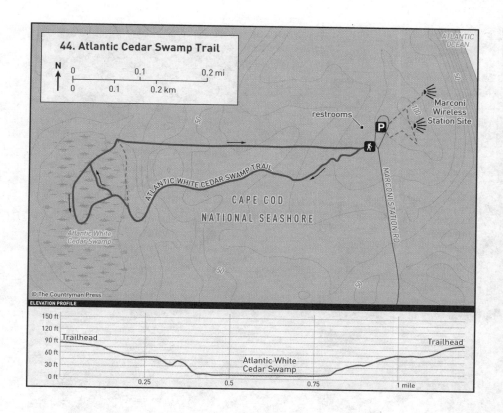

44. Atlantic Cedar Swamp Trail

N

0   0.1   0.2 mi

0   0.1   0.2 km

ATLANTIC OCEAN

Marconi
Wireless
Station Site

restrooms

P

ATLANTIC WHITE CEDAR SWAMP TRAIL

CAPE COD
NATIONAL SEASHORE

MARCONI STATION RD.

Atlantic White
Cedar Swamp

© The Countryman Press

ELEVATION PROFILE

150 ft
120 ft
90 ft Trailhead
60 ft
30 ft
0 ft

Atlantic White
Cedar Swamp

Trailhead

0.25   0.5   0.75   1 mile

GETTING THERE

If you're driving from the Salt Pond Visitor Center in Eastham after hiking Nauset Marsh (see Hike #47), continue heading north on Route 6. At the stop light near Southfleet Motor Inn, turn right off of Route 6 toward Marconi Area. Then follow the brown roadside signs to the parking area for the Marconi Site and White Cedar Swamp.

THE HIKE

Though the coastal bluff the Marconi Site is perched on is just across the parking lot, we'll save that for a reward at the end of this nature walk. This trail is indeed more of a nature walk than a full-blown hike, and that is the quiet beauty of it. Begin by entering the trailhead at the beginning of the parking lot, just a few feet down the road from the seasonal restrooms. Here, the jagged pitch pines surrounding you have created a soft blanket of rusty orange needles underfoot. The trail soon becomes sandier, and you'll enjoy easy walking all the way down to the swamp. Black huckleberry and broom crowberry flank the trail as curvy, Dr. Seuss-like scrub oaks and pitch pines hover overhead.

What's black and white and red all over? The Atlantic White Cedar Swamp. You'll soon approach it on the left. Start down the boardwalk to begin a one-of-a-kind journey into the swamp, where you'll spot not only

CURVING PITCH PINES FLANK THE SANDY PATH

A BOARDWALK FLOATS OVER THE SWAMP

white cedars, but black and white oaks and red maples. Keep left at the fork in the boardwalk to walk a full circle around the swamp. The journey feels almost like a fairy tale, thanks to the meandering walkways that seem to cut through the thick grove of cedars. Sunlight pokes through the trees in some areas, splashing the wooden walkway with patches of light. (Note: Parts of the boardwalk are being repaired and replaced in 2019.)

Loop around the swamp as many times as you'd like, and when you're ready, head up into sandy grounds once again. Though short, the path back to the parking lot is slightly uphill. You'll know you're close when you begin to hear the waves crashing at Marconi Beach. Before you end your trip to the National Seashore, make a trip across the parking lot to the Marconi Wireless Station Site. It's where Italian inventor Guglielmo Marconi sent his first transatlantic radio signal to Cornwall, England, via a group of antennae attached to four wooden towers on January 18, 1903. The towers are no longer there, but a few remains are still visible in the sand. The bluff where you're standing overlooking the sea is not just beautiful, but also windy. Gales and sea spray make the spot a harsh environment for plants, though patches of beach heather, bear oak, and broom crowberry are able to weather the conditions.

45

Great Island Trail

WHERE: Wellfleet

ADDRESS: 2–6 Griffins Island Road, Wellfleet, MA 02667

TOTAL DISTANCE: 6.8 miles

HIKING TIME: 4 hours

ELEVATION GAIN: 230 feet

DIFFICULTY: Strenuous

RESTROOMS: Yes

DOGS ALLOWED: In some parts

WHAT TO EXPECT: A long but stunning journey along the beach and through pitch pine forests, often in direct sunlight

The Great Island Trail is arguably one of the best hikes in all of Massachusetts. The loop, located within the boundaries of the Cape Cod National Seashore, begins with an easy walk, tracing the shoreline of "the gut," where the Herring River lets out into Wellfleet Harbor. Then, it climbs up into a pitch pine forest, offering stunning views from cliffs overlooking Cape Cod Bay. There's also a history lesson thrown in, as a small stone monument marks the spot where a former 17th-century whaling tavern once stood. The trail emerges from the woods and traverses sandy dunes leading to Great Beach Hill, ending with a breezy walk along the beach. While Great Island is no longer a true island, it sure feels that way, with its abundance of ocean panoramas.

If a 6.8-mile trek in direct sunlight isn't in the cards for you, there's the option to shorten your walk to a 1.8-mile hike to just the tavern site, or a 2.4-mile walk to Great Beach Hill. If you're feeling fearless, there's also the option to extend your hike to Jeremy Point, a sandy spit that can only be reached when the tide is out. (Do not attempt to reach Jeremy Point when the tide is rising!) Set out equipped with sunscreen and plenty of water, and if you can, get out there in the early morning. During summertime, it gets quite hot around midday, but that's nothing a quick dip in the ocean can't solve.

GETTING THERE

From US-6 E. in Orleans, take the second exit in the roundabout to stay on US 6-E. After 11.2 miles, turn right onto Main Street in Wellfleet, then after 0.7 mile, turn left onto Holbrook Avenue. Turn right onto Chequessett Neck Road, and stay left to stay on Chequessett

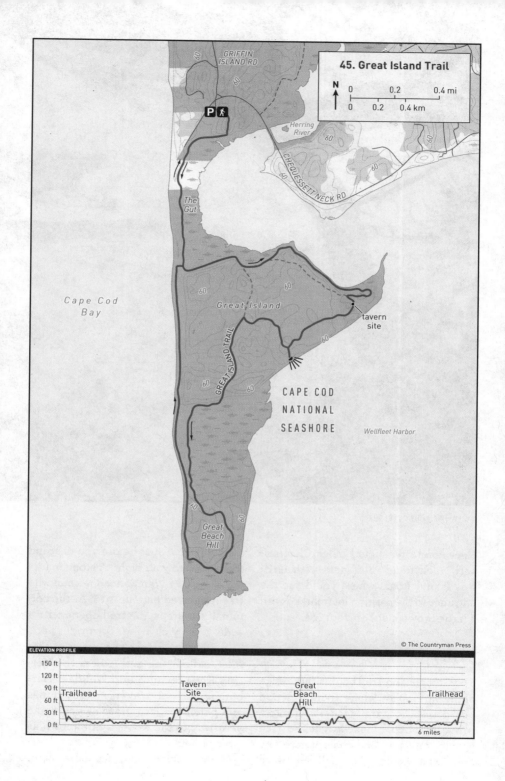

GRIFFIN ISLAND RD

45. Great Island Trail

N

| 0 | 0.2 | 0.4 mi |
| 0 | 0.2 | 0.4 km |

Herring River

CHEQUESSETT NECK RD

The Gut

Great Island

Cape Cod Bay

tavern site

GREAT ISLAND TRAIL

CAPE COD NATIONAL SEASHORE

Wellfleet Harbor

Great Beach Hill

© The Countryman Press

ELEVATION PROFILE

150 ft
120 ft
90 ft
60 ft
30 ft
0 ft

Trailhead

Tavern Site

Great Beach Hill

Trailhead

2   4   6 miles

A VIEW FROM THE OVERLOOK

Neck Road after about 2 miles. Chequessett Neck Road intersects with Griffins Island Road, where you'll see the entrance to the parking lot (marked with a large brown sign) on your left.

THE HIKE

The Great Island Trail begins at the edge of the parking lot, where an information board marks the trailhead. Enter into a grove of pitch pines—a beloved tree species on Cape Cod characterized by their twisted clumps of needles—toward a set of steps. Just before you descend them, look to your right. A stone marks the grave of a Wampanoag woman who was reinterred here in 1976. At the bottom of the steps, the trail opens onto a wide, beachy clearing. Turn right here. The dirt path traces the curve of this inlet, called "the gut," where the Herring River lets out into Wellfleet Harbor. You'll soon traverse sandy dunes and patches of sea grass as you make your way to the wooded hill known as Great Island.

As you skirt along the shoreline of

opening into the woods, as it's easy to miss. The pines, oaks, and bayberry make for a shady respite from the sunny beach. Keep along the path, which is not clearly marked in some parts, until you reach a sign with photographs from an archaeological dig at the former tavern site. Turn right here to reach the tavern site. While there's no foundation, the spot is marked by a sign and some stones. Settlers from Plymouth moved to the Outer Cape in the mid-1600s, and fished, whaled, traded, and farmed to make their livings. This site, sometimes called the Samuel Smith Tavern Site, was active from 1690 to 1740, according to the archaeological dig there. Back in the day, hardworking whalers frequented the tavern for a drink and a smoke, allowing themselves the privilege of not having to travel all the way back to the mainland for a break.

After paying your respects to the whalers of yesteryear, take this time to explore the area. A spur trail leads to a nearby sea cliff, where twisting branches frame views of the sandy spit in the distance. A few other offshoots lead to more scenic overlooks. It's worth spending a few minutes drinking in the views. When you're ready, head back to the tavern site and venture beyond it, walking down a hill and a set of steps. When you arrive at an intersection in the trail, turn left at the sign. Here, the trail widens, making for an easy jaunt through the pines. A stone marker on your left highlights the spot where a descendant of William Bradford, an early governor of Plymouth Colony, lived from 1939 until 1962. Keep on this wide trail until you emerge from the forest and back onto the beach. Turn right here, and notice once again the small crabs burrowing into their holes in the mud, then

the marsh, see if you can spot horseshoe crab and oyster shells on the beach. (Wellfleet is renowned for its oysters.) You'll see tiny fiddler crabs scurrying to and fro in the tidal zone, and if you pause, you'll be able to hear their little legs pounding the sand with soft taps. Continue along the beach as the gentle bay laps at the shore, steering clear of the erosion to your right. When you approach the trail's first instance of signage, keep left to head to the tavern site. You'll cling to the marsh's edge for a while longer until turning up into the pitch pines. Keep an eye out for this

SPEND A SUMMER'S DAY WINDING THROUGH THE DUNES

resurfacing. You'll begin to climb up and down the dunes of Great Beach Hill, with the sand underfoot giving your leg muscles a nice workout.

The sandy path flanked by seagrasses poses one small threat: fire ants. Make sure not to go barefoot in this area. As you enter into another pitch pine forest, you'll be able to hear the waves of the National Seashore echo around you. When you exit this forest and round the bend, you have the option to extend your hike if the tide is out. (Ensure you have enough water, snacks, and sunscreen if you choose to do this.) You could walk a bit further out to the tip of Jeremy Point, but make sure not to do so when the tide is rising, as the spot is only accessible at low tide. If you'd rather head back, continue on a straight shot down the beach. You could follow my lead and stop for a swim in the Cape Cod Bay, in case the sun beating down you mandates some cooling off. Provincetown's famed landmark, the Pilgrim Monument, pokes out of the land curving toward you in the distance.

You'll follow this beach, to get back to the beginning of the trail. Seals and other critters can be glimpsed in the shimmering waters beside you. The sandy beach will transition to a rockier one for a time, and tidal pools will expose themselves on the shore. You'll know you're nearing the end of the trail when you see the beachy mansions from the beginning of your trip in the distance. Keep your eyes peeled for the trail as it turns right into the dunes—it's roped off on each side for bird nesting. This leads you back to the marsh trail you started on. Follow it back to the first pitch pine forest, and ascend the steps back up to the parking lot.

Lovells Island

WHERE: Boston Harbor

ADDRESS: Lovells Island, Boston Harbor

TOTAL DISTANCE: 1.5 miles

HIKING TIME: 1 hour 15 minutes

ELEVATION GAIN: 38 feet

DIFFICULTY: Easy

RESTROOMS: Yes

DOGS ALLOWED: No

WHAT TO EXPECT: A salty jaunt around a historic fort boasting views of Boston Light and the Boston skyline

Lovells Island is one of Boston's best-kept secrets. Because it's only accessible via an interisland ferry, it remains far less crowded than some of the more popular Boston Harbor Islands, imbuing the sandy shores with a quiet beauty. Beyond that, it offers a spectacular view of the skyline. From Lovells' western shores, you feel like you could almost reach out and touch one of the city's skyscrapers. To the east, Boston Light flickers in the distance.

Tracing the coastline of Lovells Island is the perfect way to escape the heat of the city in the summer. You'll explore the ruins of Fort Standish, named after military officer Myles Standish (flip to Hike #25 for a hike in Myles Standish State Forest). Constructed in 1907, its use was short-lived. After World War II, the fort was deactivated. Its crumbling gun batteries, foundations, and bunkers have sat unused since the late 1940s.

There's a good chance of spotting a European hare in these ruins. The bunnies are not native to the island, and some speculate they were brought here by soldiers or island caretakers in the 1940s or 1950s. And though you won't be able to see them, plenty of shipwrecks lie under the waters between Lovells and Georges Islands. The shallow, rocky passage was once the main waterway into Boston, much to the anxiety of scores of sea captains over the years.

Be sure to bring plenty of water before you hop on the ferry, or fill up your bottle at Georges—there is no running water on Lovells Island. (If you're staying the night at a campsite, bring double what you think you might need.)

GETTING THERE

From Long Wharf in Boston, take a seasonal Boston Harbor Cruises ferry to

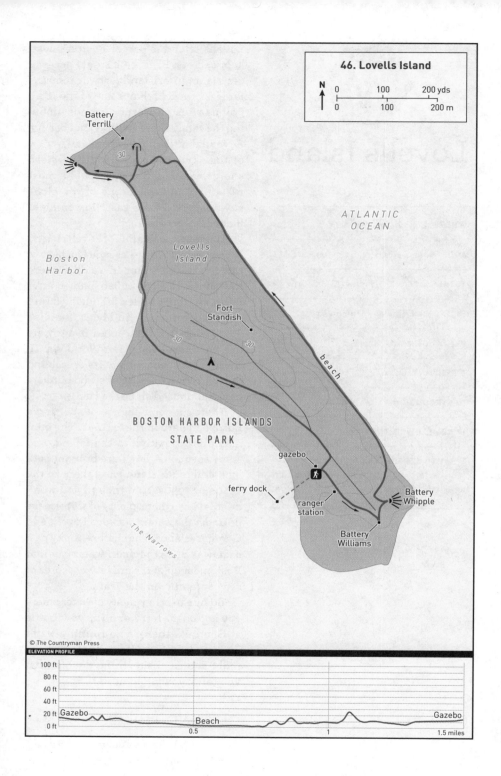

46. Lovells Island

N
0   100   200 yds
0   100   200 m

Battery
Terrill

30

ATLANTIC
OCEAN

Lovells
Island

Boston
Harbor

Fort
Standish

30   30

beach

BOSTON HARBOR ISLANDS
STATE PARK

gazebo

ferry dock

ranger
station

Battery
Whipple

Battery
Williams

The Narrows

© The Countryman Press

ELEVATION PROFILE

100 ft
80 ft
60 ft
40 ft
20 ft   Gazebo   Gazebo
0 ft   Beach
         0.5   1   1.5 miles

FORT STANDISH RUINS AND BOSTON LIGHT IN THE DISTANCE

Georges Island, then hop on a free inter-island ferry to Lovells. Small boats also run from Hull and Hingham.

THE HIKE

After stepping off the ferry, amble up the dock toward the gazebo. Take a good look at the signs in the gazebo to see times for returning ferries, then continue on. Just a few steps ahead, there's a sign introducing Lovells Island and a small path on its right. Take this path to begin your hike.

The sandy trail almost immediately flattens out to a paved one. The ranger station appears on your right, where the park ranger overseeing campers stays the night. Then, as you round the bend, the crumbling remnants of Fort Standish come into view.

This grassy courtyard inside the fort is where group camping occurs, hence the compost toilet. There are several other courtyards like it on the island, but there is no running water. Explore the ruins of the fort. You'll find old brick fireplaces inside them, plus some more modern cairns and graffiti.

Cross the courtyard to climb the steps of the ruin that's farthest from the ranger station. Be careful, however, as the steps are decaying and some are missing completely. At the top, you'll find a picnic table situated in the circular outline where artillery once sat. The blue expanse of the outer harbor also lays before you as a reward. Enjoy

THE BOSTON SKYLINE FROM LOVELLS' WESTERN SHORES

a sweeping view from Graves Light, the outermost lighthouse in the harbor, all the way to Boston Light, the second-oldest lighthouse in the country at more than 300 years old, and the tip of Hull. Georges and Peddocks Islands (see Hike #49) can be glimpsed, too.

When you've seen enough of the picturesque lighthouses, descend the same deteriorating steps you came up. Turn right toward the compost toilet, then turn right again up the paved path near a grouping of old lobster traps. In summertime, wildflowers and shrubs like bittersweet nightshade flank the trail. There are also thick patches of milkweed across the island, attracting many monarch butterflies. You'll find no shortage of wild blackberries either, which grow sweet and plump along most of the trails.

Cross a mound of rocks to reach the beach below, then turn left. Here, you'll trace the shore for about a half mile. See

by the ruins of a small brick structure. This little house was used to store the oil that lighted the Lovells Island range lights. These beacons were torn down in 1939, when Fort Standish was expanded.

Follow a narrow pass through the grass as it turns right into the trees. An almost hidden stone archway pokes through the leafy branches up ahead. It's worth taking a detour to explore this less-traveled part of the fort, where shadows dance across rotting doors and walls. Be careful making your way back out—head back the way you came and cross the mound of rocks to the water.

Hello there, Boston skyline. Civilization, it seems, is startlingly close. To the right is Logan Airport (as evidenced by the constant sound of planes overhead) and Deer Island, home to a sewer treatment plant. Look down to see bricks scattered along the rocky beach. Trace the shoreline on this side of the island, too, using your arms and your legs to climb over the huge cement blocks standing between you and the rest of Lovells. Once you've made it, you'll see a broken tunnel above you. Erosion snapped off the endcap of this underground walkway, opening it to the harbor for all to see. Continue to walk along the beach until you can turn into the trees on the left. Two individual campsites sit on both sides of the trail here. Climb the rocks to go between them, then follow the paved path through the other campsites. The path leads back to where you started—turn right to take a shade break under the gazebo.

more ruins of Fort Standish here, such as its former fortifying wall and lookout station. Continue to walk along the beach, past a patch of trees on your left. Turn left up into the rocks before reaching the second group of trees. A grassy meadow appears before you, interrupted

Nauset Marsh Trail

WHERE: Eastham

ADDRESS: Cape Cod National Seashore Salt Pond Visitor Center, 50 Nauset Road, Eastham

TOTAL DISTANCE: 1.4 miles

HIKING TIME: 45 minutes

ELEVATION GAIN: 73 feet

DIFFICULTY: Easy

RESTROOMS: Yes

DOGS ALLOWED: No

WHAT TO EXPECT: A breezy walk along a tidal pond and through a coastal marsh on the National Seashore

While Cape Cod is most famous for its pristine beaches, the hooked arm of Massachusetts is also rich with another, often underappreciated, landform: kettle ponds. Formed by receding glaciers in the last Ice Age, the area is dotted with them. On this hike, you'll get up close and personal with Salt Pond, a kettle of salt water (rather than freshwater) connected to Nauset Marsh.

When Nauset Marsh was first charted by French explorer Samuel de Champlain in the early 1600s, it was a navigable bay. According to the Cape Cod National Seashore Park Service, the native Nauset peoples built beehive-shaped homes on the fields surrounding the marsh, which de Champlain noted in his journals. Over the years, as settlers moved onto the land and the ocean continued to run its course, a narrow sandy spit was carved out by the tides. The spit curved around to protect the waters inside of it, creating Nauset Marsh as we know it.

The persevering ocean also made its way to the freshwater kettle pond of Salt Pond by creating its own narrow channel. Today, Salt Pond is still connected to the ocean, and sees tides come in and out twice a day. The pond's inhabitants—mussels, oysters, quahogs, fish, birds, and other types of shellfish—thrive in the former freshwater basin.

For a complete look at the species dwelling in the pond, and the changes in the seashore over time, stop inside the Salt Pond Visitor Center before setting out for your walk. The center's museum contains a larger-than-life map illustrating the Cape's glacial movement history. You'll also find a gift shop, a theater, and restrooms.

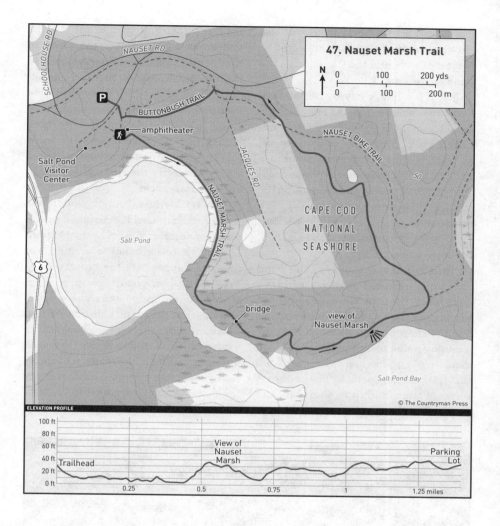

47. Nauset Marsh Trail

ELEVATION PROFILE

GETTING THERE

From MA-6 E. in Eastham, turn right onto Nauset Road at the traffic signal. (It's marked by a sign for the Cape Cod National Seashore.) The entrance to the parking lot is on your right.

THE HIKE

Begin your stroll around the marsh by exiting the visitor center and heading left toward the amphitheater. The trailhead begins just to the right of the amphitheater's stage, where there's a box of trail maps handy. Start along the gravel path, on which you'll soon be met by a sweeping view of Salt Pond, a former kettle pond the Atlantic Ocean has claimed as its own. The pond, like all the Cape's kettle ponds, was formed after the glaciers of the last Ice Age receded. But with Salt Pond, the ocean demolished the barrier separating the freshwater kettle pond from the sea. Now, the body of water is connected to Nauset Marsh, and the tides enrich the pond twice a day.

You'll likely see kayakers, canoers, and birds including swans enjoying the calm waters. On some Sundays, shell-fishers are permitted to enjoy the pond as well. It's no wonder the pond is a favorite among clammers. While you'll spot plenty of people and animals on the surface of the water, there are many more species lurking in the waters below. Salt Pond is home to oysters, mussels, fish, scallops, and quahogs.

Turn left at the shores of the pond and walk toward the grove of black oaks lining the trail. Here, a sandy path skirts the seagrass-laden shores of Salt Pond. A short boardwalk leads you over a muddy patch to a population of black locust trees and salt spray roses. Then the trail turns up into the woods. A series of steps leads up a short hill, and glimpses of Nauset Marsh peak through the trees. Descend another set of steps and cross a bridge over the channel that connects Salt Pond to the greater Nauset Marsh. Ahead, there's a charming little boathouse. It's part of a private property, so turn left (following the trail signs) to keep within National Seashore boundaries. Another set of steps leads to a fragrant grove of bayberry—see if you can identify the small blue berries as you continue on.

The trail winds through woodlands for several hundred feet before it opens onto a panoramic view of Nauset Marsh. Luckily, there are benches inviting you to sit and appreciate the quiet, watery expanse. When you're ready, pick up the path again to see more views of the marsh from different vantage points. Then, meander through sea grasses for a moment—and stop to notice if you see anything hiding in the reeds. A discerning eye will spot a cement roller lying in the grass. A small sign next to the trail indicates it's left over from when the

A HERON STANDS IN THE MARSH

A BRIDGE OPENS TO NAUSET MARSH

land served as a golf course. Indeed, the higher lands along the marsh were home to the Cedar Bank Links golf course from 1928 to 1935. Its sand traps, putting greens, and open fairways are no longer visible, however. The land was first filled in by red cedars, and later, white and black oaks took over.

Round the bend to start the latter half of your journey. While there's the option to take a detour to the Doane Memorial and Coast Guard Beach overlook, the hike outlined here does not cover that. Turn left to continue meandering through pitch pines—you'll likely smell them when breezes blow through. Here, you can foster an appreciation for the sandy, scrubby, salty landscape that defines Cape Cod.

Ahead, cross two sections of a nearby bike path, then enter into a grove that feels almost tropical. It's populated by trees of heaven, which are invasive tree species native to China. They are highly tolerant of poor soil conditions like Cape Cod's and give off a distinctly unpleasant smell in early summer. Your hike ends by walking along a portion of the Buttonbush Trail, an accessible trail with a guide rope and Braille signs. The signs have interesting tidbits about the trees surrounding you—like how white oak trees were used by Native Americans for food, and then by the colonists for building ships and houses. Take a peek at the signs before arriving at the amphitheater. A short walk up to the sidewalk leads to the parking lot.

48

Nickerson State Park

WHERE: Brewster	
ADDRESS: 3488 Main Street, Brewster, MA 02361	
TOTAL DISTANCE: 3 miles	
HIKING TIME: 2 hours	
ELEVATION GAIN: 151 feet	
DIFFICULTY: Moderate	
RESTROOMS: Yes	
DOGS ALLOWED: Yes	
WHAT TO EXPECT: A sunny hike around a Cape Cod kettle pond with no beach crowds in sight	

One look at the featured photos for this hike and you might never guess that it's on Cape Cod. Nestled in Brewster, Nickerson State Park is quite the gem—and a stress-free change of pace from the bumper-to-bumper beach traffic of Route 6A. Its landscape looks nothing like the dunes of the Cape; rather, the wooded area resembles something more like the Berkshire Hills. But no, Nickerson is a preserved pocket of freshwater ponds and woodland. It boasts more than 1,900 acres to explore, making it one of the largest state parks in Massachusetts.

The area was once owned by a man named Roland C. Nickerson and his wife Addie. The Nickersons were a prominent family on the Cape in the late 1800s and early 1900s. Roland's father Samuel Mayo Nickerson was native to the Cape but made his family's fortune by working as a liquor distiller in Chicago and becoming one of the founding officers of the First National Bank of Chicago.

The Nickersons' estate was huge, and according to the DCR, they were the largest private owner of forest land on the Cape in the 20th century. They spent their summers in Brewster, hosting lavish parties and hunting on the shores of Cliff Pond. Their mansion burned down a few days before Roland's death in 1906, and another (even larger) one was built in its place. The nearby mansion still stands, and is now home to Ocean Edge Resort.

Years later, in 1934, Addie Nickerson and her daughter Helen donated some 1,700 acres to the state. They named it in honor of Roland C. Nickerson Jr., who died in the 1918 flu epidemic. According to the DCR, the Civilian Conservation Corps swooped in to build roads, parking lots, picnic spots,

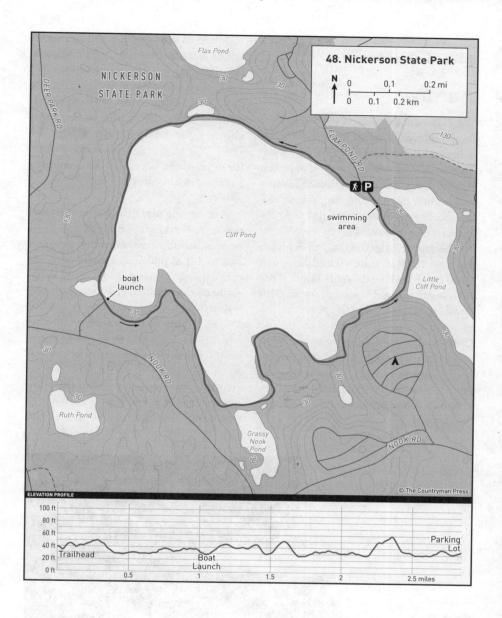

ELEVATION PROFILE

and campsites in 1935. They blazed trails and planted tens of thousands of spruce trees, white pines, and hemlock to boot. The park's kettle ponds and natural beauty have been enjoyed by countless swimmers, picnickers, campers, and hikers since.

GETTING THERE

From US-6 E, take exit 12 for MA-6A toward Orleans/East Brewster. Turn left onto MA-6A W. Follow the road for 1.7 miles, until you see the entrance to Nickerson State Park on the left. A park ranger will collect an $8 fee for a parking pass near the entrance.

THE HIKE

The shores of Brewster's sparkling Cliff Pond feel worlds away from the nearby beloved sandy beaches of Cape Cod. This nugget of wilderness is a welcome respite from fluorescent-hued floaties and boogie boards, offering peace and tranquility to those who dip into its waters or hike around it.

The entrance to the trail opens from the parking lot sandwiched between Cliff Pond and Little Cliff Pond. This hike leads around the entirety of Cliff Pond, a 204-acre kettle pond in the heart of the park. The trail encircling Cliff Pond is marked by easy-to-follow yellow blazes. Though the path is generally very easy, high water levels can flood it after heavy rains. Begin the hike knowing you might have to skirt around flooded parts.

A bed of orange pine needles kicks off the straightforward Cliff Pond path. Immediately, you can drink in views of the crystal-clear pond, seeing straight down to its soft, rippled bottom. Watch minnows dart by in the water, their slight figures skimming along the sand. The path hugs the shore tightly for most of the hike, with some mucky patches in the more heavily wooded areas.

Among the plant life along the trail, you'll find wild strawberries and blueberries, wildflowers, lady slippers, and quite a bit of poison ivy. Take care not to brush up against the poison ivy, especially as the trail curves away from the water.

The beauty of the walk around this pond is that there's no Cape commotion. Gone are the blasting stereos and neon-colored toys you might see on crowded beaches. Instead, it's a tranquil retreat of sorts, with a stillness to the water that sharply contrasts the

A BOULDER DIVIDES THE POND FROM THE TRAIL

THE CALM WATERS OF CLIFF POND

waves beating the beaches in Harwich and Chatham.

As you continue along the path, you'll pass by the recreational facilities for Department of Youth Service's Forestry Camp. Just after the halfway mark, about a mile into the hike, the terrain becomes hillier. You'll climb uphill and away from the shore for a bit, past some trees clad in Spanish moss. This part of the trail lets out at Nickerson State Park's boat launch. Cross the parking lot to continue into the lush green forest. For a few hundred feet, the pond is barely visible from the woods. Continue following the yellow markers.

Round one more cove and the trail meets up with the Little Pond trail, which loops around Cliff Pond's kid brother. The hike concludes with a leisurely walk along the beach again until you reach the swimming area at the end of the parking lot.

Peddocks Island

WHERE: Boston Harbor	
ADDRESS: Peddocks Island, Hull, MA	
TOTAL DISTANCE: 4 miles	
HIKING TIME: 2 hours	
ELEVATION GAIN: 30 feet	
DIFFICULTY: Easy	
RESTROOMS: Yes	
DOGS ALLOWED: No	
WHAT TO EXPECT: A diverse island hike with harbor and skyline views	

As one of the largest islands in Boston Harbor, Peddocks Island is also one of the most fun. It's only accessible via an interisland ferry from the city, which makes it feel more remote than Spectacle and Georges Islands.

The curving hunk of land is about 210 acres at high tide. It's made up of four headlands connected by sand and gravel bars known as tombolos. Peddocks is the most diverse island in terms of wildlife and history, and many people have called it home over the years. The island was farmed in the mid-1600s, before American soldiers used it to defend Boston from the British during the Revolutionary War. About a century later, Fort Andrews was built on the island. Opened in 1900 and named for Civil War general Leonard Andrews, it was used for coastal defense and training. The fort was given caretaker's status in 1927, according to Boston Harbor Islands National Park. It reopened in 1940 when part of America's National Guard was federalized as the country entered World War II.

While Fort Andrews sprang up on one end of the island, Portuguese fisherman settled on the other. Many of the island's quaint, colorful cottages can be traced back to a population of Portuguese fishermen and lobstermen who floated their homes to Peddocks in 1887 after the city took control of their original settlement on Long Island.

Today, the buoy-clad cottages serve as homes for a lucky few—some of whom are descendants of the Portuguese fishermen. When the state of Massachusetts purchased the island in 1970, it required the inhabitants to pay a yearly fee for use of the public land beneath the structures. Once these inhabitants pass away or move away, however, they relinquish their rights to the cottages, and

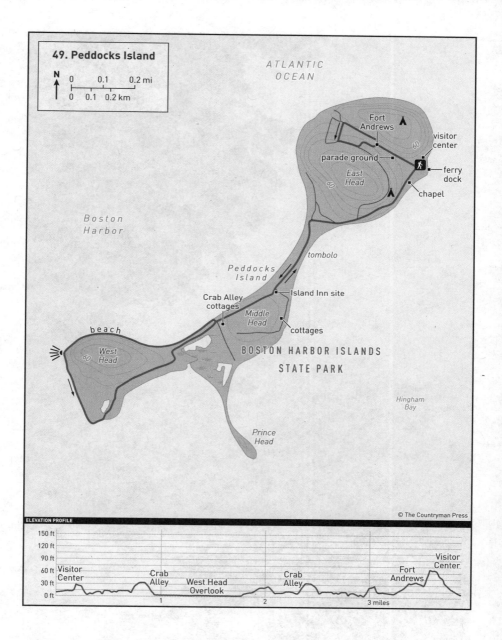

49. Peddocks Island

N

| 0 | 0.1 | 0.2 mi |
| 0 | 0.1 | 0.2 km |

ATLANTIC OCEAN

Fort Andrews

visitor center

parade ground

ferry dock

East Head

chapel

Boston Harbor

tombolo

Peddocks Island

Island Inn site

Crab Alley cottages

Middle Head

cottages

beach

West Head

BOSTON HARBOR ISLANDS STATE PARK

Hingham Bay

Prince Head

© The Countryman Press

ELEVATION PROFILE

150 ft
120 ft
90 ft
60 ft
30 ft
0 ft

Visitor Center

Crab Alley

West Head Overlook

Crab Alley

Fort Andrews

Visitor Center

1   2   3 miles

they aren't able to be passed on to next of kin. A few cottages have already been turned over to the state, and some are dilapidated and decaying. The future for the former Portuguese village is uncertain, as the cottages could be removed from the public land.

The island harbors plenty of other secrets, too. From drunken parties in a notorious inn to bootleggers stashing bottles in Peddocks' coves, there's plenty to be learned, glimpsed, and discovered. This walk around the island only skims the surface of the place's rich history.

VEGETATION CREATES A TUNNEL TO WALK THROUGH

GETTING THERE

From Long Wharf in Boston, take a seasonal Boston Harbor Cruises ferry to Georges Island, then hop on a free interisland ferry to Peddocks. Small boats also run from Hull and Hingham.

THE HIKE

This hike puts Peddocks Island's diverse range of wildlife on full display. It starts with a walk through forests, then along the coastline, and around the paved paths of Fort Andrews. When you disembark from the ferry, head to the visitor center before setting out, as you'll want to grab a map and maybe chat with a ranger about the island's history. With a map and perhaps a copy of the *Harbor Islands Times* in hand, exit the 1910 brick building on Peddocks' East Head, formerly Fort Andrews' guardhouse, and head straight toward the white chapel. This nondenominational chapel is one of hundreds like it built during World War II, but it's thought to be the only one of its design still standing. The 1941 chapel fell into disrepair starting in the 1950s, after the fort was decommissioned, but it was restored by the Massachusetts Department of Recreation and Conservation in 2014.

The wide-open parade ground on your right was created by the partial filling of a freshwater pond. It was the site of drills and inspections when Fort Andrews was operational, as well as soccer, baseball, and football games. Sidestep the goose poop along the trail and continue on. The stairs on your right lead to a group camping site. Camping is a popular Peddocks activity for city dwellers during summertime. There are additional campsites behind the visitor center, as well as yurts for rent.

You'll soon hear gentle waves crashing ashore below as the trail leads you to your first tombolo, then Middle Head. When the leaves are filled in, they create a tunnel-like atmosphere for part of the hike as you duck under the cool shade of the trees. Through the branches, you can see the shores (and homes) of Hull and Hingham.

Once you emerge from the tree tunnel, you'll notice a white cottage on your right. This is the first of a handful of seasonal homes you'll spot during your hike, some of which were built by Portuguese fishermen. After this first white cottage, you'll see a sign showing the history of a former hotel on the island called the Island Inn. In the early 1900s, it was the site of alcohol-fueled parties featuring gambling and prostitution, and the place was nicknamed the Headache House Hotel. Bear right here and walk through field-like lands until you reach woods (and another leafy tunnel) once again. More seasonal homes will peek through the trees here. The trail lets out at a cluster of cottages called Crab Alley. Be mindful of the private homes as you make your way onto the rocky beach, which offers stunning views of the Boston skyline and other harbor islands from afar.

This portion of the hike, along West Head, will trace Peddocks' coastline. While the beach isn't an ideal spot for sunbathing, there are quite a few good swimming spots to cool off mid-hike. Unfortunately, trash litters the rocks along the coast, though it's interesting to see what washes ashore from the city. Round the next bend to get even better skyline views, along with up-close ones of Quincy, Weymouth, and Hingham. The coast leads you to the other side of the drumlin. Trace the water's edge, and look out for tugboats, small barges, and

THE CITY APPEARS CLOSE, BUT FEELS WORLDS AWAY

other industrial seafaring vessels. After about a mile, the trail takes you up to the first tombolo once again. You'll want to return to this trail to make your way to the other side of Peddocks, where Fort Andrews is situated.

Retrace your steps until you reach the parade grounds, then turn left to explore. A series of paved paths weave in and out of Fort Andrews' stately brick buildings. Though the buildings are not open to the public, they once were part of an active coastal defense and training camp during World Wars I and II. In addition to defending the coast, the fort held Italian prisoners of war from 1944 to 1945. The prisoners were moved to Peddocks after the surrender of Italy in 1943, and according to *Discovering the Boston Harbor Islands* by Christopher Klein, they weren't viewed as a threat.

This meant that when they were done working in the Charlestown Navy Yard during the day, they were free to enjoy the island at night. They also visited Boston in groups, and could often be found in the North End on Sundays. Some POWs fell in love with Bostonians— Klein writes that there were about 50 marriages between prisoners and daughters of "sponsor families" in the North End.

Head down whatever paths suit your fancy at the fort, and try and picture life at the fort in the 1940s. A few offshoots lead to scenic overlooks, and others up to the campground on the northern part of the island. When you're sufficiently tuckered out, head back toward the docks to kick back in one of the multi-colored Adirondack chairs along the beach.

50

Wellfleet Bay Wildlife Sanctuary

WHERE: Wellfleet	
ADDRESS: 291 US-6, South Wellfleet, MA 02663	
TOTAL DISTANCE: 3.5 miles	
HIKING TIME: 1.5 hours	
ELEVATION GAIN: 58 feet	
DIFFICULTY: Easy	
RESTROOMS: Yes	
DOGS ALLOWED: No	
WHAT TO EXPECT: A winding walk through marshes and woodlands sprinkled with stunning bay views	

This hike described in one word? Serene. Wellfleet Bay Wildlife Sanctuary teems with unparalleled natural beauty in all of its 937 acres. There's a diversity of landscapes to be enjoyed, too, from salt marshes to beaches to pine forests. You're guaranteed to see fiddler crabs poking around in the marshes and great herons plucking fish out of Goose Pond.

But just a mere 150 years ago, you would have seen neither crabs nor great herons. That's because the land where the sanctuary stands now used to be open fields for farming. Asparagus and turnips thrived here, while dairy cows mooed and fishermen scanned the waters of Wellfleet Bay.

The origins of the sanctuary can be traced to Dr. Oliver Austin, the recipient of the first doctorate in ornithology from Harvard University. The distinguished scholar opened the Austin Ornithology Research Center in Wellfleet with his father in 1929, which went on to become one of the largest private birding stations in the world. The station was sold to the Massachusetts Audubon Society in 1959, yet Austin's legacy is everlasting.

GETTING THERE

After crossing the Sagamore Bridge onto Cape Cod, stay on US-6 E. for just over 36 miles. The Sanctuary is located along US-6 on your left, just after Wellfleet Cinemas.

THE HIKE

After a spin through the exhibits in the Nature Center, begin your journey by passing through its double doors and past the pergola. This hike consists of several trails: the Bay View Trail, the Goose Pond Trail, and the Try Island

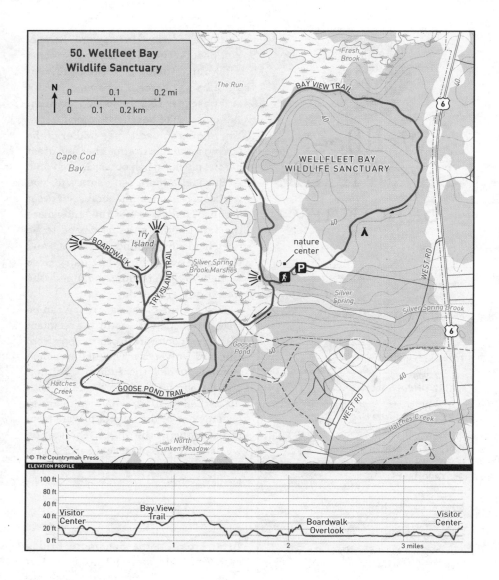

50. Wellfleet Bay
Wildlife Sanctuary

N

| 0 | 0.1 | 0.2 mi |
| 0 | 0.1 | 0.2 km |

The Run

Fresh Brook

BAY VIEW TRAIL

Cape Cod
Bay

WELLFLEET BAY
WILDLIFE SANCTUARY

Try
Island

BOARDWALK

TRY ISLAND TRAIL

Silver Spring
Brook Marshes

nature
center

P

Silver
Spring

Silver Spring Brook

WEST RD

Goose
Pond

Hatches
Creek

GOOSE POND TRAIL

WEST RD

Hatches Creek

North
Sunken Meadow

© The Countryman Press

ELEVATION PROFILE

| 100 ft |
| 80 ft |
| 60 ft |
| 40 ft |
| 20 ft |
| 0 ft |

Visitor
Center

Bay View
Trail

Boardwalk
Overlook

Visitor
Center

1   2   3 miles

Trail. To start on the Bay View Trail, take the first right on the path, and continue straight on the clearly marked walkways.

Immediately you're met with a sweeping view of the salt marsh. Next, duck under the cover of pitch pines, where the path is carpeted by rust-colored pine needles. As the trail turns up into the woods, notice how the pitch pines tent over the path. Turn left to stay on the Bay View Path, and take in more panoramic views of the marsh. This trail truly lives up to its name, framing views of majestic great herons and other birds. It juts out onto the beach again, where you'll notice the shells of horseshoe crabs and other fallen critters. You'll see a bench

A PORTION OF THE BAY VIEW TRAIL

up ahead—stop here to sniff the salty air for a moment before turning right to continue on the trail. Here, you'll bypass Fresh Brook as you walk into the woods. At low tide, you can smell the brine of the marsh.

Views of the bay fade away behind you as you begin to approach the woods along Route 6. For a few moments, instead of the quiet stillness of the salt marsh, you'll hear cars whizzing by. The hike then winds through the sanctuary's campground before returning to the starting point. It's here that you'll begin the next trail.

Pass by the pergola once again to embark on the Goose Pond Trail, dubbed the sanctuary's most popular trail. Turn left instead of right this time, and pass over a bridge at the edge of Silver Spring Brook. Once you reach the edge of the marsh, turn right, and drink in views of Goose Pond.

At the next juncture in the trail, veer right to start the Try Island Trail. This small piece of land jutting into the bay is covered with a grove of oak trees. At the top of a small hill, turn left, and the trail will offer the option to follow a spur out to Fresh Brook Bay. The boardwalked

A SEEMINGLY NEVER-ENDING BOARDWALK

spur offers beautiful vistas, not to mention glimpses of sandpipers and other beach-loving birds. The winding boardwalk—which appears seemingly never-ending—makes for a lovely photo opportunity.

When you're ready, turn around and head back the way you came on the boardwalk to pick up the Goose Pond Trail again. You'll veer into woodlands once more, passing by a private residence and catching views of the other side of Goose Pond on your way back to the Nature Center.